Roots in Reverse

Richard M. Shain

ROOTS IN REVERSE

Senegalese Afro-Cuban Music and Tropical Cosmopolitanism

Wesleyan University Press Middletown, Connecticut

Wesleyan University Press
Middletown CT 06459
www.wesleyan.edu/wespress

Manufactured in the United States of America
Designed by Mindy Basinger Hill
Typeset in Minion Pro

The Publisher gratefully acknowledges the support of the AMS 75 PAYS Endowment of the American Musicological Society, funded in part by the National Endowment for the Humanities and the Andrew W. Mellon Foundation

Library of Congress Cataloging-in-Publication Data

Names: Shain, Richard M. (Richard Matthew), 1949– author.
Title: Roots in reverse : Senegalese Afro-Cuban music and tropical cosmopolitanism / Richard M. Shain.
Description: Middletown, Connecticut : Wesleyan University Press, 2018.
Series: Music/Culture | Includes bibliographical references and index.
Identifiers: LCCN 2018023906 (print) | LCCN 2018025256 (ebook) | ISBN 9780819577108 (ebook) | ISBN 9780819577085 (cloth : alk. paper) | ISBN 9780819577092 (pbk. : alk. paper)
Subjects: LCSH: Popular music—Senegal—History and criticism. | Popular music—Senegal—Cuban influences. | Popular music—Social aspects—Senegal—History.
Classification: LCC ML3503.S38 (ebook) | LCC ML3503.S38 S53 2018 (print) | DDC 780.89/96972910663—dc23
LC record available at https://lccn.loc.gov/2018023906

5 4 3 2 1

FOR WOODIE BROUN

1918–2001

"You recall most often . . .

[the] people who were kind to you."

Remember Me | Heywood Hale Broun

Son is the most perfect thing for entertaining the soul.

Ignacio Piñeiro, founder of Septeto Nacional

C'est trés simple . . . On danse.

Luambo "Franco" Makiadi, "Cooperation"

It stays fresh as long as we catch the pattern.

Baloji, "Karibu Ya Bintou"

CONTENTS

ACKNOWLEDGMENTS

This book has its origins in a presentation I gave to the Cuban Student Association at Rutgers University–Newark in 1994. The attendees' enthusiastic response inspired me to take my inchoate ideas and mold them into something more substantial. As I did so, I realized I owed a great debt to my intellectual "fathers," Robert Christgau and the late John Storm Roberts. I never met either man, but they both have had a significant impact on my life and my current research. As a teenager, I discovered both Latin and African music through Robert Christgau's reviews in the *Village Voice*. Many years later John Storm Robert's inimitable catalogs for his Original Music tutored me in the finer points of global musical traditions. A number of phone conversations with him furthered my training, and his books and cassettes were vital in my intellectual growth.

I would like to thank the provosts and the vice presidents of academic affairs at Philadelphia University for their support over the years, allowing me to attend numerous conferences on three continents at which I was able to present my research. Many of these presentations enabled me to deepen my thinking about Afro-Cuban music. I especially would like to thank Lee Cassanelli and Ali Dinar at the University of Pennsylvania; the members of the Puerto Rican Studies Association and the Afro-Latino Research Associations; EHESS in Paris; Richard Fardon and Graham Furniss of the School of Oriental and African Studies at the University of London; and Ousmane Sene and Omar Ndongo of the West African Research Centre in Dakar for their astute commentaries on my work.

I am grateful to three European colleagues who played a significant role in helping me complete my research. Hauke Dorsch, the director of the African Music Archives at the Johannes Gutenberg University in Mainz, Germany, literally gave me the key to the extensive offerings of this outstanding collection. Karin Barber's editing of an article I published in *Africa* was so scrupulous and insightful, it necessitated my rethinking important parts of my arguments. Denis-Constant Martin at the University of Bordeaux has provided years of intellectual camaraderie and stimulation. He has clarified a number of issues for me through our conversations and his own research on South African music.

In the United States, many colleagues have made this a better book. Ariana Reguant Herńandez of *EthnoCuba* and *Cuban Counterpoints* has championed my work, not least by reading some of my chapters and making valuable suggestions. Charles Ambler also commented on my work with his characteristic acuity. Salvador Mercado has patiently tutored me on the nuances of Puerto Rico culture. Jean Hay "commissioned" me to write my "Roots in Reverse" article and offered much needed encouragement in the early stages of this book's development. Bob W. White pushed me to think more rigorously about my work when I was contributing a chapter to his edited collected *Music and Globalization*. Tsitsi Jaji alerted me to the significance of *Bing* magazine. Robin Moore supported my work through its many stages. Eric Charry, the eminent scholar of Mande music, has improved this book in many ways, especially through his cogent comments as an external reader. Indeed, the ethnomusicology academic community has welcomed this disciplinary interloper and has been exemplary in accepting this work on its own terms while always helping to better it. An example of this intellectual generosity is the extremely constructive comments I received from my other, anonymous reader, for which I am grateful. Selma Cohen was invaluable in addressing some technical issues with my manuscript and in many other ways as well. I would like to express my thanks to Ken Braun of Stern's Music. Ken is a legendary "good guy" in the world music scene. He opened many doors for me when I was a neophyte researcher in this field and always has been available to help. He was willing to read my work and correct errors of fact and interpretation.

My gratitude to the Fulbright Program knows no bounds. A Fulbright dissertation grant financed my dissertation research in Central Nigeria, and another grant in 2002–2003 made it possible for me to spend a year teaching and doing research in Dakar. Those of us who do African cultural history have few potential sponsors. Without a Fulbright grant, it would have been impossible for me to undertake this project.

Indeed, I completed most of my research for this book when I was a Fulbright professor at Université Cheikh Anta Diop in Dakar in 2002–2003. Professor Mamadou Gaye, then head of the English Department, made certain that I had a productive and memorable year. The entire department was welcoming, and I always will remember the intellectual exchanges I had with my colleagues there, especially Professor Omar Ndongo. Professor Mamadou Kandji was doyen of the Faculté des Lettres et Sciences Humaines during my time at the university. He worked closely with Professor Gaye to ensure that I had a marvelous year as a Fulbrighter. He has become a good friend, although I have no hope of ever equaling his scholarly productivity!

A number of individuals were helpful to me in Dakar. I owe special thanks to Ibru Iba, proprietor of Chez Iba, and his staff for the many unforgettable evenings I spent there. Aminata Sy, then of Centre Baobab, gently oriented me toward Senegalese culture during my first months in Dakar. Alioune "Juan Carlos" Diop invited me to be a guest on his RTS television show several times and graciously accommodated me at his house in Thiaroye. He also gave me rare footage of the first Cuban tour by Senegalese Afro-Cuban musicians. I spent countless enjoyable hours in Sacré Coeur with Antoine Dos Reis, who connected me with Dakarois active in the Afro-Cuban scene and the Senegal-Cuba Friendship Association. My thanks to him. The celebrated impresario Daniel Cuxac gave me many computer discs from his personal archive of Cuban music and shared his inexhaustible knowledge of Cuban and Senegalese music. The late famous record producer Ibrahima Sylla permitted me to attend two Africando recording sessions and spared time from his frenetic schedule to let me interview him twice. The late Cheikh "Charles" Sow, author and librarian at the West African Research Centre, directed me to many essential sources for my work. Judy Dusku and Lew Shaw, the directors of the Dakar campus of Suffolk University, provided me with a luxurious second Dakar home, enabling me to extend my period of research. Finally, the friendship and hospitality of John and Papu McIntire sustained my family and I during our year in Dakar and beyond, for which we remain grateful.

As anyone who has interacted with them knows, Senegalese Afro-Cuban musicians are a special breed. I rarely have encountered a more convivial, refined, and articulate group. They were profligate in sharing their knowledge and experiences with me and welcomed me into their world with typical Senegalese *teranga*. The great *sonero* Mar Seck was unusually open with me. Camou Yandé always made me feel at home, and his sense of humor kept me laughing. The late Laba Sosseh, who was averse to being interviewed, still agreed to meet with me. We ended up having a wonderful conversation reminiscing about the New

York salsa scene. Lamine "Lemzo" Faye, formerly of Super Diamono, and I spent many delightful hours at the now unfortunately shuttered Central Park, discussing *m'balax*. My biggest debt, however, is to Pape Fall, the illustrious *salsero* and leader of African Salsa. Monsieur Fall invited me to many private performances and immeasurably aided me. He truly personifies all the admirable qualities of Senegalese Afro-Cuban culture

I owe special thanks to many friends whom I met in Dakar. François Richard, then a graduate student at Syracuse University, initiated me into the mysteries of Université Cheikh Anta Diop and alerted me to the importance of generations in Senegalese history and culture. Drs. Ibrahima and Mariéme Thiaw have been wonderful listeners and lavish hosts. They have supported me emotionally and intellectually through every phase of this project. I learned much from the late Ahmadu Ndoye of the Department of Spanish and Portuguese at Cheikh Anta Diop, and he was unfailingly kind to my family during my year as a Fulbright Professor at Cheikh Anta Diop University. I greatly miss his companionship and his intellectual example. Serigne Mbacké Fall of Groupe Walfadjiri has been stalwart in his backing of my project. He reproduced for me his *entire* remarkable archive of Orquesta Aragón. Becoming friends with him was one of the high-points of my time in Senegal. The late Garang Coulibaly took me under his wing, as he has done for so many other scholars of Senegalese music, and unselfishly shared all his research materials. He became a good friend whom I still miss.

I was extremely fortunate that the internationally respected Senegalese photographer Djibril Sy was willing to join me in visually documenting the Dakar salsa scene. His brilliant images appear in this book and on its cover. Djibril quickly earned the trust of the Senegalese Afro-Cuban musicians, and he photographed them with great sensitivity. I thank him for allowing his work to be reproduced here.

I couldn't have asked for a more accommodating press than Wesleyan. Marla Zubel and Suzanna Tamminen have been a pleasure to work with: responsive, courteous, and cooperative. My thanks to them.

I was fortunate to have two remarkable individuals working with me on my research. Mody Sidibé started helping me when he was a graduate student in the department of English at Cheikh Anta Diop University. A brilliant scholar in his own right, he took time out from his studies of Scottish literature to explore what was for him the new universe of Senegalese salsa. His intelligence, humor, resourcefulness, and work ethic contributed immeasurably to the completion of this project. Yahya Fall is a legend in the Senegalese music world. A renowned guitarist, he also has superb managerial and human relations skills. He was uncannily quick in grasping my research goals and methods and seemed to have a better idea of where my work was heading at times than I did. He taught me a great deal about music, Senegalese culture, and life. Getting to know and work with him and Dr. Sidibé was an unanticipated dividend of undertaking this research. My profound thanks to them both.

In addition, I am grateful to the following businesses, individuals, and institutions for their permission to reproduce texts and images in this book: Ken Braun of Stern's Music for the Africando CD cover; Art Resources and the Agence Photographique de la Reunion des Musees Nationaux for the Brassai photograph; the University Press of Virginia for the Senghor poem "Comme Je Passais" in its English translation by Melvin Dixon; and Editions Seuil for the original in French.

I owe a great debt to my adopted family: Hob, Jane, and Woodie Broun. In high school, Hob shared my enthusiasm for the music of Eddie Palmieri and Willie Colon; later, in the 1980s, he introduced me to the music of Laba Sosseh. We were close friends until his tragically early death. His mother and father, Jane and Woodie, became my surrogate parents in my twenties. Until they died, they cheered me on, offered me endless hospitality at their home in Woodstock, New York, and even gave me crucial financial support. Their lives embodied the qualities that so many Senegalese admire: warmth, intellectual erudition, dignity, integrity, and generosity.

Finally, like all authors, but perhaps more than most, I have to thank my family. My daughters, Sam and Abbie, embraced Senegalese life during their year abroad and made many friends. As they have become adults, they have lovingly kept my spirits up during the many years of this project and always been great sounding boards for my ideas and arguments. I know they are relieved that the book is finished. My wife, Marcy Schwartz, willingly sacrificed her own research on Latin American literature to come and live in Dakar. Though she despaired of my idiosyncrasies as a salsa dancer, she still accompanied me occasionally on my 1:00 a.m. forays to Chez Iba. She earned the respect and affection of every Senegalese who crossed her path. She has been my partner in everything, and this book would not exist without her love, humor, zest, emotional succor, intellectual acumen, and incomparable linguistic prowess. To her, I owe more than I can express.

NOTE ON SPELLING OF SENEGALESE NAMES

Transcription of names from Senegalese languages and Arabic into Roman script can be imprecise. As a result, it is not unusual for Senegalese names to have inconsistent spellings. I have incorporated these variations in my text.

INTRODUCTION
Sound Track for a Black Atlantic

If a traveler goes to Cuba today to search for the burial sites of such renowned Afro-Cuban musicians as the bandleader and singer Beny Moré, the classic sonero Abelardo Barrosso, or the flutist Pancho Bravo, they will find beautiful stone markers for the graves, only recently erected. If they were to examine the markers more carefully, they would be drawn into one of the more fascinating histories of the black Atlantic. It wasn't the Cuban government or the families of these artists who commissioned these impressive monuments. Rather, it was an admirer of these musicians from the West African nation of Senegal who financed the gravestones and insisted on their installation.

These renovated burial sites attest to the continuing passion that many Senegalese have for the music of Cuba. It is an enthusiasm that has deep roots in Senegal and has played a significant role in Senegalese history for over eighty years. By examining this francophone West African preoccupation with *Cubanidad*, this book extends the borders of the black Atlantic to include the Hispanic Caribbean and francophone Africa. In so doing, it documents overlooked local modernities and expands our knowledge of the different forms of resistance that Africans used to contest European cultural and political hegemony in the twentieth century.

This book is based on the premise that "people think through music, decide who they are through it . . . [music] is less a 'something' than a way of knowing the world, a way of being ourselves."[1] As Denis-Constant Martin points out, "music is an inextricable combination of audible elements and social processes."[2] From this perspective, the history of Afro-Cuban music in Senegal is more than an analysis of a marginal and "exotic" aesthetic form. Since the 1930s Senegalese have used music to imagine a new social order and engage in discussions about citizenship, cosmopolitanism, authenticity, masculinities, consumption, and the creation of local modernities. By looking at how the Senegalese deployed Afro-Cuban music in various cultural and political spheres, this book provides a history of taste and generational friction in twentieth-century Senegal and reveals the tensions involved in the Senegalese creating a postcolonial national culture.

In Senegal, listening and dancing to Afro-Cuban music created structures of feeling that united generations and bridged ethnic differences.[3] In the 1930s Afro-Cuban served as a catalyst for bringing African and Caribbean intellectuals together in the negritude movement, which sought to insert African narratives into universal history and create a space for Africa in the global "republic of letters." From the 1950s through the 1960s the movement helped the first postcolonial generation in Senegal define its cultural mission; in the 1990s it contributed to a revitalization of Senegalese cosmopolitanism. Today it helps mend frayed diasporic connections between Senegal and the Caribbean.

This abiding Senegalese affection for prerevolutionary Cuban music has an important story to tell. During the twentieth century consumption of Afro-Cuban music was integral to the imagining and embodying of Senegalese modernities. The discovery of Afro-Cuban music in Paris in the 1930s by Senegalese students inspired an entire generation of Senegalese intellectuals like Léopold Senghor to find their voice. Later in the 1950s and 1960s Senegalese youth, through the creation of Afro-Cuban record clubs, experimented with new forms of "modern" sociality. In the 1960s and 1970s nightclubs in Dakar and other Senegalese cities featuring live performances of Afro-Cuban music were laboratories for decolonizing Senegalese culture. In the 1980s Senegalese Afro-Cuban music spearheaded a growing diasporic cultural transnationalism anchored in the tropical world. In the 1990s the international impact of Senegalese Afro-Cuban music continued when one song by the group Africando became a radio hit in Latino New York and throughout the Hispanic Caribbean. During most of the twentieth century and into the twenty-first, Afro-Cuban music has played a critical role in Senegalese debates about sociality, cultural authenticity, and cultural citizenship.

MYTHS ABOUT AFRO-CUBAN MUSIC IN SENEGAL

In spite of its significance, until recently Afro-Cuban music in Africa has largely been overlooked as a research subject. A number of pervasive myths about this music explain this neglect. Many believe, even in Africa itself, that Afro-Cuban music was exclusively the preserve of "Westernized" African elites in the 1950s and 1960s, listened to by only a prosperous few for a limited period of time. It also is an article of faith in some circles in Africa and abroad that Afro-Cuban music in Africa has been aesthetically stagnant, locked into clichéd covers of a handful of Cuban classics like "El Manisero" and "Guantanamera." Perhaps most damagingly, many commentators have categorized Latin music in Africa as culturally inauthentic and inherently colonial.

This book dispels these myths. Latin music has never been limited to a privileged cadre in the capital. Its appeal for much of the twentieth century transcended class and ethnic boundaries in both urban and rural Senegal. The local musicians playing Afro-Cuban music, few of whom came from prominent Senegalese families, were attracted to it in part for its aesthetic possibilities. Over time they retained its musical structure and repertoire but remained open to artistic experimentation. After mastering the Cuban style in the early 1960s, for example, they proceeded to sing in Wolof, one of Senegal's major languages, and integrated indigenous traditions of instrumentation, singing, subject matter, and rhythm into their performances. These musicians and their public never viewed Afro-Cuban music as "foreign," a "Western" import. They were aware that the music arose out of the "forced migration" of Africans to the New World and that it incorporated many African elements. In playing, hearing, and dancing to it, they heard and felt their history and culture echoing from across the Atlantic Ocean. By embracing the music, they were reforging diasporic ties and proclaiming their autonomy from exclusively Western models of modernity.

PLACE(S) DE L'INDÉPENDANCE

Tracing the trajectory of Afro-Cuban music in Senegal illuminates many dimensions of that nation's cultural history, such as gender relations, generational competition and conflict, debates over cosmopolitanism and hybridity, the role of nostalgia in Senegalese national culture, and shifting diasporic identities. The music also has provided new forms of enjoyment, a template for cultural citizenship, and a tool for creating a public sphere free from European and North American cultural hegemony. It is all too easy when writing about popular music in Africa to overlook the essential truth that its primary purpose has been to provide pleasure. For some scholars of popular culture, incorporating pleasure into their analysis would be tantamount to arguing that popular music is frivolous and devoid of significant cultural and political content. In this book I argue that examining the ways the Senegalese have experienced pleasure is crucial to understanding how they have imagined modernity and defined cosmopolitanism. The Senegalese historically have responded to Afro-Cuban music on a number of levels. In talking about their attraction to this music, they emphasize how much it has stirred them physically and mesmerized them aurally and visually. By drawing on so many of their senses, it has led them to embody new codes of behavior and new modes of enjoyment. As a consequence, in listening to how the Senegalese have listened to Afro-Cuban music, we can trace the genealogies of a modern Senegalese sensibility.

While Afro-Cuban music has been a source of enjoyment for many Senegalese, it also has been a tool for moral instruction and a means for thinking about alternative varieties of citizenship from French colonial models. Since the 1930s the Senegalese have equated Afro-Cuban music with "modern" forms of sociality and leisure. Integrating women into previously all-male social domains was intrinsic to these new practices, as was patronizing cabarets and music clubs. Dancing to Cuban music with a partner of the opposite sex became for men and women a symbol of sophistication. Innovative patterns of consumption were even more important as Senegalese acquired the latest European male fashion and, by the 1950s, LPs of Cuban music. The new forms of sociality emphasized that being *correcte* was a path to modernity. Self-discipline, affability, tolerance, erudition, an elegant appearance, and a general air of savoir faire became characteristics of the well-ordered, morally grounded life. Changes in consumption relating to Afro-Cuban music enabled young Senegalese to claim "rights of difference" within the context of the Franco-Senegalese state.[4] They appropriated power consumer goods from abroad, like shoes, shirts, jackets, sunglasses, pens, and Cuban records, to assert and create cultural spaces beyond French domination. Though grounded in cultural practices, these patterns of consumption had significant political ramifications. They solidified new ways of defining and actualizing themselves and helped lay the foundations for a Senegalese national culture in tune with but subtlety different from the official negritude version propagated by President Léopold Senghor.

THE ORAL AND THE AURAL: RESEARCHING THE HISTORY OF SENEGALESE POPULAR MUSIC

The Senegalese have valued Afro-Cuban music both for its artistic worth and for the sensibility and conduct linked with it. Because the music and its cultural complex have been intertwined with so many major social and cultural issues in the Senegalese past and present, any research methodology for studying its changing roles and meanings must be multidisciplinary and attuned to the multivocality of the nation's Afro-Cuban music scene. Monographs on African popular music tend to either focus exclusively on recordings and musicians in a "maps and chaps" narrative or reduce music to its sociological and historical dimensions where context overrides content. Neither one of these approaches can account for Afro-Cuban music in Senegal. The story of this music has involved intellectuals, musicians, members of record collecting clubs, amateur dancers, music club habitués, broadcasters, club owners, impresarios, and world music executives. Its geographical expanse is equally vast, taking in Cuba, Puerto Rico, Colombia, Peru, New York, Miami, Paris, Abidjan, Dakar, and a number of smaller Senegalese cities. Only a multifaceted research methodology can capture this complexity.

I began my fieldwork by immersing myself in the recorded music of Cuba, Puerto Rico, and the Senegalese Afro-Cuban ensembles. The advent of CDs in the 1980s led to the reemergence of large amounts of previously unavailable music. Small record labels in Europe, especially in the Netherlands, Germany, and Greece, pioneered the re-release of Senegalese music. The owners of these labels traveled to Senegal, bought old discs or tapes, remastered them, and then repackaged them as CDs, often with excellent liner notes. Sometimes these re-releases were "pirated," but in most cases the original musicians were compensated for their work.[5] Without this newly available invaluable archive, it would have been almost impossible to conduct my research. The records in and of themselves constitute a treasure of oral histories. with proverbs, historical references, and interpretive "takes" on cultural change. Moreover, by the time I interacted with the musicians who made these recordings, I already had a rough understanding of their artistic development. I also had an extensive familiarity with recorded Latin music from the Caribbean and the United States. If I had been without this expertise, the Afro-Senegalese music community in Dakar would have dismissed me as an amateur who was not worth their time. With that knowledge came not only mutual esteem but also camaraderie. We all were initiated members of an exclusive club of enthusiasts and experts.

Attending concerts and recording sessions in New York was another valuable research activity. Before I began my research in Dakar, I was able to attend a performance by the Senegalese Afro-Cuban group Africando at Lincoln Center in New York in 1997. I also had the privilege of being present at some of their recording sessions for two of their albums and engaging in extensive conversations with one of the album's arrangers, the Malian/Nigerian arranger and flutist Boncana Maïga, and with the late Senegalese producer Ibrahima Sylla. These experiences gave me a solid grounding for my work in Senegal years before I arrived in Dakar in the fall of 2002 to spend a year as a Fulbright professor at Cheikh Anta Diop University.

I originally conceived of my project as being based on a series of interviews I planned to do with Afro-Cuban musicians in Senegal. I thought these oral histories would supply me with everything I needed. I soon discovered I was wrong in two respects. I started off well enough in January 2003. Two of the most prominent salsa musicians in Dakar, Pape Fall and Mar Seck, readily agreed to be interviewed. They couldn't have been more accommodating and were articulate and well informed. However, after this promising start my work ground to a halt. I made appointments with musicians, but they didn't show up. I realized I had proceeded too rapidly. I needed to work at establishing a relationship of trust and respect with the musical community. Regularly attending their performances at clubs around Dakar, like Chez Iba, and visiting them during the day facilitated this. Over a period of four years and a number of research trips, I attended hundreds of these performances in a variety of venues, ranging from elegant private parties to working-class neighborhood bars. Participant observation became part of my research tool kit. The musicians turned out to be welcoming, frank, open, and eager to talk about their work and lives with insight and eloquence. They appreciated that I had become a semipermanent fixture in their world, as I was able to make annual research trips to Senegal for a number of years.

Once I had established myself in the Afro-Cuban musical community, I resumed my formal interviews. These interviews gave the musicians an opportunity to be taken seriously as artists, something they clearly relished (and merited). If an interview proved particularly fruitful, I would schedule several more sessions with that individual. As I created a place for myself among the musicians, I realized that I had too narrowly conceived my research. These artists were part of extensive overlapping networks in Dakar that went well beyond the walls of a music club or recording studio, taking in the realms of academia, the media, politics, commerce, and government. In order to comprehend the Afro-Cuban music world, I needed to chart these networks. This aspect of my research brought me into contact with a remarkable coterie of aficionados of Afro-Cuban music in Dakar (retired civil servants, journalists, recording engineers, broadcasters, media executives, record collectors, academics, and entertainment entrepreneurs). The depth and breadth of this group's knowledge of the development of Afro-Cuban music both in Cuba and Senegal is astonishing. Fortunately they were as generous as the musicians in sharing what they knew—and they made themselves even more available when they recognized my expertise in Caribbean music (which in truth was much less extensive than theirs). Here, too, I was able to establish satisfying relationships that continue until this day. I wasn't doing research *on* them but *with* them.

My research also involved archival work at the Senegalese national archive, perusing back issues of Dakar newspapers and looking through scrapbooks kept by local fans of Afro-Cuban music. Friends at the Senegalese broadcasting service, RTS, also made available to me tapes and DVDs of past programming or their own visual coverage of the Senegalese Afro-Cuban community at home in Dakar and on tour in Cuba.[6] The colonial archive on urban nightlife was thin, showing that the French felt they had little to fear from the bourgeoning Afro-Cuban "scene." Newspaper clippings showed that Senegalese journalists were highly proficient in writing about Afro-Cuban music. The tone of their articles was serious, and their coverage of musicians was dignified and professional. However, as a source this material was more useful for background than for detail. The visual documents from RTS, by contrast, provided essential, accurate, and detailed material unavailable elsewhere. The difference between the utility of these two sources stems from the fact that the individuals responsible for the RTS documents were long-standing participants in Senegal's Afro-Cuban community, who were personally invested in the stories they were covering, whereas the journalists writing on Afro-Cuban musicians were more generalists.

The richest print sources for this project were representations of Afro-Cuban music in Senegalese fiction and poetry, starting in the 1930s. These sources uncover a "silenced" history of Afro-Cuban music: its role in the formation of negritude. They also illuminate some of the circuits through which Afro-Cuban music reached Senegal. Perhaps most significantly, they reveal how Afro-Cuban music has been linked with Senegalese debates about cultural (and political) citizenship and modernity since before World War II. Either through its conspicuous presence or its explicit exclusion, this music has shaped how the Senegalese have defined republicanism and cosmopolitanism. Today it has little place in contemporary literature. However, as long as negritude in one form or another remains influential in Senegal, Afro-Cuban music will continue to resonate in the nation's intellectual life.

MAPPING ROUTES IN REVERSE

This book reconstructs the history of Afro-Cuban music in Senegal from the 1930s through the beginning of the twenty-first century. The first chapter briefly surveys the history of Afro-Cuban music and identifies which of its musical traditions have most appealed to Senegalese listeners and performers. Chapter 2 begins by showing how Afro-Cuban music became a global phenomenon in the 1920s. It then analyzes how Latin music contributed to the formation of negritude in Paris in the 1930s. It concludes with Senegalese explaining in their own words why they have felt so drawn to Caribbean music. The third chapter examines the rise of a new type of cultural citizenship in Senegal in the 1950s, informed by both consumerism and Afro-Cuban music. This linkage was especially evident in Dakar's record clubs. Made up of young men, these clubs collected Latin music discs and staged carefully organized parties. These groups pioneered innovative ways of enjoying leisure time and developed new forms of sociality tied to their conception of modernity. The fourth chapter focuses on the establishment of a Senegalese tradition of performing Afro-Cuban music. By the late 1960s Senegalese ensembles had mastered the Cuban style, and they began to incorporate indigenous languages and musical elements into their performances. The chapter also considers how new technologies and new audiences shaped the development of Senegalese Afro-Cuban music in the 1970s and 1980s. The result of these changes was an urbane style, well suited to a rapidly changing and decolonizing Dakar. The chapter concludes by telling the story of the singer and bandleader Laba Sosseh, who became one of the first Pan-African music stars and then a salsa musician in the United States. The fifth chapter surveys the debates in 1980s Senegal about authenticity and cosmopolitanism. During this period younger Senegalese began to see Afro-Cuban music as irrelevant and dated, and the music went into a temporary eclipse. Many began to buy cassettes of their favorite *m'balax* bands and attend their performances, participating in Afro-Cuban music and dancing. The chapter analyzes the forces that led to the music's survival and then its resurgence in the early 1990s. Chapter 6 examines a number of recent attempts to market Senegalese Afro-Cuban ensembles as "world musicians." These marketing campaigns reveal the diverse ways different parts of the world imagine Africa in the twenty-first century. Africa and the Caribbean have generated some of these images, but the dominant global vision stems from "Western" fantasies of tropical decay. The chapter next deals with the first tour of Cuba in 2002 by a Senegalese Afro-Cuban group. The tour was a mixed success, demonstrating how diasporic identities can become entangled in ideological conflicts and divergent institutional priorities. The chapter ends by exploring how certain musical riffs have resonated in the black Atlantic. As these riffs circulate, they acquire new meanings in different contexts. Their itineraries map the aesthetic contours of the black Atlantic. They demonstrate that the cultural conversation between Senegal and the Hispanic Caribbean endures in productive and unpredictable ways.

Roots in Reverse

ONE

Kora(son)

Africa and Afro-Cuban Music

When I listen to Cuban music, I feel there is a part of me in that music. I think I'm right because when Orquesta Aragón came here, the *chef d'orchestre* said they had to come back to Africa because that is where the music is from, especially Senegal. Every time I hear that music (hums a song), I hear "El Manisero." You see—it's the same culture.

Pape Fall, leader of the group African Salsa[1]

Though Cuba has a population of less than twelve million, its cultural and political prominence in the twentieth century has far exceeded its modest size. Its impact has been particularly pronounced in the realm of music. Cuban music throughout its history has absorbed elements from numerous cultures and in turn has helped shape popular culture in many parts of the world, including the rest of Latin America and the United States. However, its influence has been most pronounced in twentieth-century Africa. Cuban music, with its variety and complexity and its profusion of genres, encouraged Africans to imagine new cultural identities and experiment with innovative forms of leisure. Indeed, it provided a template for modern popular music for most of Africa, from Guinea to the Congo to Tanzania. The guitar bands of Conakry, the rumba orchestras of Kinshasa, and even the Taarab ensembles of the Swahili coast and Zanzibar all found some of their musical roots in this small island nation. To understand why Cuban music has held sway so far from its shores, it is useful to explore its origins and examine its development. This chapter analyzes some of the most conspicuous features of the Cuban style and looks at the factors shaping the development of the Cuban genres that have had the most appeal in Africa in general and Senegal in particular.[2]

ROUTES OF ROOTS

Many New World musics incorporated African features as a result of the forced migration of tens of millions of Africans to North America, the Caribbean, and Central and South America during the era of plantation slavery. However, what makes Cuban music so unusual is its range of African influences, their intensity, and their revitalization through African migration throughout most of the nineteenth century. Cuba's African population arrived in waves from different parts of the continent, starting in the sixteenth century. Each of these unwilling African immigrants brought with him or her techniques, beliefs, aesthetic preferences, linguistic practices, and types of knowledge from the "home" culture. The immigrants found themselves in a situation in which they encountered other Africans who came to Cuba with related but sometimes significantly dissimilar conceptual "tool kits." In their struggle for survival, Afro-Cubans had to construct a culture out of bits and pieces from the "Old World," mostly African but sometimes Spanish, using shared organizing principles.[3]

It is probable that creating a common musical tradition was one of the first tasks undertaken by the uprooted migrants. "Music has no frontiers" is an expression often heard in contemporary Senegal, and given the commonalties that exist among many African musical cultures, fashioning a music for their oppressive existence in colonial Cuba must have been one of the less daunting tasks facing the black Cuban community. In the process of undertaking this cultural project, the first black Cubans made one of the hallmarks of their emerging musical tradition an aesthetic conservatism that maintains aspects of the old while layering on the new.[4] This tendency made the inclusion of unfamiliar musical cultures from incoming populations a much easier proposition. Because of this aesthetic conservatism, Afro-Cuban musicians frequently have staged conversations between the established and the innovative in their work, rather than submerging or eliminating older ways of playing music in the name of novelty or "progress" as is done in many other parts of the world. They may play old rhythms on new instruments; have a chorus sing in a "traditional" nasal timbre while the soloist performs in a more modern melodious style; or incorporate old instruments in new settings, as the bandleader Arsenio Rodríguez did in the 1940s when he brought conga drums previously exclusively used in religious observances into a popular music ensemble.[5] This practice has meant that informed listeners from Africa can hear the many separate elements that comprise Cuban music much more distinctly than in other more streamlined New World musics. Afro-Cuban music is not only part of Cuban history; it seeks to contain as much of that history as possible within many of its compositions. As a result, the sound of Africa insistently comes through.

There is some debate about whether Central or West Africa supplied the bulk of the first forced migrants to Cuba in the sixteenth and seventeenth centuries. Ned Sublette, a musician, music producer, and writer who is a respected expert on Cuban music, insists that most of the first Afro-Cubans were from what is now the Congo and Angola. His argument relies more on negative evidence than on substantial proof. Sublette cites a *cédula* (royal edict) issued by the Spanish king Carlos in 1526 barring the importation of Muslim Wolof speakers (*Geofes* in the original document) from present-day Senegal to the New World.[6] However, it was common for settlers in the Hispanic Caribbean to flout royal decrees because these edicts were difficult to enforce under even the best of circumstances. Moreover, the cédula only banned the Muslim Wolof from being sold as slaves. That left the Portuguese and later French traders considerable latitude to traffic in Serer, Mandinka, Diola, and other captives from Senegambian regions immediately to the south of the zone of the Wolof speakers. It is likely that following the usual pattern in the Caribbean, the first Spanish settlers in Cuba filled their slave quarters with both Senegambians and Congolese/Angolans. The slaveholders believed, with good cause, that a slave population of only one language group was more prone to rebellion than a mixed group, which would find mounting a unified insurrection more challenging.

Musically, it is possible to hear traces of both Congolese and Senegalese music deeply embedded in Cuban song. The *sanza/likembe*, a Congolese instrument on which metal prongs are mounted above a sound box and plucked, took root on the island, and its descendant, the *marímbula*, supplied the bass lines for the earliest recorded *son* groups, like Septeto Habanero in the 1920s.[7] Soon the contrabass replaced the marímbulas, and bass players have retained their prominent position in Cuban popular music ensembles ever since. It is their role to articulate the basic beat of any piece so that the dancers know which rhythm to follow. Their crucial musical role led Cuban bassists to become some of the first virtuosos on their instruments in the twentieth century.[8]

Though conclusive proof is lacking, the Senegambia region might have provided one of the basic building blocks of Cuban music, the *clave*. The clave is both an instrument (two wooden sticks) and a syncopated rhythm that has become the bedrock of the Cuban sound. Lucy Duran, an ethnomusicologist who has studied both Cuban and West African music, argues that the clave rhythm originated in the Mandinka/Maninka area of West Africa.[9] The Mandinka, one of the major population groups in the Gambia River valley, were among the first to supply captives to the Caribbean. Since the Mandinka were forced to migrate to other areas of the Caribbean and the Caribbean Basin, a significant number must have ended up in Cuba, perhaps bringing the clave with them. Certainly the clave abounds in the contemporary Mandinka *kora* repertoire, although modern Mandinka musicians actually may be borrowing this rhythm from Cuban records.[10]

In the centuries that followed the initial forced migration of Congolese/Angolans and Senegalese to Cuba, other regions of Africa supplied numerous captives. The peoples of the Calabar River valley in Nigeria (who were called Carabali, Ñáñigo, or Abakuá in Cuba) were one important source of enslaved manpower,[11] as were those from the Fon- and Ewe-speaking areas of present-day Dahomey and Togo (who were called the Arará in Cuba).[12] In addition, Akan speakers from present-day Ghana (called the Mina); groups from present-day Côte D'Ivoire, Liberia, and Sierra Leone (called the Gangá); and even some captives from Mozambique in Southern Africa were forced to migrate to Cuba. In the eighteenth and nineteenth centuries there was another influx of captives from the Senegambian region, mostly Mande speakers, as well as a huge wave of Yoruba speakers (called Lucumí) from what is now Nigeria.[13] By the nineteenth century Cubans with links to Yoruba-speaking areas of Nigeria comprised the largest percentage of black Cubans, followed by the Congolese and the Cross River peoples.[14] Not surprisingly, the influence of these three groups became dominant in Afro-Cuban music by the dawn of the twentieth century. Nevertheless, reflecting the aesthetic conservatism of Afro-Cuban culture, elements from other African traditions like the clave remained an important part of the "mix."

The diverse origins of Cuba's African population were not historically unusual. However, what was remarkable was how the Spanish allowed their African captives to preserve aspects of their culture like drumming and even encouraged them to organize themselves into ethnic mutual help organizations, called *cabildos*.[15] This limited cultural accommodation by the Spanish helped keep African musical expression alive in Cuba. What was even more extraordinary, though, was how Cuba drastically expanded its African population in the nineteenth century with new enslaved laborers. Elsewhere in the New World, with the conspicuous exception of Brazil, *direct* African cultural influence largely subsided during this period, as first the importation of captives from Africa and then slavery itself ended.[16] In Cuba the opposite occurred. The incoming migrants re-Africanized aspects of Cuban music making, especially drumming and dancing. This revitalization of the African roots of many Afro-Cuban cultural forms only two generations before the first recordings of Cuban songs served to make Cuban music especially appealing to African listeners in the twentieth century. The sound of Africa came through loud and clear to them.

Africa, of course, was not the only force molding Afro-Cuban music. Other global influences were at work. Many of the original Spanish settlers of Cuba, for example, were from Andalusia, a part of Spain deeply effected by its interactions with Arabs, Berbers, and sub-Saharan Africans. They brought with them such song forms as the *décima*, which can still be heard in Cuba. Black Cubans appropriated such song forms and made them part of their cultural repertoire. After the Haitian revolution in the closing decades of the eighteenth century, large numbers of French planters migrated to eastern Cuba with their enslaved Africans. The Haitian captives introduced black Cubans to their rhythms, many of which derived from Fon culture.[17] The French planters popularized the French *contradanse* in Cuba and introduced Cubans to their flute and violin ensembles, which were embraced by both criollos and black Cubans.

Another new musical element came to Cuba from Europe. One of the little known cultural repercussions of the Napoleonic age was the revamping of the European military marching band. The bands started to have better trained musicians and grew larger, with more varied instrumentation such as cymbals, adapted from Ottoman military orchestras. The new style military bands caught on with the Cuban public, and many towns formed their own brass ensembles, which exist to this day. Black Cubans were as fascinated with these new musical groups as were other Cubans. Indeed, a number of the early major black and mulatto Cuban musicians and composers had had experience playing in such ensembles.[18]

MI GUAJIRA: CUBAN MUSIC GENRES AND SENEGALESE MUSICAL TASTE

By the end of the nineteenth and early twentieth centuries, these disparate musical elements from Africa and Europe had coalesced into five major Cuban music genres—rumba, bolero, *guajira*, son, and *danzón*—which either alone or in combination with one another organized Afro-Cuban musical expression in the twentieth century. The boundaries between these genres have not been rigid, and Cuban musicians have moved freely from one to the other. Africans have found some of these genres more appealing than others. Indeed, they have shown no interest in perhaps the most African of all Afro-Cuban musical forms, the rumba. The rumba has been the music of black Cuban "street people" and other marginalized Afro-Cuban groups in Cuban society since the nineteenth century. Its instrumentation is exclusively percussion. Most of its rhythms have their origin in Afro-Cuban religious ritual. Euro-Cubans until recently regarded the rumba as disreputable and not worthy of serious attention. Recordings of it were extremely rare until after the Cuban Revolution (1953–1959), when the Castro regime designated it as "folklore" and an important part of the national cultural patrimony.[19] Because of this neglect, other than a few cognoscenti, African listeners outside had little opportunity to hear authentic rumba recordings throughout most of the twentieth century. When many Senegalese finally did encounter the rumba in the 1980s, their aloof response to it mirrored that of Euro-Cubans in the prerevolutionary era. Both musicians and the listening public found the music too atavistic and unrefined for their taste.[20] In Senegal, a nation of exceptional percussionists, the drumming of the *rumberos* failed to impress listeners. Along with most Africans, the Senegalese mostly ignored this form of Cuban musical expression.

The bolero has been the most popular genre of Cuban music in Cuba itself and in the rest of Latin America. Mexicans particularly have an affinity for it. Boleros are romantic songs, performed with smooth intensity by mostly male performers. In most instances melody trumps rhythm, and the musical arrangements tend to be lush. The main public for this type of music in Latin America has always been women, with a significant cohort of gay men.[21] Paradoxically, this type of Cuban ballad has not especially resonated with African audiences. African listeners have preferred to embrace the term and the concept (languorous beats, romantic lyrics) rather than the genre itself. A well-paced evening of Latin dancing at a social gathering always includes slow ballads, which Africans, following practice elsewhere, label boleros, even if these numbers are stylistically far from the original Cuban model.[22] A number of factors account for Africans' relative lack of interest in this variety of Cuban music. Classic Cuban boleros usually lack an obvious African tinge.[23] Moreover, French music has its own tradition of sentimental love songs. From the 1930s through the 1960s such French performers as the Corsican Tino Rossi (1907–1983) were beloved in Africa.[24] The

Cuban bolero was not sufficiently different from the French romantic song to wean African audiences away from a musical tradition that already had entranced them. Perhaps the emphatic feminine orientation of bolero also made young African men uncomfortable before the sexual revolution of the1960s. Even as African tastes have shifted in the last twenty years, African audiences of Cuban music have yet to explore this deep well of Cubanidad.[25]

A greater number of African listeners have been attracted to rural Cuban genres like *tonados* and *puntos*. Cubans associate these cultural forms with the peasants and small ranchers of the Cuban interior, *los guajiros*, who have been mostly descendants of migrants from Spain. Guajira musicians like the guitarist, *tresero*, and singer Eliades Ochoa like to stress their rural background, sometimes wearing the Cuban equivalent of cowboy hats.[26] The unadorned but powerful style of guajira singers like Guillermo Portabales appealed to African sensibilities much more than the exaggerated fervor of bolero crooners.[27] The instrumentation of a typical guajiro group, with guitar, *tres*, bongos, and sometimes a bass, combined for many Africans listeners the best of African and European musical traditions. "Guantanamera," the most famous guajira song, became an anthem of African Latin musicians as early as the 1960s and is still extensively performed.[28] While in Cuba guajiro music resonates with nostalgia for an idyllic rural past, in Senegal it has been associated it with elegance and urbanity. Indeed, guajiro rhythms have become one of the bedrocks of Senegalese salsa and remain extremely popular today.[29]

Son is the most expansive of all Afro-Cuban musical genres. Musicians have found it malleable and easy to combine with foreign music like jazz. It also has worked well in a wide array of musical settings, from guitar trios to small ensembles to large brass orchestras. An intricate interweaving of African rhythms and vocal styles with European melodies and harmonies, son is a celebrated example of *méttisage*. The Cuban ethnologist Fernando Ortiz, who was among the genre's first champions, described it as "Cuban counterpoint" and argued that it was a perfect metaphor for Cuban history and culture.[30] In a similar vein, the ethnomusicologist Robin Moore pointed out that son was able to link "the culture of the Afrocuban underclasses with that of mainstream society . . . [widening] the syncretic sphere mediating between realms of African- and Iberian-derived culture."[31] This adaptability and cultural inclusiveness enabled son to have the greatest international impact of all Cuban musical forms.

Arriving at a definition of the son form is difficult because of its protean nature. However, Moore has successfully managed to describe its main elements.

According to him, a basic son piece has seven musical characteristics. It is in duple meter and employs simple European-derived harmonic patterns (I-V-I-IV-V). It alternates between verse and chorus sections, and it usually contains short instrumental segments, often played on either a tres or trumpet. The three most distinctive features of the son are the use of African-type percussion instruments, the *montuno* section, and the clave. From the time of the earliest son conjuntos, ensembles used bongo drums to provide propulsive syncopation. Though there doesn't seem to be any African antecedent for the two small high-pitched drums that make up bongos, black Cuban musicians played them in a style derived directly from African drumming traditions.[32] The montuno is the final section of a son, in which the accompanying musicians start playing at a brisker tempo, and the chorus and the sonero take turns rapidly singing strongly rhythmic improvisations. The clave is the heart of the son. Musicians playing in clave emphasize the fourth beat of the 4/4 measure more strongly than the first and lay down a unique bass rhythm, emphasizing the "and-of-2" (the upbeat falling between beats 2 and 3) and "4," which is generally described as an "anticipated bass."[33]

Son emerged as a cultural form sometime in the nineteenth century in eastern Cuba. Its early history remains obscure. By the first decades of the twentieth century it began to spread to other parts of Cuba, including Havana. Dislocations in the sugar economy in the last part of the nineteenth century and political turmoil spurred the migration of rural black Cubans from the eastern end of the island to the capital. In their new home the migrants introduced their Havana neighbors to the music from their part of Cuba. Isabelle Leymarie, a French writer on Cuban music, suggests that the shifting of Cuban troops in 1909 by then president José M. Gómez was another factor in the diffusion of this regional musical form. Afraid of a coup, Gómez switched the companies stationed in Havana and Oriente (Eastern Cuba). Some of the soldiers who had been garrisoned in Oriente played son; once in Havana, they introduced their music to a whole new audience.[34] Initially, the only audience for son music was the poor people living in the roughest Havana barrios. Gradually, however, it gained acceptance from other Cuban social classes and enlarged its listenership. The advent of recording in the first decades of the twentieth century and the rapid growth of Cuban radio in the 1920s were crucial to bringing son to groups who otherwise never would have been exposed to it on a regular basis. By the 1930s it had become one of the national musics of Cuba.

Son's success in serving as an artistic bridge between black and white Cubans helps explain some of its appeal to Africans in the 1920s and 1930s. They, too, were trying to reconcile the universalist ethos of the colonial European regimes with their more locally based cultures. Just as significantly, by the 1920s son music had become a sign of modernity in avant-garde circles, first in Havana and then in Europe. Though many in the United States have regarded Afro-Cuban music as an inconsequential folkloric style, produced by marginalized Hispanic immigrants from the Caribbean, by the late 1920s increasing numbers of European listeners regarded son music as an important art form, on the same level as other distinguished types of popular music like jazz. In 1929, for example, one of the first famous son groups, Septeto Nacional, won a major prize for a performance at the Exposición Ibero-Americana in Seville, Spain. This European embracing of son music as a prestigious cultural form was not only gratifying for black Cubans. Many Africans also took pride in an Africanized *modern* form of cultural expression's being equated in the colonial metropole with sophistication and advanced artistic taste.

However, the attraction of son went beyond its lofty role as a mediator between civilizations. The structure of a son piece resembled many African musical traditions, and the montuno, with its improvised call and response between a chorus and a leader, has counterparts in many types of African musical expression. The rhythms of sons also encouraged dance styles compatible with African practice. The clave encouraged the shifting of weight from one leg to another in such a way as to generate a gentle swaying of the hips. While in many African dance traditions hip movements are more accentuated, the dance styles associated with son music clearly had their origins in Africa, not Europe. Because of such shared cultural characteristics, according to the Malian/Nigerien flutist Boncana Maïga, son music provided a mirror for Africans and gave them the aesthetic jolt of hearing familiar rhythms from a new perspective.[35] Hearing and dancing to this music that straddled Europe and Africa became a pleasurable way to be at home in the modern world.

On first hearing it, one would think that danzón, the fifth Cuban popular music genre, would hold little interest for African listeners. The style appears to be a by-product of the European ballroom culture: demure, dignified, and slightly formal. Although a connection with an African musical tradition is not immediately apparent, it is there. For at least three decades, starting in the 1950s, a variation of this musical form captivated the Senegalese public, who considered it a fount of sophistication. Even in the twenty-first century there is still a sizable audience for this style of music in Dakar and St.-Louis, where crowds pack the concerts given by touring ensembles, such as Cuba's Orquesta Aragón, that still include danzones in their repertoire.

To better understand the allure of danzón for the Senegalese, it is useful to analyze the development of the form.[36] A closer look reveals that danzón for much of its history has been a distinctly Africanized and Gallicized form of musical expression, as popular with black Cubans as with Iberian Cubans. Since at least the middle of the nineteenth century, African and French influences have shaped its evolution. Given the abiding impact of these influences, it is not surprising that Senegalese listeners (and other Francophone audiences in places like the Congo) have felt so comfortable with this genre. Moreover, the fact that Cubans for two centuries have associated this type of music with sociality and respectability has heightened its appeal for Senegalese. It has provided a model for forging a modernity that incorporates pleasure, civility, and embracing global cultural connections.

The origins of danzón lie in the Haitian revolution at the turn of the nineteenth century. With the dismantling of the plantation system there, a number of French planters took refuge in Cuba. They brought with them many of their slaves and their French cultural practices. Included in their cultural baggage was a dance music form, the *contradanza* (in the Spanish spelling). In some respects similar to US square dances, the contradanza was performed in a fast-paced 2/4 meter. The accompanying musicians often were of African ancestry and, according to Ned Sublette, gradually syncopated the European-derived music by adding such features as the tango rhythmic cell.[37] The contradanza quickly found favor with well-born Ibero-Cubans. It became a fashionable leisure time activity, even though it meant that the Cuban elite began dancing in between the beat in African fashion rather than on the beat, which was more characteristic of European ballroom music.

By the 1830s Cubans had indigenized the contradanza by creating a related dance music, *danza*. The danza had an ABAB form and was danced by couples facing but not touching one another. It began with a *paseo*, a repeated 8 measure that was good for chatting or resting. A section in 2/4 followed the paseo, and a danza piece would conclude with a section in 6/8. Perhaps in recognition of the humid Cuban climate, the pace of the danza was significantly slower than the contradanza's. By the 1880s the danza had grown into an immensely popular cultural form, the danzón, which many Cubans in the twentieth century regarded as the true national music of Cuba. The danzón has an ABACAD form (rondo) and is danced by couples, which was a daring innovation for socially conservative nineteenth-century Cuba. Traditionally, it was played at an even more majestic pace than the danza, allowing for a full evening of dancing without exhaustion.[38]

Originally the instrumentation for danzónes involved woodwinds, brass, and violins, with clarinets and trombones dominating. However, in the first decades of the twentieth century a different kind of orchestra, the *charanga francesa*, gradually became the preferred ensemble format for playing this genre of Cuban music.[39] In these musical groups, led by artists such as Antonio María Romeu (1876–1955), brass instruments disappeared, with their part being taken by the violin section. The woodwinds contracted to just a couple of five-key wooden flutes, and the orchestras featured pianos for the first time.

There is some debate over why Cubans considered this new type of musical organization more French than that of other types of ensembles. The great Cuban flutist José Fajardo maintained that charangas francesas were characteristic of prerevolutionary Haiti and were brought to eastern Cuba by fleeing French planters. Others have pointed out that the addition of a piano made danzón groups more refined, with refinement being associated by Cubans with anything French. Still others have argued that the new emphasis on flutes and violins led to an elegant lightness, qualities the Cubans also connected with the French.[40] All these hypotheses are equally plausible. Certainly when Senegalese listeners discovered this Cuban musical tradition after World War II, they found this music as elegant, light, and refined as had the Cubans half a century earlier, and they, too, connected these qualities, in part, with French culture.[41] Moreover, they associated the prominence of pianos, flutes, and violins in this type of Cuban music with the prestige of classical music.[42]

The rise of son music in the 1920s posed a challenge to danzón's popularity. Faced with diminishing audiences, the leaders of the danzón orchestras began to experiment with modernizing their nineteenth-century sound. In 1929, for example, Aniceto Díaz (1887–1964) devised the *danzonete*, which deemphasized such traditional rhythms as the *cinquillo* and added singers to what previously had been an overwhelmingly instrumental form. Most important, however, is that Díaz added a montuno in the danzón's final section that allowed his musicians to improvise. By so doing, Díaz broke down some of the barriers separating danzón and son and prepared the way for even more important departures from tradition in the 1940s.

In 1937 the flutist Antonio Arcaño (1911–1994) formed a charanga orchestra that was destined to permanently change Cuban music. The musical advances pioneered by Arcaño's ensemble created a more fluid and percussive sound that was especially appealing to African listeners. Arcaño's orchestra was pathbreaking in a number of respects. It allowed its players, especially its flutists, to improvise much more freely than was the custom during that period. Most of the charanga's musicians were dark-skinned Cubans, and Arcaño made it a band policy to play frequent engagements at Afro-Cuban social clubs for low fees, or, occasionally, even for no fee at all. Arcaño further grounded his charanga in Afro-Cuban culture by being among the first *charangueros* to add conga drums to his percussion section.

This immersion in *Afro-Cubanismo* endowed his ensemble's music with textures and timbres that were new to Cuban music (the combination of congas, strings, and flutes) but that Senegalese audiences later found familiar and satisfying. Among the many language communities existing within present-day Senegal's borders, there have been widespread string and flute traditions. A number of groups, especially within the last one hundred years, have given a prominent musical role to the kora, a twenty-one-stringed African harp. The *riti*, a one-string bowed instrument with a violin-like sound, has also been musically significant in many areas. The *xalam/hoddu*, a plucked string instrument, has occupied a central place in Wolof and Pulaar/Tukolor musical culture. The Pulaar/Tukolor, who mainly reside in northern Senegal, are also famous for their wooden flutes. In all regions a diverse array of drumming styles continues to flourish. Though Arcaño's music does not seem to have reached Senegal while he was alive, his influence on other Cuban string and flute orchestras was profound. Unwittingly, by augmenting the instrumental mix of danzón ensembles he paved the way for the vast popularity of Cuban charanga music in Senegal and other parts of Africa in the 1950s.

Arcaño's revamping of the danzón genre was only one revolution among several that occurred in the 1940s in Cuban music. The blind tres player Arsenio Rodríguez (1911–1970) was similarly transforming son. Other Cuban musicians, like the *conguero* Chano Pozo (1915–1948), helped initiate bebop jazz in the United States.[43] Reveling in their instrumental virtuosity, Cuban musicians delighted in intricate rhythms, dense sonic textures, and dissonant key changes. The music that grew out of this creative ferment, like the mambo, was artistically distinguished but increasingly difficult for Cubans to dance to, not to mention the tourists from the United States who were becoming big consumers of Cuban music. This may have been the reason that the mambo never became hugely popular in Senegal, although its brass-heavy arrangements also may not have been as appealing to Senegalese listeners as the string and flute charangas.[44]

The violinist Enrique Jorrín (1926–1987), who briefly played in Arcaño's ensemble before becoming musical director of the charanga Orquesta America, noticed that dancers were having trouble adjusting to the complicated new syncopation of music like the mambos of Beny Moré. Rather than shifting their weight between the beat, they were moving on the second and fourth beats of the bar, out of sync with the music. Jorrín resolved to create a new offshoot of the danzón tradition that would be easier for dancers to master but that would still preserve some of the rich sonority and rhythmic complexity of the 1940s style.[45] His *nuevo ritmo* came to be called *cha-cha-chá,* supposedly from the sound of dancer's feet shuffling on the dance floor and the rhythmic accompaniment of the *güiro* and the timbales.[46] In 1950 Jorrín wrote "La engañadora," which became the first big cha-cha-chá hit. The song initiated a global boom for Cuban music similar to what had transpired with "El manisero" when it became a worldwide hit in 1930.[47] The cha-cha-chá became a sensation in New York, Paris, London, and Dakar, where its popularity continues to this today.

For many Senegalese who came of age in the 1950s, the cha-cha-chá and later its variant, the *pachanga*, exemplified modernity. The musical forms sounded sleek and smooth, the aural equivalent of the smartly tailored uniforms the Cuban charanga musicians wore on their record covers. Even the dance attached to the music was streamlined, shorn of extraneous movement (and easy to learn). More than listeners elsewhere, the Senegalese were aware that the cha-cha-chá and the pachanga were the result of a centuries-long interaction among Spanish, French, and African music. It was a global cultural "movement" wherein African culture met European "civilization" on equal terms, without being peripheralized or exoticized. In the words of the noted Dakar recording engineer Aziz Dieng, the cha-cha-chá "is a mix of African music and classical music. It has the ambience of classical music."[48]

Just as significantly, the cha-cha-chá / pachanga phenomenon combined contemporaneity with decorum. In so doing, it inspired young Senegalese to create a "local" modernity that allowed them to be polished, worldly, *and* resolutely African.[49] In subsequent eras, first US soul music and funk and then hip-hop similarly created spaces where African publics could explore new ways of being in the world. However, none of the subsequent waves of popular music had the enduring influence of Afro-Cuban music. It ultimately constituted a foundation that other musical genres could build on but never totally displace.

TWO

Havana / Paris / Dakar

Itineraries of Afro-Cuban Music

The history of modern Cuban music in Senegal begins with the song "El manisero" ("The Peanut Vendor"). It re-creates a Havana street peddler's chant advertising the peanuts he has for sale. While the piece's lyrics are not particularly memorable, its melody, rhythm, and key changes have fascinated musicians and listeners from many cultures ever since its composition in the 1920s by the Cuban musician Moisés Simons. The song's impact was especially strong in colonial Francophone Africa and continued to resonate throughout the early phases of postindependence as well. This chapter focuses on what the Senegalese have heard in Afro-Cuban music, beginning in Paris and then in Dakar, from the 1930s onward. It examines the influence of Latin music on pre– and post–World War II Senegalese debates about the fashioning of an autochthonous modernity. Afro-Cuban music, for example, played a major role in the formation of negritude in the 1930s among Senegalese intellectuals in Paris, a relationship that many of negritude's founders, like Léopold Senghor (1906–2001), who later became the first president of an independent Senegal, either ignored or obscured once they became prominent politicians and literary figures after World War II. This chapter also reveals why the nightclub became a site where Senegalese could formulate and contest different conceptions of negritude, the black Atlantic, and cosmopolitanism. As liminal spaces free from colonial hegemony, nightclubs allowed Senegalese to combine erotic adventure and intellectual exploration in unprecedented ways. At all points in this process of developing a modern cultural identity, Afro-Cuban music had a crucial role to play.

"El manisero" first became a hit in 1929. In that year the Cuban zarzuela singer Rita Montaner (1900–1958) traveled to Paris for her second French tour.[1] France during the 1920s was cosmopolitan in its musical tastes. The French discovered jazz after World War I and were enthusiastic participants in the Charleston dance fad. Argentinean tango also acquired a sizable following. However, until Rita Montaner's tour in 1928 and her recording of "El manisero," Cuban music was relatively unknown to French listeners. Her first appearance at the Olympia the previous season, where she was accompanied by the dancing duo of Julio Richards and Carmita Ortiz, had piqued the Parisian public's interest.[2] Her 1928 recording of the song, released after her show at the Olympia, had raised her profile in France, and she wanted to build on her triumph there.

Montaner's second concert in Paris, in 1929, was both a critical and popular success and brought Afro-Cuban music to the fore just as she had hoped. A highpoint of her act was "El manisero." Her performance of the song made her the talk of Paris and promoted sales of her record. There was already a sizable community of Cuban artists, intellectuals, and musicians in Paris, and it is likely that their activity laid the groundwork for an escalating French interest in Cuban culture.[3] Before long the disc circulated widely throughout France and the Francophone world.[4] It ignited an enthusiasm for Cuban music in Paris that resulted in the establishment of a number of nightclubs featuring Cuban bands filled with Afro-Cuban musicians.[5] These clubs formed the hub of a bohemian culture in Montmartre and the Latin Quarter in the 1930s that attracted the Antillean and Francophone African students who had come to France to obtain advanced academic training unavailable in the French colonies

The popularity of "El manisero" had ramifications even further afield. On Saturday, April 26, 1930, in New York, a sellout crowd at the Palace Theatre, the premiere venue for vaudeville in the United States in the early days of the Great Depression (1929–1939), viewed a spectacle that no local audience had seen before. The Palace had transformed its stage into a fanciful Havana streetscape. As the orchestra led by the Cuban musician Don Azpiazú (1893–1943) started playing "Mamá Inez," one of the most famous songs in the Cuban repertoire, the audience heard instruments that were still exotic to US listeners: maracas, claves, güiros, and bongos. Then a crew of Cuban dancers bounded onto the stage, in the first documented exhibition of authentic rumba dancing in the United States. Though they created a commotion with their energetic movements, it was the orchestra's third song, "El manisero," sung by the Afro-Cuban sonero Antonio Machín that drove the Palace crowd wild, just as it had when Montaner sang it the year before in Paris.[6] Azpiazú's arrangement of the song, which combined complicated Cuban time signatures (the clave) with sophisticated American-style big band orchestration, immediately struck a chord with the public.[7] Indeed, "El manisero" became such a hit, it sparked a passion for Cuban music that swept through North America and then Europe,[8] especially after Azpiazú and his ensemble recorded the song later that year for RCA.[9] By 1931 the 78 rpm recording of the song reached Africa, selling extremely well throughout the continent, especially in Francophone Africa, where it reached a far wider public than just a few African intellectuals in Paris.[10]

LA NOCHE CHEZ CABANE CUBAINE: LÉOPOLD SENGHOR, OUSMANE SOCÉ DIOP, AND AFRO-CUBAN MUSIC, 1930S–1960S

I feel the Other, I dance the Other, therefore I am.

Léopold Senghor[11]

By the late 1920s Paris had become one of the international centers of Latin music. The vast Colonial Exposition in Paris in 1930–1931 contributed to the music's burgeoning popularity by further whetting the French appetite for "exotic" foreign cultures like Cuba's. This Afro-Cuban boom in Paris occurred during a period of decline on the island. The end of prohibition in the United States in 1933 resulted in a precipitous drop in US tourists traveling to Havana right at the time that the global Depression began to devastate the island nation. As the Cuban economy contracted, opportunities for Afro-Cuban musicians dried up.[12] Faced with grim professional prospects, some Afro-Cuban musicians migrated to Paris, where a network of Latin music clubs had opened up to capitalize on the craze for Cuban music.[13] There the musicians found the work and respect that had eluded them at home.[14]

This influx of Caribbean musicians coincided with the rapid expansion of the population of Antillean and African students in Paris. The 1930s saw a gradual opening up of the French higher education system to the most gifted students from throughout the French empire. The French motives in providing university education for their colonial and "overseas" subjects and citizens were complicated, a mixture of the pragmatic and the idealistic.[15] There was a need for middle echelon manpower in many colonial bureaucracies, and local personnel often were cheaper to employ. In addition, both French assimilationist policy and republican ideals called for at least some non-European French speakers with university training and respectable positions in colonial governments. Financial aid for these students in France was insufficient, and their level of academic preparation was often inadequate. Furthermore, they had to contend with the racism of the French academic establishment and the "glass ceiling" that limited their advancement after they obtained their degrees. For many of these students, their experiences in the French educational system were stressful and alienating. For support, they turned to one another and the few places in Paris where they were welcomed with no ambivalence. Latin music clubs provided one such refuge for them.

The most famous and influential of these clubs was La Cabane Cubaine in the Place Blanche in Pigalle. The Cuban musician and entrepreneur Eduardo Castellano opened the club at 42 Rue Fontaine in 1930. The club featured cabaret shows with both large Cuban *orquestas* and small son and rumba ensembles.[16] Its success appears to have been instantaneous. Probably because the poet and surrealist theorist André Breton lived upstairs, the club soon became a surrealist haunt. Jean-Paul Sartre and Simone de Beauvoir were also habitués. Bohemians and intellectuals of all sorts flocked to the club to hear "authentic" Cuban music and see professional Cuban rumba dancers. The club was simultaneously seedy and stylish, a mix many Parisians found exhilarating.

For somewhat different reasons, African and Antillean students frequently visited the club as well. The club was a place where individuals from the black Atlantic could meet one another, recognize their cultural diversity, and find common ground in Afro-Cuban music. The Senegalese writer Ousmane Socé Diop (1911–1973), in his novel *Mirages de Paris*, described it as an "ethnographic museum": "In the throng of blacks gathered at the Cabane Cubaine so similar in appearance, Fara introduced Jacqueline to Africans, Haitians, and Mauriciens. People said this nightspot was an ethnographic museum of the black world, to which each nation had sent a specimen."[17]

The club was a cultural contact zone, one of the few places in the world at that time where blacks and whites could socialize on a basis of relative social equality. An image by the photographer Brassaï, "En La Cabane Cubaine," shot around 1932, captures the special ambience of the club. The photo immediately draws the viewer's eye to how racially integrated La Cabane Cubaine was in its heyday. There are racially mixed couples as well as all-black and all-white couples, everyone obviously at ease at the club. In the photo's foreground is a table at which are seated a white couple deep in conversation with one another and a nattily dressed

A La Cabane Cubaine, Montmartre, ca. 1932 Brassaï (Gyula Halasz, called, 1899–1984) © Estate Brassaï-RMN. Photograph PL.473. Photo: Michèle Bellot. Private Collection. © RMN-Grand Palais/Art Resource, NY

black man lost in thought, smoking a cigarette. Movement is an important visual component of the image. At the center of the image a laughing black man dances with a smiling white woman. The delight they take in each other's company is palpable. Other dancing couples surround them, equally enjoying themselves. Indeed, pleasure and desire, rather than racial diversity, is the image's dominant feature. Brassaï's photo references Paris as a city of erotic adventure where taboos that impede sexual intimacy elsewhere evaporate.[18] During the Harlem Renaissance, European American men went to Harlem to hear Duke Ellington and court black mistresses in segregated nightclubs like The Cotton Club. La Cabane Cubaine offered an altogether different experience. It was a combination of a nodal point for people of color in Paris, a space where whites and blacks could freely interact, and a space where desire from *all* its patrons could be displayed publicly. Most of all, it was a site where young Africans connected Afro-Cuban music, movement, and blackness with modernity.

One of the patrons of La Cabane Cubaine in the early 1930s was a young Senegalese student in Paris, Léopold Sédar Senghor, a major figure in the cultural and political history of Senegal. Senghor was born in 1906 in Joal, a coastal maritime village in a region where Kru and Cape Verdean sailors had been exposing the Senegalese inhabitants to Caribbean music for centuries. After spending his early years in an agricultural village with his mother, Senghor began attending a Catholic mission school as a boarder when he was eight years old. He proved an extraordinary student, and when he was seventeen he entered a newly established Catholic seminary in Dakar. Disenchanted by the racist condescension he encountered there, he withdrew and enrolled in a new lycée in Dakar in 1926. He excelled in his studies and in 1928 received a half scholarship from the colonial regime to study literature in Paris.

Senghor found academic success difficult to achieve in France in the 1920s. His colonial education had not adequately prepared him to excel at the university level. Moreover, many of his Parisian professors were not receptive to teaching African students, no matter how outstanding. One of his biographers, Janet G. Vaillant, also suggests that he found much of the teaching about literature at the Sorbonne hidebound and out of date.[19] To make himself better able to withstand the rigors of the French university system, Senghor withdrew from the Sorbonne and became a student at a famous lycée, Louis-le-Grand, where he formed a close lifelong friendship with fellow student Georges Pompidou, later president of France. By the early 1930s Senghor had reenrolled at the Sorbonne, this time as a student of grammar. During this period he took up residence at the Cité Universitaire, a dormitory for French speaking students from around the world. It was there that he met Antillean students like Aimé Césaire (1913–2008) and began to get a sense of the global dimensions of African civilization. Despite his plaintive letters to colonial administrators complaining about his life of unrelieved drudgery in Paris,[20] it was during this period that he first started visiting La Cabane Cubaine, sometimes in the company of Césaire. A New World opened up to the previously reticent and withdrawn student as he began to socialize with intellectually gifted youths from the Caribbean and elsewhere in Africa at Paris's Afro-Cuban music nightclubs. Though an awkward dancer, by the late 1930s he was teaching newly arrived Senegalese students in Paris the latest steps.[21]

Out of this sustained intellectual and social interaction between African and Antillean students and the explosively creative climate in Montmartre/Pigalle and the Rive Gauche emerged the famous cultural movement negritude. Pioneered by Senghor, Césaire, and the Guyanese Léon-Gontram Damas (1912–1978), "*négritude* was a rejection of assimilation, an identification with blackness, and a celebration of African Civilization."[22] The movement advocated a reverse racialization of colonial knowledge, privileging an African "emotional" way of knowing over an arid European "rationalism." According to negritude theorists like Senghor, Africans and people of African descent, through intuition and sensory perception, could see through surfaces to the essence of an object or behavior. This ability to get to the heart of the matter was something invaluable that African culture could bring to world civilization. At its inception, negritude tried to strike a balance between cosmopolitanism (universal ways of knowing) and cultural authenticity (validating particular African methods of producing knowledge). In so doing, it addressed philosophically many of the same challenges of being modern and African that Afro-Cuban music did on a more everyday level.[23]

At least in their early phases, the histories of negritude and the Senegalese embrace of Afro-Cuban music were intertwined, involving some of the same individuals. The initiators of negritude and those who saw the path to African modernity illuminated by Afro-Cuban music believed that African modernity must have a prominent aesthetic dimension. The two groups equally underscored the significance of rhythm and movement in defining blackness. The theorists of negritude and the aficionados of Afro-Cuban music also argued that any modern black identity had to be transnational, "not simply constructed in opposition to Europe but in relation to it."[24] Both argued that these identities had to be performed publicly to counter dominant European cultural models. Each saw cafés and nightclubs as important laboratories for incubating ideas and developing modern forms of sociality.

By the late 1930s, however, the trajectories of negritude and the linking of Afro-Cuban music with Senegalese modernity began to diverge. This fissure grew out of a number of debates that began in Paris in the 1930s during the formative period of negritude and still resound in Senegalese academic and artistic circles. Senghor and his allies saw negritude as a "high-culture," modernist project in dialogue with important contemporary trends in French literary and philosophical thought, like surrealism and phenomenology. He recognized that for his generation Paris was the world capital of modernity and cultural prestige.[25] It was also, despite its imperial ambitions, a global repository of republican values and political liberalism.[26] Taking these facts into account, Senghor's strategy for the political and cultural liberation of his nation was to simultaneously pursue full citizenship in the French Republic and "the world republic of letters" centered in France.[27]

The realization of Senghor's vision of cultural citizenship entailed the creation of a mandarin literary class, similar to France's. By definition, such a group would dominate the imagining of modernity in Senegal and, as a result, would benefit the most from it. While this position was intellectually coherent and politically viable, it had ramifications that some Senegalese found disturbing. Their reservations revolved around the elitist assumptions of Senghor's position. In addition, Senghor's variety of negritude, despite its efforts to strike a balance between universalism and cultural nationalism, still seemed to favor cosmopolitanism over cultural authenticity, thus potentially limiting the scope and significance of intellectual decolonization. Some Senegalese felt it was too accommodating of French intellectual hegemony. Moreover, Senghor's model left little room for serious consideration of the role of popular culture in creating Senegalese modernity. That meant a dismissal of the cultural importance of Afro-Cuban music (and even of African music) and, with it, an implicit repudiation of an embodied modernity.

Two literary texts dealing with this era—Senghor's famous poem "Comme Je Passais" and a much less known novel by Socé Diop, *Mirages de Paris,* articulate these differing early visions of negritude. Afro-Cuban music plays a crucial role in both texts. However, in Senghor's poem, references to Afro-Cuban music are so oblique that many distinguished literary scholars have completely overlooked them. By contrast, Socé Diop's novel gives pride of place to Afro-Cuban musical expression and shows how it served as one of the foundations of an African modernity. Senghor's poem hints at his future distancing from Latin music, while Socé Diop's novel suggests why this music would have such a powerful attraction for postwar Senegalese youth. Not surprisingly, Senghor was critical of the novel when it was published in Paris in 1937.[28] His disapproval, however, could not prevent the ideas expressed in the novel from having a long life in Senegalese discussions of what sort of modernity would best suit the Senegalese.

It is possible to generate many readings of the extraordinary "Comme Je Passais," but the analysis here focuses exclusively on how the poem illuminates Senegalese debates about music, cultural identity, and modernity.[29] The poetic voice recounts the thoughts and sensory sensations he experiences as he walks past La Cabane Cubaine on the Rue Fontaine in Paris:

Comme je passais rue Fontaine,
Un plaintif air de jazz
Est sorti en titubant,
Ébloui par le jour,
Et m'a chuchoté sa confidence
Discrètement
Comme je passais tout devant
La Cabane cubaine.
Un parfum pénétrant de Négresse
L'accompagnait.

Voilà des nuits,
Voilà bien des jours au sommeil absent.
Réveillés en moi les horizons que je croyais défunts.
Et je saute de mon lit tout à coup, comme un buffle
Mufle haut levé, jambes écartées,

Comme un buffle humant, dans le vent
Et la douceur modulée de la flûte polie,
La bonne odeur de l'eau sous les dakhars
Et celle, plus riche de promesses, des moissons mûres
Par les rizières.

As I was walking by Fontaine Street,
I heard a jazz song stagger about,
Dazzled by the day,
And it whispered its secrets to me
Discreetly.
And just as I walked in front of
The Cuban Cabana
The penetrating scent of a black woman
Became its accompaniment.

Here come the nights,
Here come the days without sleep.
Horizons I thought had gone
Have reawakened in me.
And suddenly I bound from my bed
Like a buffalo with its muzzle raised high,
Legs spread, like a buffalo

Sniffing the wind
And the modulated sweetness of the polished flute,
The good smell of water under the *dakar* trees
And the aroma, richer in promise,
Of ripe harvests from the rice fields.[30]

In a number of respects, this poem constitutes a daring sequence of appropriations by Senghor. Most saliently, Senghor creates a new African subject. In the poem he veers away from representing Africans as the exoticized objects of the European gaze, positioning Paris as the object of desire and fantasy. The poet's tool for fashioning this new subject is French, the language of the imperial dominator. He uses this language to assert his cultural "citizenship" in the "lettered" imperial city. Senghor's adroit use of French literary style, infused with his knowledge of French literary history, further supports his case for cultural citizenship.[31] His poem pays homage to Baudelaire through oblique references to such poems as "À une passante."[32] A key element in the poem is the textualization of urban space. Though a colonial subject, the speaker moves comfortably around the capital of the country that has conquered his nation, proclaiming his freedom of movement. The speaker in this poem is an African flaneur marveling at but not being intimidated by the semiotic spectacle of Paris. This poem demonstrates that the speaker is at home abroad, cosmopolitan without being French.

Senghor explicitly links the poem to negritude through his emphasis on sensory perception. The poem engages the body and many of the senses: seeing, smelling, and hearing. Senghor's flaneur uses his head (eyes, nose, and ears) to know the world. The poem also references negritude through its identification with black music and rhythm. Here Senghor introduces music stripped of its specificity. There is only a vague association in calling it "jazz." When the speaker passes by La Cabane Cubaine, he detects "Un parfum pénétrant de Négresse" (the penetrating perfume of a black woman). Similarly, later in the poem, when he encounters "la douceur modulée de la flûte polie" (the soft and refined modulations of a flute), it awakens his sense of smell: "La bonne odeur de l'eau" (the beautiful smell of water). The music as a symbol of blackness induces nostalgia. He keeps on walking and resists responding to the music physically. However, it continues to resonate for him. Later that night he is finally affected by it, perhaps involuntarily and subconsciously, in the privacy of his room.

The poem reveals more of Senghor's complicated feelings about Afro-Cuban music than he perhaps intended. His African flaneur is not sauntering down the

Champs Élysées or wandering through the arcades. He is strolling around Pigalle, a district famed in the first part of the twentieth century for its bohemianism and artistic modernity. The sonic environment of this area, so associated with advanced artistic production, was saturated with Afro-Cuban music during this period. Senghor thus, consciously or not, links Afro-Cuban music with African modernity by locating the poem in this quartier. This link, however, is fraught with ambivalence. The speaker passes by La Cabane Cubaine but does not go in. Moreover, he misrepresents the type of music that was played there in the 1930s, calling it "jazz." While it is true that there are numerous instances of African musicians and listeners referring to Afro-Cuban music as jazz, especially in the Congo, it is much more unusual for an African resident in Europe to conflate the two musical traditions.[33] Senghor listened to Duke Ellington in Paris and undoubtedly heard other US jazzmen. As an urbane sophisticate, there is little chance that the speaker would have incorrectly identified the music that was wafting out of the club. Senghor's veiling of his experience with Afro-Cuban music demonstrates that he already considered it as lacking in cultural prestige. In his view, it was not a suitable sound track to accompany the Senegalese quest for modernity and potentially could undermine his yearning for full cultural citizenship.

In Senghor's later years this belief grew even stronger, especially after the launching of his political career in the 1940s. As he enjoyed increasing political success, his version of negritude shifted from being primarily a literary movement with political ramifications to a political philosophy with a cultural dimension. Shaped by the exigencies of becoming a state ideology, Senghor's negritude became intertwined with his doctrine of "African socialism." It now had to coexist with cultural nationalism in Senegal and humanism and neocolonialism in France. It also had to compete in West Africa with the conscientism of Ghana's Kwame Nkrumah and the African Stalinism of Guinea's Sékou Touré. Under pressure from these two new political philosophies, Senghor shifted his position and began to propagate *Africanité* instead of blackness. Simultaneously, his negritude evolved from a tool for achieving cultural and political citizenship into an instrument for garnering international cultural prestige, especially important for newly independent African states struggling to become full-fledged members of the international community. Promoting Afro-Cuban music had no place in this new orientation, which relied on African culture to gain global recognition. In fact, in his "state of the arts," in which up to 30 percent of the national budget in the early 1960s went to the Ministry of Culture, Senghor relegated any type of musical expression to the background.[34] Literature and "high art" painting fit much more securely into his cultural program. As new artistic forms for Senegal, they were much easier to control through state patronage and drew much more serious international attention than did African or Cuban music at the time.

In the 1960s Senghor's hostility toward the Cuban Revolution also had an impact on his attitude toward Afro-Cuban music. Although he was an admirer of Hispanic civilization and mandated the teaching of Spanish in Senegalese schools through the university level, Senghor abhorred Fidel Castro.[35] His promotion of *latinité* stopped short of embracing the Cuban Revolution. His antipathy toward Castro had several roots. Senegal's neocolonial ties with France in the period after independence made establishing diplomatic ties with Castro's communist Cuba an impossibility. Furthermore, Castro's alliance with Sékou Touré of neighboring Guinea complicated matters. As previously mentioned, Senghor and Touré were fierce rivals for regional influence, and Senghor resented Cuba's military support of his enemy. Though the Senegalese public's love of Cuban music almost entirely lacked any "revolutionary" political content, Senghor largely prohibited Afro-Cuban music from being performed at the premier Festival Mondial des Arts Nègres (FESMAN) in 1966 on political grounds. Sizable demonstrations occurred in Dakar over Senghor's musical policy, but the president stood firm.

Senghor's public retreat from Afro-Cuban music (which according to his son he continued to listen to privately) meant that the development of Afro-Cuban music in Senegal had to proceed without state sponsorship, in marked contrast to neighboring Guinea and Mali.[36] Whatever interest Senghor had in music during this period he devoted to jazz, which had a significant following in the Western European and North American art and literature worlds.[37] During this same era the prestige of Latin music declined in Western intellectual and artistic circles outside of Africa as well, despite its continuing artistic excellence. With the possible exception of Tito Puente's band in the 1950s, Afro-Cuban music lost whatever cultural cachet it had once had outside the Latin community in Paris and New York.

Observing Afro-Cuban music's diminished status and its potentially controversial association with the Cuban Revolution, Senghor shifted from his previously ambivalent attitude toward the music to a more actively censorious stance once he became head of state. He sought to erase from his personal history his early involvement with Afro-Cuban culture. Where once he was at least willing to write about his bohemian past, with its wild nights at La Cabane Cubaine, he increasingly appeared embarrassed by it. From the postwar period onward, in his essays and poetry, Senghor replaced the few references to Afro-Cuban music with abstract paeans to rhythm and dance and passing nods to jazz. In his autobiographical musings and the reminiscences of his friends and allies during this era, Afro-Cuban music receives scarcely a nod. Senghor's close associate Birago Diop's four-volume autobiography, which documents both their sojourns in Paris, contains few mentions of Afro-Cuban music.[38] A pervasive silence has come to envelop the important role of Afro-Cuban music in Senghor's cultural and political development.

However, many of his countrymen did not share his increasingly negative attitude about the cultural significance of Latin music. For them, Cuban music was far from disreputable. On the contrary, they saw it as integral to the embodiment of modernity that was culturally suitable for their society. Ousmane Socé Diop's *Mirages de Paris*, for example, looks at the relationship between Afro-Cuban music and modernity from a much different vantage point than Senghor's.[39] In Socé Diop's work, Afro-Cuban music awakens the protagonist Fara to the beauty and power of his African roots and alerts him to the cultural richness and significance of the black diaspora. It accompanies him as he courts a white French woman, Jacqueline, and it underlies many of his philosophical reflections. His life in Paris would be unthinkable without it.

Socé Diop was a close associate of Senghor's in Paris and was present at the creation of negritude. He received a scholarship to study veterinary medicine in Paris around the same time that Senghor obtained his scholarship to study literature. They studied together at the Lycée Louis-le-Grand and worked together in forming the Association of West African Students (both were among the original ten members). In 1934 Socé Diop helped Senghor and Césaire publish the short-lived journal *L'Étudiant Noir*. Later in his career, he was a politician and diplomat. In the 1950s he was the publisher of the important Senegalese magazine *Bingo*.

Mirages de Paris appeared in 1937 and is one of the earliest African novels. It is a foundational text in Senegalese literature, exploring issues such as cultural hybridity and the quest for a tropical cosmopolitanism. The book is especially significant for its explicit linkage between nightclubs, Afro-Cuban music, and Senegalese modernity. The text is a mélange of descriptions of the 1931 Colonial Exposition, philosophical discussions between Fara and his African friends, and a recounting of the troubled relationship between him and Jacqueline. It is both an African appreciation of Gustave Flaubert's *L'Éducation sentimentale* and a novel of ideas, establishing a novelistic template that has been used by many other African writers, most strikingly by the Senegalese Cheikh Hamidou Kane in his

L'aventure ambiguë.[40] Socé Diop's plot revolves around the experiences of Fara, a Senegalese who travels to Paris in the early 1930s. He gets a job at the Colonial Exposition and one day meets Jacqueline, a white French woman. They start dating and frequent Afro-Cuban nightclubs. Ultimately, they move in together despite her parents' opposition to the relationship. She becomes pregnant, and problems ensue. A despondent Fara ultimately commits suicide by jumping off a bridge into the Seine.

The novel is perhaps most notable for depicting a typical evening's entertainment at La Cabane Cubaine and for containing one of the first detailed descriptions of modern Afro-Cuban music and dance in any language (over ten pages long). Just as important, it documents the emotional response of a young Senegalese student to hearing the music, providing a unique glimpse into what the music meant for Senegalese in the 1930s. The first thing that Fara and his French girlfriend notice upon entering La Cabane Cubaine is its remarkable (for the time and place) ethnic diversity. There is an orchestra playing Latin dance music, and the dance floor is filled with couples. When the orchestra takes a break, a small Cuban combo takes the stage, performing a son number. A rumba dance display that thrills Fara completes the evening. Later, Fara holds forth on why he prefers Afro-Cuban music to jazz. His discourse establishes a framework for the Senegalese appreciation of Afro-Cuban music that remains relevant to the present day: "Rumba was softer than jazz. The latter has a charm and fascination that was measured in kilowatts. Dizzying contagious, jazz had a direct effect on the nerves like an electric current while rumba echoed with the heart. When jazz is unleashed it evoked planes taking off, the frenetic turning of a transatlantic propeller. Rumba evoked a black girl swinging in her hammock at nightfall, rocked by the plaintive sounds of a guitar."[41]

Fara makes it clear that he considers both jazz and Afro-Cuban music emblematic of modernity. However, for him jazz is cerebral, almost neurological. It is the music of a frenetic industrial society, powered by the most advanced technology. In contrast, Afro-Cuban music fits a developing tropical world: soft, soulful, and evocative but still modern. It appeals to the heart as well as the head and culturally straddles continents. Revealingly, jazz doesn't strike him as particularly "black music," while Afro-Cuban music does. Jazz may be the product of the black diaspora, but Fara implies that it has only limited "pull" outside of Europe and North America. Afro-Cuban music, he thinks, could gain popularity with a potentially much wider public in the black world. The image of a black woman in a hammock resonates in many more African cultures than the metaphor of airplanes taking off. As the subsequent history of Afro-Cuban music in Senegal and Africa demonstrates, Fara's words were prophetic. Outside of South Africa, jazz has been a cult music appreciated by small coteries in Africa's capital cities, while Afro-Cuban music has gone on to be the foundation of many African nations' popular music.[42]

In other respects as well, Socé Diop's novel foretells the future significance of Afro-Cuban music in Senegal. The explanation the book offers for the allure of Afro-Cuban music for Senegalese abroad in the 1930s still holds true for many Senegalese at home today. Socé Diop's protagonist in the 1930s and the salsa musicians in 2003 express their fascination with Afro-Cuban music in much the same terms. For both groups, Afro-Cuban music, the product of méttisage, bridges the diaspora, bringing Africa and the Caribbean closer together culturally.[43] Both groups also share an intense emotional connection to Afro-Cuban music. Perhaps most strikingly, both groups agree that the emphasis on dance and movement inherent in Afro-Cuban music promotes a type of modernity appropriate for Senegal.

A DISTANT MIRROR: LISTENING TO SENEGALESE LISTENING TO AFRO-CUBAN MUSIC

Cuban Music truly belongs to us.

Camou Yandè, sonero and conguero[44]

When asked to describe their relationship with Afro-Cuban music, Senegalese Latin music connoisseurs and musicians respond by declaring that Cuban music is deeply pleasurable, emotionally direct, and aesthetically powerful. It is important both as a source of enjoyment and for what it signifies and symbolizes. Afro-Cuban music for them has been representative of a cosmopolitanism that is rooted in the black internationalism of the diaspora without undermining "local" norms and aspirations. It also has inculcated "correcte" modern social behaviors such as self-control and a ritualized respect for women. As a consequence, in addition to constituting a highly satisfying form of leisure, the music has been a guide to how an urbane *citoyen* should behave in public in a modern African state in terms of etiquette and personal style. This section explores what Senegalese have heard in Cuban music beneath its evocative melodies and compelling rhythms. Though its focus is on musicians, broadcasters, and Latin music connoisseurs, the sentiments expressed are shared by nearly anyone in Senegal who listens and dances to Afro-Cuban music.[45]

For many individuals in preindependence Senegal, listening and dancing to Afro-Cuban music anchored them more securely in the cultural universe of the black Atlantic. When asked why Afro-Cuban music appealed to them, Senegalese repeatedly stressed its diasporic dimension. By linking Senegal with distinguished artistic expression in the Caribbean, the music first served as a bulwark against the racial arrogance of colonial French society. Later, during the Cold War era of the 1960s, when cultural nationalism was rife, the diasporic connection with Afro-Cuban music demonstrated the global reach and prestige of African civilization, especially in the Atlantic tropical world, while circumventing dominance by US popular culture. In Senegal, consumers always have viewed Afro-Cuban music as *black* music, originating in Africa. Balla Sidibè, a leading sonero and timbale player, stated: "Everything that comes from there [Cuba] comes from Africa. It's the slaves. The great Cuban musicians—they're black or *mulattos*."[46]

Djibril Gaby Gaye, a radio and television broadcaster, made much the same point: "Black people are the foundation of Latin American music and we feel that."[47] Mbaye Seck, a guitarist who played with celebrated saxophonist and bandleader Dexter Johnson in the 1960s, like many Senegalese asserted that he finds himself reflected in the music in a diasporic mirror: "Even though it's not sung in any [Senegalese] national language, it's the melody that people like. In my opinion, I find there're African roots in salsa. Africans feel salsa like they feel African music. It interests everybody."[48]

Antoine Dos Reis, a retired journalist and radio personality, further developed this diasporic line of thinking: "This is not a music that came out of nothing. It was transplanted to Cuba, Brazil and other places from its native land. So this music came back to us. When you hear this music, you really feel something, the Africanness. This music is not foreign to us."[49]

Pierre Gomis, a Latin music radio announcer, perhaps put it most succinctly: "In Afro-Cuban music, I find my roots."[50]

For a portion of the Senegalese Afro-Cuban music public, the music has linked Senegal with other tropical societies like Cuba that face somewhat similar challenges of cultural and social development. This group views both Senegal and Cuba as products of cultural méttisage: a mixing of European and African cultural materials. For these listeners, Afro-Cuban music exemplifies a cultural "counterpoint" that illuminates a path to modernity. It enables its Senegalese audience to celebrate African civilization's contributions to world history without lapsing into cultural chauvinism. This group regards cultural "purity" as an illusion. Instead, they believe a "modern" society selectively blends elements from a number of global "traditions." By orienting themselves toward black Atlantic nations such as Cuba (and to a lesser extent Brazil), they have been able to practice their own form of cultural nationalism, simultaneously rooted in the African diaspora and in an expansive cosmopolitanism. Pierre Gomis, for example, declared: "In Afro-Cuban music . . . there's the rhythmic inspiration of Africa, French dancing and the Spanish language. There's nothing that can rival it. You rediscover yourself in this music—whether you're in Havana, New York or here [Dakar]."[51]

Orchestre Baobab's Rudy Gomis said to the researcher Aleysia Whitmore: "We needed something that wasn't our folklore but that was close to our folklore. That's why *cha-cha-chá* came here to Africa. . . . Before you could go to a bar and you danced tango, waltz, pasa doble. It was too white, too *toubab*."[52]

Pascal Dieng, who was a singer with the group Super Cayor for many years and now leads his own ensemble, articulated why the cultural mélange of Afro-Cuban music is so important for many Senegalese: "Afro-Cuban music is a music of blacks and whites. It's a music of *méttisage*. With salsa, there's no apartheid. It's for whites and blacks. Our grandparents who left Africa for slavery in the Americas—they sang in the sugar cane field. They mixed with white people so salsa is a music that mixes and joins white skin and black skin."[53]

For the generation that came of age in the 1950s and 1960s, those who could dance well to Afro-Cuban music gained a reputation for cultural refinement. Dance for this group has been more than just social leisure. Along with expertise in Latin music, it has been a means for achieving social distinction, accumulating social capital, and embodying modernity. For this generation of Senegalese, Afro-Cuban dancing is modernity in motion. The late El Hadj Amadou Ndoye, a professor of Hispanic literature at Université Cheikh Anta Diop in Dakar, recalls: "Dancing and Cuban music go together. . . . Ibrahima Fall—he became Minister of Foreign Affairs—we were students then—he was a great dancer. There was a contest to see who was the best dancer. He was Dean of the Law School, a great intellectual—and he won a bunch of those dance contests. It [Afro-Cuban music] is, in fact, associated with modernity, class, education. It's urban, modern and it goes with what's chic and the latest style."[54]

Many Senegalese of this generation that straddles the colonial and postcolonial eras associate the fluid steps and swaying motion of Afro-Cuban dance styles with a modernity that they have found culturally comfortable. The cabaret singer Aminata Laye remarked: "I started dancing to salsa music. That was the beginning of my loving the music—the rhythm. Whether it's two-step, three step, four step—you feel at ease. There's less noise in the music."[55]

Mas Diallo, a radio announcer of Afro-Cuban music, has had a similar response to the music: "I love salsa and I find it's one of the best musics. For the very simple reason, I choose salsa because it's accessible and flexible (*souple*). As a music, it has no equal."[56]

Senegalese from this generation of the 1950s and 1960s have viewed Afro-Cuban dancing as dignified and respectable as well as modern. Indeed, because it emphasizes proper comportment and courtesy toward women, many see it as having a moral dimension. The guitarist Mbaye Seck observed: "Everyone dances not only because of the rhythms—it's the morals. It's their [Afro-Cuban music] calm morals. They're sensible morals. It's a music of deep feeling and everyone loves it."[57]

Seck's observations about why so many Senegalese have loved Afro-Cuban music points to another reason for its enduring popularity: its role as a catalyst for creating a "community of sentiment" for Senegalese "entering modernity" in the last half of the twentieth century. The anthropologist Arjun Appadurai argued in *Modernity at Large* that mass media have been especially effective in fostering the formation of such communities. Through film, sports, or, in the case of many nations in Africa, music, "a group . . . begins to imagine and feel things together."[58] In Senegal, a shared enthusiasm for Afro-Cuban music has allowed the generation that came into its own after independence to coalesce and create its own cultural identity. The singer and bandleader Pape Fall commented, "when I listen to Cuban music, I feel there is a part of me in that music,"[59] an experience shared by many others in the Senegalese Afro-Cuban music public. The guitarist Baye Sy talked of his engagement with Afro-Cuban music in similar terms: "To love something is a sensation. You listen to something and it touches you and you don't even know why. As soon as I heard this music, right away I loved it."[60]

Nicolas Menheim, a sonero and bandleader, has an equally emotionally charged relationship with Afro-Cuban music: "We identify with this music. It's almost as if it was in the water."[61] Cheikh "Charles" Sow, the late writer and librarian, also pointed to the emotional immediacy of Afro-Cuban music and its ability to create "communities of sentiment": "It's something that people sense right away. People feel it spontaneously regardless of the fact that it comes from far away. It's not the same thing with jazz. People love it but it's, let's say, something intellectual or for people who have lived a long time in France. It's not a music that is as instantly appreciated . . . I don't even understand why people love it so much. Old people love Cuban music and so do young people."[62]

Sow's statement demonstrates that for the Senegalese of his generation (those who reached adulthood in the 1950s), involvement with Afro-Cuban music was not primarily cerebral. It was not just an exercise in salon cultural politics or an intellectual gesture. Instead, it entailed a profound emotional and, through dance, physical connection with the Hispanic cultures of the African diaspora, the méttisage/*mestizaje* of the Caribbean and a modernity as much based in the Atlantic tropical world as in the cooler climate of Western Europe. It engendered a community of sentiment based on lived experience that has lasted for three generations and shows few signs of disintegrating.

Communities of sentiment, though, as Appadurai has observed "are capable of moving from shared imagination to collective action."[63] This potential capacity is in part responsible for this group of music lovers' often tense and complex relationship with the Senegalese state, even though the music has never been associated in Senegal with a political position. When Senghor became head of state, negritude became the semiofficial cultural policy of Senegal until the 1980s, a period coinciding with government neglect of Afro-Cuban music. Those in power during this era regarded the Afro-Cuban music community as being potentially at odds with negritude. By depriving it of state patronage and recognition, the Senegalese government inhibited the community of Afro-Cuban listeners from developing their aesthetic preferences into a political ideology.

This official disregard did little to quiet debates about what type of modernity was best suited for Senegalese society. In new contexts with new participants, discussions continued, informed by Senghor and Socé Diop's differing models of negritude. Afro-Cuban music lay at the core of both these models; conspicuous in one case for its absence and in the other for its animating presence. In the 1950s Senegalese urban youth took up as their generation's *bandera* both Afro-Cuban music and a form of negritude closer to Socé Diop's version. This mixture made Senghor uncomfortable, but he was powerless to prevent it. For him, the path to full cultural citizenship, both domestically and internationally, involved securing an esteemed position in the global "republic of letters," requiring that he mask his interest in Afro-Cuban music. In the 1950s and 1960s, however, for many youthful Senegalese the struggle for full cultural citizenship entailed engaging in new patterns of consumption and mastering new forms of sociability. For this generation, Afro-Cuban music continues to embody modern sociability in a unique and powerful way.

THREE

Son and Sociality

Afro-Cuban Music, Gender, and Cultural Citizenship, 1950s–1960s

Where there is consumption there is pleasure,
and where there is pleasure there is agency.
Arjun Appadurai[1]

Mbelekete was a well-known figure in the Kinshasa (Léopoldville) of the early 1950s, despite his lack of any particular trade or talent. He stopped traffic with his acrobatic stunts on his unicycle. He delighted in cycling into areas where Congolese normally were unwelcome by the Belgian colonial state and was famous for circling around stalled traffic at busy Kinshasa intersections. Occasionally Mbelekete would take it upon himself to direct traffic, much to the amazement of his fellow Kinois. Mbelekete became a fashion leader and tastemaker in Kinshasa before his premature death in the mid-1960s as a result of a traffic accident. His attendance at a club where a band was playing always ensured a full house. Indeed, his freewheeling attitude toward colonial authority influenced such youths as the famous musician Luambo "Franco" Makiadi. Fifty years after his death, Congolese from his generation still celebrate Mbelekete as the "No. 1 Kinois," an avatar of modernity and an author of the Kinois urban style that has so attracted international attention.[2]

Mbelekete's antics, using modern products like bicycles in a culturally transgressive manner, were not unique in postcolonial Africa. This chapter looks at how in Senegal urban youth similarly rehearsed "modern" identities by purchasing newly accessible goods like radios, sunglasses, and Western clothes and listening to and dancing to recorded music. These young Senegalese were less socially disruptive than their counterparts elsewhere in Africa, such as the "Buffalo Bills" of Kinshasa or the "cowboys" of Enugu, Nigeria. However, they were just as culturally significant. Starting in the 1950s, young men in Dakar and other communities congregated in courtyards or small sitting rooms to drink tea and listen to Afro-Cuban music on portable phonographs.

These casual gatherings rapidly crystallized into clubs with distinctive identifying names, large collections of Afro-Cuban music, and lengthy meetings. As the clubs grew, they staged elaborate parties. Clubs initially vied with one another over who had the most current Cuban discs. Over time, though, competition increasingly revolved around perceived expertise and the ability to project a distinguished mien. What started out as the pursuit of sociality evolved into new ways of being in the world that departed from both the dominant local and colonial French models.

These informal associations of urban youth, like their counterparts in Nigeria, Angola, and Tanzania, constituted innovative ways of defining masculinity in Africa, "fueling the imagination of nation" in a rising generation.[3] As was the case elsewhere in Africa, Senegalese record clubs grew out of the coming together of new gender constructions, patterns of consumption, and imagining of communities. However, while young Dakarois men longed for the same prestige goods and were preoccupied with the same issues of cultural "sovereignty" as their counterparts elsewhere in Africa, their reformulation of manhood revolved around different axes. Reflecting local cultural practice, their modern masculinity emphasized sociality over aggression and cosmopolitanism over ethnic or regional particularism. As a consequence, in place of public displays of male power typical of Enugu and Kinshasa, Dakarois engaged in semisecluded enactments of elegance and sophistication. Rather than carve out alternative zones of male refuge and withdrawal like the *musseque* clubs in colonial Luanda, Dakar's young men created arenas where they prepared for future societal leadership roles, enlarging social networks through demonstrating the latest Latin dance moves.

The Senegalese clubs were especially significant in how they pioneered modern social behaviors for men. Members at all times had to be *correcte*. In Senegalese terms, this word has multiple meanings and dimensions. It refers to neat and fashionable clothes, a punctilious concern with etiquette, flawless self-discipline, and a general air of refinement. Together, these qualities denote an individual with an unblemished moral reputation, as internally clean as he is externally elegant. Whether consciously or not, club members were using Afro-Cuban music to fuse elements of "traditional" Wolof/Serer/Tukolor cultures with French bourgeois mores to devise a new standard of behavior for a modern Senegal.

The clubs themselves were a bricolage of French, Cuban, and Senegalese social institutions. The club members overtly appropriated the French salon and soirée, for example. They were not the first Senegalese to do this.[4] However, by holding salons and soirées far removed from the elite precincts, democratizing them, and adding Spanish to French as the languages of "high" culture, they were departing from tradition. From Cuba, the young Dakarois borrowed the idea of the rumba session in which music and dance enhanced solidarity and congealed new identities. From their own cultures, the Afro-Cuban club members recontextualized age grades and initiation ceremonies and in a altered form made them relevant to urban life. By linking expressive culture with modernity and generational differentiation, they provided fresh frameworks for thinking and feeling. These linkages created modern ways of associating with one another and their community that the club members felt were congruent with a progressive society.

CONSUMPTION, SOCIALITY, AND CULTURAL CITIZENSHIP

The record clubs thus served as workshops where Senegalese youth of the late colonial era could experiment with new forms of sociality that drew on local, Caribbean, and French traditions. For these youths, this new form of sociality with its transnational basis and its emphasis on tolerance and refinement provided a pathway to modernity that bypassed the usual colonial circuits. Consumption was central to this new notion of sociality. The young Senegalese in the Afro-Cuban music clubs consumed goods like phonographs and records to encode popular experience into self-consciously "modern" cultural forms. For them, "consumption was good for thinking," for conceptualizing and enacting a form of cultural citizenship that would enable them to be modern and African in a postcolonial world.[5]

Ever since Karl Marx made commodity fetishism a centerpiece in his analysis of how capitalism shapes culture, researchers have studied how the consumption of commodities by individuals and groups transforms consciousness and alters social relations. In African and Latin American studies, researchers have often connected consumption with the global expansion and penetration of a Western-dominated capitalism.[6] In this line of analysis, Africans or Latin Americans become modern through their acquisition of European industrial products. Their modernity stems both from their newly conceived desire for these goods and the ways purchased items such as bicycles, furniture, and clothes change their daily lives, their self-perception, and their worldview.

Consumption can play a vital role in the creation of identities independent of the cultural meanings originally attached to specific goods. Soap, for example, may have one meaning for the European or South African producers and quite another for Zimbabwean consumers. For the manufacturers, their merchandise is a device for becoming "clean but for the Zimbabweans, the toiletries were a tool for defining and refining personhood."[7]

In the Argentine sociologist Néstor García Canclini's work, consumption can be a means for claiming "rights to difference," enabling a group to gain recognition "as subjects with 'valid interests, relevant values and legitimate claims.'" By consuming, we can "distinguish ourselves . . . and [find] ways to combine pragmatism with pleasure."[8] Canclini maintains that consumption can have political ramifications, whether intended or not. Clusters of individuals, by preferring one commodity to another, can be both part of a society and distinct from it. How and what they consume establishes their "cultural citizenship" and has an impact on their status. For Senegalese youth growing up in 1950s and 1960s Dakar, the idea of cultural citizenship galvanized their generation. Straddling the colonial/postcolonial divide, they asserted themselves culturally and politically as a generation that was both African and modern.[9]

A new form of sociality provided the foundation for the cultural citizenship they were advocating. The concept of sociality has a long history in Western thought. Definitions abound, from Lord Shaftsbury to Georg Simmel. The definition that best typifies the Senegalese situation comes from the anthropologist Richard Fardon's work on Western Cameroon. Fardon explains that sociality (or as he prefers, "sociability") "is the behaviors and attitudes anticipated in different relationships . . . a framework of knowledge and organization of feeling about the way people impinge upon one another."[10] Fardon makes the important point that "since sociability identifies and models personal relations, it is related both to the conceptual and moral ordering of societies."[11]

By linking the emotional textures and rhythms of daily life to the organization of societies and states on a wider scale, Fardon's model of sociability illuminates the cultural significance of Dakar's Latin record clubs. The sociality that typified the clubs reflected the complex realities of postwar African Dakar. New French colonial policies and internal economic changes within Senegal itself reshaped the city's social landscape. There was an expansion of Western educational opportunities and an increased rate of migration from the rural hinterland into the capital city. These developments necessitated new "frameworks of knowledge and feeling" for young Dakarois. At the very moment when the colonial authorities were slowly easing their access to *evolué* status, the influx of new inhabitants from the interior who were relatively unexposed to classic French culture transformed their city. Some of the new arrivals regarded the clubs as insufficiently Islamic because of their overt secularity and kept their distance. However, many of the migrants, especially those who were students in colonial schools, joined and were welcomed. Indeed, many children of migrants established their own record clubs. The sociality of the Latin record clubs enabled their members to simultaneously embrace the culture of the wider Atlantic world represented by their European education while affirming their Africanité in solidarity with their newly urban Senegalese neighbors.

This sociality also furthered the growth of a Senegalese civic society embedded in local practice but reflecting French republican ideals. In the English-speaking world the state and civic society are separate. Civic society provides a space for individual liberty, and the state legally guarantees that freedom.[12] In French republicanism, by contrast, the state is an *extension* of civil society. What happens in civic society shapes the state and is of great significance. In this model, civic society emerges out of citizen participation in many different realms, the cultural and social as well as the political. Indeed, "sociability and citizenship [presuppose] each other."[13] Citizenship doesn't just entail involvement with political institutions. The *correcte* attitudes and behaviors arising out of intensive participation in the public sphere are also essential in defining citizenship. In fact, in the Francophone tradition, cultural citizenship lies at the heart of the republican project.

From this perspective, the Senegalese record clubs as voluntary cultural and social associations had an implicit political dimension. The behaviors and *mentalités* the clubs fostered were similar to the republican virtues of being immersed in public life and bringing an informed, critical perspective to significant issues facing society. By creating the record clubs, the young Senegalese Latin music enthusiasts were establishing new patterns of consumption and new models of sociality. In so doing, they were rehearsing citizenship in a free African polity, organized around republican principles. However, in order for these changes to occur, Dakar in the 1940s and 1950s had to develop the physical, economic, and social infrastructures that could sustain cultural enterprises like the record clubs.

URBAN GROWTH AND CULTURAL CHANGE IN POSTWAR DAKAR, 1940S–1960S

Dakar, like many other urban areas in sub-Saharan Africa, experienced rapid growth from the 1940s to the 1960s. According to some estimates, between 1945 and 1960 the city doubled its population. Already by 1950, approximately one out of every ten Senegalese lived in Dakar.[14] Such growth led to improvements in the city's infrastructure and altered its urban identity. Dakar developed into one of the major cities south of the Sahara and the de facto cultural capital of Francophone Africa. The city became one of the major transportation centers of Africa in the 1950s, the focal point of far-flung sea, rail, and air networks. Although other African metropolises like Lagos and Kinshasa surpassed it as a business and industrial hub, Dakar's markets and shops were filled with consumer goods of all types, sold at a price an increasing number of African customers could afford. It was indisputably the educational capital of Francophone Africa. Its population was sophisticated and multiethnic. In 1945, 43 percent of the city's African population was Wolof; 13 percent was Tukolor; and the remaining 44 percent consisted of sizable communities of Pulaar, Serer, Cabo Verdeans, Hassaniya-speakers, and Bamana. It is likely that the city's ethnic composition preserved this diversity ten years later.[15] In addition, there were thirty-eight thousand French residents and a large concentration of Lebanese and Syrians. With its large expatriate population and its sizable communities of migrants from many parts of West Africa, Dakar had become one of the continent's most cosmopolitan and culturally complex cities.

From the time the Free French under Charles de Gaulle wrested control of Dakar from the Vichy regime in 1943, Dakar's economy began to revive from the doldrums of the Depression and the early years of World War II. The Free French, knowing that the city had one of the best natural harbors in Africa, undertook improvements of the port's infrastructure. Simultaneously the Dakar airport, established in 1937, became a major refueling stop for air traffic to Africa and the Allies stationed large numbers of French and US troops in the city. The soldiers freely spent money, stimulating local commerce; but even more important, the colonial authorities strengthened the manufacturing capacity of Dakar by creating import-substitute industries.[16] By 1945 Dakar had become "a naval and air base of global importance"[17] and a crucial center of trade and manufacturing.

After the war Dakar developed even more rapidly. Always wary of the British, de Gaulle became concerned in 1945 that the British-controlled city of Accra in the then Gold Coast (contemporary Ghana) was overshadowing Dakar as the leading port in West Africa. To counteract this perceived threat, the French leader resolved to make the city into an imperial showcase through enlightened urban planning and an extensive public works program. De Gaulle's plans entailed dividing Dakar into spatially distinct zones with areas reserved for administration, industry, commerce, and residential housing. His planners envisioned six residential sectors, accommodating various populations including a growing African presence. As is often the case with urban master plans, this ambitious undertaking never received a big enough budget to realize all its objectives. However, the French did spend enough money to make the port one of the leading cities in Africa, and the spatial model they imposed still shapes contemporary Dakar.

Other changes in French colonial policy promoted Dakar's growth as well. In 1946 France established FIDES (Fonds d'Investissement pour le Développement Économique et Social), supposedly to develop their African colonies rather than exploit them.[18] Between 1946 and 1956, 64 percent of FIDES' budget went to infrastructural improvements in France's African colonies, especially transportation.[19] These improvements made the movement of goods to and from Africa more efficient, reducing costs and encouraging investment. The French also worked to improve urban housing for Africans, although their efforts fell far short of meeting local demand. At the end of World War II they founded SICAP (Société Immobilière du Cap Vert) to provide housing for both Dakar's growing middle class and its large working-class population. In its first year of operation, it built 150 houses and 4 *cités ouvrières*.[20]

During this same postwar period, French business interests found Dakar and Senegal increasingly attractive areas for investment. French capital came in two waves. Between 1946 and 1949 francs flowed into Dakar from France because investors in the metropole feared a communist takeover of the French government. Two years later, in 1951, as the French commercially disengaged themselves from Indochina, there was another significant flow of capital into Senegal, which the French business class regarded as more politically stable. Initially, French investment in Dakar provided funds for the enlargement of already existing manufacturing concerns and the establishment of new ones, a change in strategy from the 1930s, when the French had been more likely to invest in trade in agricultural commodities. By the mid-1950s French merchants and bankers were especially drawn to projects that made more consumer goods like radios, phonographs, textiles, and soft drinks available to Africans at lower prices. While Dakar never became an industrial powerhouse like Abidjan in

Côte d'Ivoire, its industrial zones in the late colonial period were bustling with a number of beverage and textile concerns.[21] It is not clear how many new wage jobs were added in the immediate postwar period, but given that gainful employment has always been scarce in Senegambia, the creation of these manufacturing jobs had a marked impact on Dakar's hinterland and beyond. Hopeful job seekers from all regions of Senegal flocked to the city in search of work in the 1940s, forming a multiethnic labor force.[22] The fact that most of these migrants were disappointed did not reverse the flow. Even if they were frustrated in their search for work, the migrants felt that ultimately there were more opportunities for them in Dakar than elsewhere in Senegal.

Many migrants dreamed of their children attending a colonial school. They were aware that in addition to its emphasis on economic development, French policy in Africa during the postwar period also sought to expand "Western" educational opportunities for Africans. The effect of this policy change was dramatic. In 1937 enrollment in Senegalese schools was only fifty thousand, a figure that included students from other parts of French West Africa.[23] By 1960, 28.8 percent of the school-aged population in Senegal was receiving a French colonial education.[24] In French West Africa "expenditure on education rose from 3% of the total budget in 1935 to 4% in 1947, and to 13% of a much expanded budget in 1957."[25] As a result of this increased expenditure on education, it became possible for more Africans to receive a postprimary education in the 1950s, although educational opportunities still remained restricted. During this period the French built a number of new lycées in Dakar, and in 1950 they opened the Institut des Hautes Études de Dakar, which offered a postsecondary degree. In 1957 the University of Dakar opened with 575 students from throughout French West Africa. Affiliated with the universities of Paris and Bordeaux, it was established as the eighteenth French public university. With its renowned lycées and postsecondary institutions, Dakar became a magnet for ambitious Senegalese youth.

The Dakar these students inhabited was a much different place from the provincial town it had been in the 1930s. Dakar's social and economic transformation into one of Africa's most culturally dynamic cities created a fertile climate for the formation of Latin music clubs and the emergence of a student subculture linked to sociability and consumption. However, it took the introduction and dissemination of new media technologies like the portable phonograph to fully stimulate the imagining of a new type of cultural citizenship for Senegal.

SOUND MADE TANGIBLE: PHONOGRAPHS AND THE COMMODITIZATION OF MUSIC

It is likely that French administrators and merchants brought the first phonographs to Senegal at the turn of the twentieth century for their personal use. During World War I improvements in sound reproduction made phonographs increasingly portable. As a result, by the 1920s phonographs were relatively common in the European quartiers of Dakar and St.-Louis, providing music for dance parties and individual entertainment. By the 1930s in major urban centers, a few prosperous Senegalese began to acquire them as well.[26] Accompanying the phonographs was an ever-increasing number of records, bringing the music of the French music hall, the US jazz club, and the Cuban cabaret to Senegalese clubs and domestic residences for the first time.

With records, music from around the world became tangible to the Senegalese, something they could hold and touch. It became a commodity that individuals bought, sold, and consumed. It began to circulate like other goods. Music furthermore became portable, transportable, and repeatable.[27] Different parts of the world like Senegal and Cuba now could hear each other's music. Music started to become despatialized and displaced for the Senegalese.[28] Individuals could carry records from place to place and play them anytime they wished, whether any musicians were present or not. No longer was it necessary to fully understand the original contexts and nuances of a piece of music. Audiences were free to fashion their own meanings and understandings. Simultaneously, music also became more private. Listeners could fashion their own subjective response to a genre of music isolated from their community, a radical departure for Africa.[29] Music as a consequence became a tool for either constructing a private aesthetic realm or transforming a public sphere, depending on individual or group behavior. All these characteristics of records had implications for how the Senegalese listened to music.

Initially in the 1920s, only Senegalese who occupied positions of privilege within colonial society gained exposure to this new media technology. Before long, however, other urban groups gained access to recorded music, even if that entailed standing outside an open window while a record was playing. By the 1930s there was a huge market for records in Africa.[30] The music historian John Collins states that the major record companies sold eight million records in West Africa alone between 1930 and 1933.[31] The flood of records into Senegal introduced new divisions into Senegalese music. For the growing Senegalese listening public, indigenous music now became "local" in comparison to the recorded "global" sounds flooding into the country. Increasingly, lack of access to "modern" communication technology made the music "local." Being unrecorded, its listenership was severely constrained and its status diminished, at least in the urban areas.

Another repercussion of the advent of "foreign" records into Senegal is that the music listening experience of the Senegalese became segmented in an unprecedented fashion. Previously, an audience hearing Senegalese music would have a shared understanding of the music, having grown up in the same culture. However, when records from France and Cuba became available, what people heard was influenced by their position in society and the intensity of their exposure to French culture. During the 1940s and 1950s, for the cosmopolitan members of the intelligentsia Cuban music was the epitome of modern verve and sophistication; for the urban artisans the music was slightly disreputable "youth" music, heralding changing social mores and roles. For Dakar's army of students, the music was simultaneously both. This audience segmentation was to last until the coming of transistor radios created a more unified national listening public in the 1960s.

Despite the sensation that Afro-Cuban records created in Senegal from the 1930s onward, their availability in the 1950s and 1960s was limited and their price remained high. Phonographs also were costly in prewar Senegal, and the French business interests concentrated on importing other items to sell. Pathé-Marconi had a monopoly on Francophone Africa on the distribution of all records and phonographs.[32] For reasons that are not clear, the company was much less aggressive in penetrating this market than its EMI counterparts in Anglophone Africa. Eventually the scarcity of recorded Cuban music, combined with its unwavering popularity among Senegalese listeners, created a situation in which the records became "prestige" goods that could easily be converted into social capital. However, while Afro-Cuban records remained rare, the machines necessary to play them became much more common after 1945. The development of a new generation of portable phonographs, smaller and less expensive than their predecessors, meant that more Senegalese could afford them than ever before, especially since French trading houses began to import consumer goods in greater quantities in the 1950s.[33] This discrepancy between the increasing availability of phonographs and the difficulty in obtaining the latest Afro-Cuban records set the stage for the emergence of Latin music clubs.

INDEPENDENCE CHA-CHA-CHÁ: THE RISE OF THE AFRO-CUBAN RECORD CLUBS

Dakar in the 1950s was a city full of young people. By 1950, for the first time in its history, birth, not migration, was the major factor in its demographic growth.[34] Unprecedented numbers of these youths, both male and female, were enrolled in French colonial schools. Given this dense concentration of students, it is not surprising that soon a student subculture, drawing on both indigenous and French elements, coalesced. This student subculture encouraged hard work and achievement, but it also led Senegalese youth to explore new forms of leisure like soccer and dancing to recorded music from abroad, and new forms of consumption like purchasing fashionable French and Italian clothes. The Afro-Cuban record clubs provided an institutional framework to experiment with these new patterns of leisure time activity and consumption, enlarging and stabilizing social networks.

At their inception in the late 1940s and early 1950s, the Afro-Cuban music clubs were specifically tied to micro-neighborhoods but not specific language communities. Their membership was largely comprised of the children of first-generation immigrants to Dakar, who felt shut out of the more established social institutions of the commune, plus a few individuals from more established Dakarois and St.-Louisien families. The clubs were a means of sharing enthusiasm and increasing knowledge through the pooling of members' nascent Cuban record collections. Meetings initially were informal and private. Some ten to fifteen young men of roughly the same age gathered on a verandah or in a courtyard to listen to and analyze Afro-Cuban music in a modern adaptation of age group socializing. While one member brewed *attaya*, Senegalese-style tea, another assumed the role of master of ceremonies. They drank glasses of sweet tea and evaluated new recordings. Members memorized the Spanish lyrics of their favorite songs and sang along with the records. The meetings were exercises in multilingualism, as the guests communicated with one another in Wolof, French, and Spanish, although at this point in Senegalese history few had expert knowledge of the third language. Politics were rarely, if ever, discussed, preserving what the members regarded as the purely social function of the club. After several hours of listening, singing, and aesthetic debate, the students would plan their next gathering and return to their studying.

By the mid- to late 1950s, Dakarois and St.-Louisien youth had considerably expanded the scope of the Afro-Cuban record clubs. The intensified appeal of Afro-Cuban music in Senegal, combined with an increased supply of Afro-Cuban records, resulted in more clubs with larger memberships. One factor promoting the clubs' growth was the worldwide popularity of the cha-cha-chá, played by such Cuban orchestras as Enrique Jorrín's (the originator) and Orquesta Aragón. In addition, Dakar now had at least half a dozen record stores run by French and Lebanese merchants. With a steady if still small supply of Latin records to expand their music libraries, the clubs could widen their range of activities for their enlarged membership. One way of doing so was by staging Cuban record parties.

Starting out as small, impromptu affairs, these occasions evolved into highly ritualized events with exacting protocol that had to be followed to the letter. Clubs competed with each other in a good-natured way over having the most young women, the best Afro-Cuban music, the most skilled dancers, and the most exclusive guest lists. The organizers issued handwritten invitations in French. They enforced a dress code and turned away any prospective guest who was improperly attired. The parties included both genders, and the members treated the women guests with exaggerated courtesy. The soirée organizers provided light refreshments but rarely alcohol. Couples danced to Afro-Cuban music played on small portable phonographs. Some men without partners danced alone, sometimes in front of a mirror.[35] The parties could become animated. In a recent novel by the Senegalese writer Boris Diop, the character Nguirane Faye recalls one such gathering from his youth: "We were playing lots of Cuban music at our parties in Le Plateau. These parties were hot and the alcohol was flowing. I can still see us shaking our bodies in complete chaos in a burning hot, dusty warehouse. Imagine dozens of girls and boys with bodies shivering as if taken by complete madness, and shouting even louder than the tumbas [sic] and the maracas."[36]

The film *Ça twiste à Poponguine* (1993) documents the activities of these clubs and some of the roles they played in their communities.[37] Though the movie takes place in 1964 in a small fishing village near Dakar, Sene Absa's depiction of the clubs could easily have been set in several Senegalese cities in the 1950s. The movie tells the story of two music clubs: the Inseparables, who champion *yéyé* French singers like Sylvie Vartan, and the Kings, who favor US rhythm and blues musicians like James Brown (interestingly, there is no Latin music in the film).[38] One of the two groups, which recruits its members from young people who work in the fishing industry, has a portable record player, while the other, which consists of students, has access to girls to invite to parties. The two groups vie for social supremacy in their village without either permanently gaining the upper hand. Eventually, after their competition becomes too heated and threatens the social cohesion of their community, they unite in staging a concert and party that features a visiting French pop singer. Though overly sentimental, the film convincingly argues that the clubs allowed their members to dream of modernity and experiment with behaviors that enabled them to be simultaneously African and cosmopolitan.

The Kings and the Inseparables in Sene Absa's film were loosely organized, typical of clubs in rural Senegal. However, record associations in major cities like Dakar frequently evolved into much more complex institutions, with members specializing in specific roles. Some club members, like Mbacké Fall "Aragon," won fame in their quartiers for their skill in dancing to Cuban music.[39] Others were celebrated for their debonair fashion sense. The more dynamic clubs had entrepreneurs like Ibrahima Sylla who used their ability to track down the scarcest and newest Cuban 78s and LPs to assemble legendary Latin music collections.[40] Still other club participants, like Garang Coulibaly and El Hadj Amadou Ndoye, gained respect for their knowledge and understanding of Cuban culture and helped hone the musical taste of their fellow members.[41] The aim of the young Senegalese in developing these areas of expertise was enjoyment and enhanced personal standing in their neighborhoods. However, whatever their original intent, their activities ultimately had wide-reaching social and cultural ramifications. In their patterns of consumption, their experimentation with new forms of sociality, and their diasporic musical sensibility, they pioneered an embodied modernity that transformed the mentalité of first, their generation, and later, their nation.

While the record clubs carved out space to listen to Afro-Cuban music, they also established semisecluded spaces where men and women could dance together. This emphasis on couples dancing by young unmarried individuals constituted a significant cultural shift in gender relations for Senegal. Before sustained European contact, dancing in Senegalese cultures usually was a public expression of community solidarity and cultural identity and often was done in a ritual context.[42] As a rule, it involved strict separation of men and women and almost always was done in large groups.[43] Though it sometimes promoted marriage between young people, "traditional" dancing generally lacked a romantic dimension. The Cuban dancing in the record clubs, by contrast, was secular. It defied gender segregation and was unattached to any ethnic identity. Although precolonial societies valued individualized dancing prowess, the record clubs' focus on dancers' *personal* style and skill represented a radical departure from prior practice. Their emphasis on creating a private milieu in which young men and women could mingle, talk, flirt, and dance without adult (or colonial) supervision was even more of a rupture with the past. Through these social innovations, the clubs helped strengthen a link in Senegal between Afro-Cuban music and modernity.

A crucial part of the clubs' mission was pedagogical. As part of their project promoting Cuban music as a pathway to modernity in Senegal, they aspired to show a generation how to dance "Cuban" in a culturally authentic way and convince them that this dancing was superior to other dances imported from abroad, such as the fox trot and the tango. As in Ghana, young people learned about European and Caribbean dances through newspapers and imported books. Dance academies even existed for those who could afford them.[44] Films also provided visual templates for how to dance in the Cuban style, and magazines were still another source of instruction. *Bing*, for example, which was based in Dakar, published visual diagrams of the steps for a cha-cha-chá or a rhumba. However, family and friends were most often the dance "professors." In her autobiography of growing up in 1940s and 1950s Dakar, *A Dakar Childhood*, Nafissatou Diallo (1941–1982) writes of her brothers guiding her into the world of foreign dance, though she couldn't figure out where *they* had gained their expertise.[45] Diallo is vague about what steps she learned. She mentions that she learned the bolero, a slow dance done to romantic ballads in Cuba, and later mentions that she could dance to *gumbe* music.[46] Interestingly, her brothers stressed fancy footwork, playing down exaggerated hip movements, probably in the cause of decorum. Diallo's relatively privileged background made it easy for her to obtain the knowledge she sought. However, few Dakarois or St.-Louisiens had the opportunities open to Diallo. For many of these young Senegalese, the Afro-Cuban record clubs filled an important void in their *éducation sentimentale* by initiating them into foreign dance. For them, the renowned dancers of the record clubs were masters of an embodied modernity.

The leading club dancers often were also fashion leaders. Dakar in the 1950s and early 1960s resembled other parts of Africa like the Congo or Zambia, where modish young men imported materials or concepts from abroad in pursuit of pleasure, prestige, and modernity. In Zambia during the 1950s, for example, young men banded together in teams of around twenty to dance the *kalela*.[47] Dressed in pressed trousers, singlets (undershirts), and highly polished shoes, the groups danced in public in a circular pattern, accompanied by loud drumming. Most of the dancers were individuals with little prospect for advancement in racially stratified colonial Zambia. Indeed, the participants in the kalela movement, according to the anthropologist J. Clyde Mitchell, used dance and clothes to construct ethnic identities and fantasize about achieving an elite status that was out of their reach.

In Kinshasa in the 1980s, the *sapeur* movement emerged at the nexus of popular music and fashion. The sapeurs were young Congolese dandies dedicated to purchasing and wearing European designer clothes, despite their modest incomes.[48] They particularly associated themselves with Congolese musicians like Papa Wemba and Koffi Olomide and attended their concerts attired in the latest European fashion. The sapeurs were subtly rebelling against the *authenticité* policies and political dominance by northern Congolese during the Mobutu regime and were fixated on foreign designer labels.[49] Whether fairly or not, many in the Congo saw the sapeurs as marginal youths with a propensity to engage in petty crime to finance their fashion forays.

The Senegalese record club members had a different agenda than their counterparts in Zambia and the Congo. They worked against reifying ethnic self-definition and were training for an elite status that they saw as soon being within their reach. Neither obsession with foreign designers nor opposition to a government-defined policy of authenticité figured in their activities. They did not perceive themselves as marginal, nor did their society regard them as so, and they rarely, if ever, engaged in illegal activities. They lived in a period when social mobility was a possibility, and many were eager to grab any opportunities that came their way.

In Dakar young men associated "proper" dress with refined conduct, modernity, and consumerism, all behaviors and qualities they equated with Afro-Cuban music. Though limited in their finances, club members still were able to project an ambience of elegance and distinction in their embrace of "sartorial modernity."[50] In the 1950s young Senegalese favored slimly cut French and Italian clothes or local imitations, often by tailors trained in Paris.[51] The frilly and flamboyant costumes of many Cuban and Puerto Rican performers of the period such as the Conjunto Casino had little appeal for club members, who regarded the musicians' uniforms more as costumes than as stylish outfits. In the early 1960s British "mod" fashion became influential, in part as a result of the rise of the Beatles, who were popular in West Africa.[52] Women guests, in contrast, dressed in European clothes less frequently. More typical attire was chic but modest "African dress" and elaborate hairstyles. The different approaches to proper dress for men and women show that the clubs, despite their new ideas about social life, still projected a pronounced gendered conception of modernity.

The individual who assembled a club's library of Afro-Cuban records was one of its most important members. To a great extent, a club's prestige rested on the size and depth of its Cuban music collection. Those who were able to expand their collections became highly respected figures among their peers. Club members believed that having a large number of Afro-Cuban records ensured a stream of attractive women as dance partners at their soirées. As the late Senegalese show business impresario Ibrahima Sylla recollected: "The one who had the biggest trunk was the one the ladies looked up to, the cat that got the cream! We used to love showing off all our new musical discoveries! We organized a whip round, each of us contributing 500CFA francs, and we made up trunks of vinyl that were to set people's dancing feet alight. . . . We were always trying to out-do each other, every man seeking to preserve the exclusivity of a rare treasure by removing the labels from the records."[53]

A "big trunk of vinyl" also attested to the strength and international reach of a record collector's social networks and his resourcefulness. Senegal's record shops carried a varied stock during this period (French cabaret and popular music; US rock and roll, rhythm and blues, and jazz; and Egyptian and Lebanese music) to appeal to as wide a customer base as possible: African, European, and Arab. Given that the shops were small, the selection of Cuban music was limited in range and quantity. When new Cuban music discs arrived in the 1950s and early 1960s, the supply rarely met the demand. In a matter of days, sometimes hours, a new release would sell out. This meant that in order to have a celebrated collection, the record clubs' music procurers had to have sources for Cuban music records beyond the record shops. A successful record "maestro" like Sylla worked at developing ties with sailors, broadcasters, and family and friends who traveled abroad—anyone who could obtain for him the most current Cuban records.[54]

The French cultural theorist Jacques Attali has associated this behavior of stockpiling music with groups that feel socially and culturally disenfranchised; this certainly was the case with Senegalese youth in the late colonial period: "Music . . . becomes a strategic consumption, an essential mode of sociality for those who feel themselves powerless before the monologue of the great institutions."[55] Consuming and listening to Afro-Cuban music became a subtle act of cultural resistance for a Senegalese generation that had to proceed through a harsh and culturally patronizing French educational system to advance socially and economically. The record club members and their French schoolmasters both listened to Cuban music but understood it differently. For the French, the music represented tropical exotica. For their Senegalese students, Afro-Cuban music enabled a record club member to establish "a mental realm over which I hold sway, a thing whose meaning is governed by myself alone. It is all my own."[56] As a consequence, the music was an aural sign of liberation and a source of new behaviors that could provide a social foundation for a postindependence Senegal.

The record collections themselves show how "consumption is good for thinking."[57] The musicologist Martin Stokes has observed that record collections can give "shape to the sheer profusion of identities and selves."[58] The young Senegalese Latin music libraries drew a portrait of their cultural and social aspirations, "giving shape" to their identities as Africans and cosmopolitans, embracing modernity and alterity on their own terms. Stokes also has argued that record collections constitute "a means of transcending the limitations of our own place in the world . . . constructing trajectories rather than boundaries across space."[59] Purchasing Latin records allowed the young Senegalese to "articulate a number of idiosyncratic sets of places"—Dakar, Havana, San Juan, New York—that bypassed the political and conceptual boundaries of the French colonial world, tracing an African/Caribbean trajectory that mirrored negritude without duplicating it.[60] Though the impulse to collect Cuban records may have arisen from a sense of powerlessness in the face of French imperial institutions, ultimately the young Senegaleses' consumption of recorded Cuban music enabled them to claim "rights to difference" from both an older generation in Senegal and the French and to gain recognition "as subjects with 'valid interests, relevant values and legitimate claims.'"[61]

The connoisseurs, the fourth type of specialists in the record clubs, were instrumental in this quest for recognition. Nearly always these connoisseurs were outstanding students who clearly were going to be intellectual leaders of their generation. Many of them, like El Hadj Amadou Ndoye, Djibril Gaby Gaye, and Garang Coulibaly, went on to become university professors, broadcasters, and cultural bureaucrats. They helped forge a national modern imaginary for their nation, consciously incorporating the ethos of the record clubs.[62] Their knowledge of Latin music is exhaustive. They enumerate the repertoire of all the major ensembles and recount the history of the sidemen on most records.[63] More important, they are aware of what to listen for in Cuban music: the subtleties of time changes, a graceful bridge, the harmonic sophistication of an arrangement. They especially excel at discerning why one ensemble is superior to another, an exercise that entails the elaboration of an aesthetic code. The characteristics they cherish in Cuban music, not surprisingly, reflect the qualities they wished to inculcate in themselves and their generation: panache, refinement, sincerity, and elegance. The connoisseurs inserted these values into the debates over the relative merits of different ensembles that were an important feature of the music clubs from their inception.[64] By so doing, they made these debates seem like intellectual dialogues in a salon.

The connoisseurs also helped situate the record clubs in their larger cultural and political contexts. The clubs faced potential opposition from two quarters: the French colonial government and the Islamic establishment in Senegal. As Gary Wilder has pointed out, the duality of the Senegalese as both *sujet* and citoyen conceptually bedeviled the French government in Senegal throughout the twentieth century, leading to vacillating policies.[65] It is not surprising, given this confusion, that French colonial governments in Africa had a deep ambivalence about cultural associations, especially ones that were not formed in response to one of their initiatives. French administrations came from a society where cultural life and civic culture were intertwined. They were attuned to how cultural participation could quickly lead to political action. However, many of them also subscribed to a "humanistic" philosophy that viewed cultural associations as "civilizing" institutions for the participants that would make them better citizens. This tension between vigilance and tolerance resulted in administrative paralysis in regard to the record clubs. Moreover, much more than their British and Portuguese counterparts, French colonial figures turned a blind eye to music as long as it remained uncritical of the imperial regime.[66] The fact that the young Senegalese were listening to Caribbean music genres that, as far as the French were concerned, had little connection to political protest or cultural nationalism, led the French to allow the record clubs to develop relatively unmolested by the colonial security apparatus. One of the responsibilities of the connoisseurs was to ensure that the record clubs retained the appearance of being purely a social and cultural phenomenon and avoided "trespassing" too overtly into political territory.

Maintaining cordial relations with the Islamic establishment was a more complex task. Many of the record club members came from Islamic families, and a significant proportion were devout practicing Muslims. A few, like Ibrahima Sylla, were even scions of prominent marabout families. Often their parents were displeased with their children's engaging in behaviors that some might construe as contrary to Islam.[67] While the intellectual cadre of the clubs had little power to placate distressed Muslim parents about the secular pursuits of their children, they seemed to have been more successful in keeping the Islamic establishment at bay. Few of the club members are inclined to discuss what compromises they might have reached with their neighborhood imams and with the local representatives of the Islamic brotherhood who have dominated Senegalese life since the colonial period. Perhaps the fact that so many of their members remained active in their mosques and developed proud, confident Islamic identities persuaded the marabout community that the Afro-Cuban music clubs didn't represent a threat to the *umma*. Indeed, a few Islamic clergy looked with favor on the clubs' project of reconciling local religious and cultural practice with changing social and cultural realities.[68] What is clear is that while the Islamic clergy as a whole were not pleased with the emergence of the clubs, they chose to tolerate their existence as long as the clubs remained semiprivate and affirmed values like civility and *correcte* behavior.

GOING PUBLIC: FROM RECORD CLUB PARTIES TO LIVE CUBAN MUSIC

Starting in the early 1960s, Latin musicians from the United States, responding to the burgeoning interest in Cuban music in West Africa, began touring Senegal and staging shows. These performances spurred the expansion of an audience for live Afro-Cuban music and encouraged the performance of new transnational identities by the concertgoers. More important, though, they enabled the spatially dispersed record clubs to coalesce as a public with common tastes and ambitions and a shared sense of purpose. Ultimately the coalescence of this public helped form a national modern imaginary for Senegal, rooted in the tropical world of the black Atlantic.

Before the early 1960s performances by Latin musicians from the Caribbean in Senegal, although not unprecedented, were extremely rare. Senegal lacked the large audience, infrastructure, personnel, and capital that would make importing notable Afro-Cuban musicians from abroad a feasible proposition. From time to time, however, live shows did take place. From the 1930s until regular service faded out in the early 1970s, the European passenger ships that plied the West African route occasionally hired Cuban ensembles to entertain those on board. When the boats docked in Dakar or St.-Louis, it appears that the musicians sometimes would stage spur-of-the-moment concerts to make some extra money.[69] The audiences of these hastily arranged recitals were mostly Dakar's expatriate community, though some Senegalese also attended. Older Senegalese Latin music enthusiasts claim that the famous Cuban son ensemble Septeto Habanero once played such a show in Dakar.[70]

By the early 1960s a number of changes made performances by US-based Latin musicians much more common. The record clubs had considerably enlarged the public for Cuban music among the younger generation. Moreover, many Senegalese returning from their studies in France had acquired a taste for Latin music while in Europe and were eager to attend the sort of musical events they had experienced while abroad. The prospective spectators for a Latin music performance now numbered in the tens of thousands. This new public was diversified in its class composition. During this period, besides the students of the record clubs, well-heeled Senegalese (civil servants and successful business people) liked to be seen in public. In addition, many young people who had recently migrated to Senegal's cities from the country's rural hinterland were looking for inexpensive diversions. They soon found Cuban music concerts an exciting alternative to sports matches.

At the same time that this new public was forming, major urban areas in Senegal began to build bigger and better concert facilities. In the 1940s and 1950s, as soccer gained in popularity, the colonial government built a network of soccer stadiums, as did the Senegalese government after independence. These stadiums could hold sizable crowds and were ideal locations for Latin music shows. By the 1960s Dakar boasted substantial international hotels with pool and garden areas that were equally well suited for entertainment events, if on a much smaller scale than the stadiums. Concert organizers arranged large shows at the stadiums for the young people in the community with moderate priced tickets and separate intimate but more expensive affairs at hotels that attracted an older, more elite audience.[71] This expanded range of performance spaces made it financially possible for the first generation of Senegalese impresarios to hire the more famous Latin musicians, such as Johnny Pacheco.

Most of these new concert promoters emerged from the record clubs. At the start, they were enthusiastic amateurs whose ambitions exceeded their managerial capacity. Unlike in Anglophone West Africa, where modern show business was well established with an institutional framework, the Senegalese Latin music concert organizers were pioneers with little access to capital.[72] They also lacked professionally trained staff, such as ticket takers and stage crew personnel.[73] What they lacked in experience, however, they made up for in energy and audacity. Daniel Cuxac was typical of this new breed of Senegalese entertainment entrepreneurs. Born in Casamance, Cuxac grew up in Dakar, where he was active in record clubs as a particularly resourceful collector. After finishing his education (including learning Spanish), he became one of the first stewards on the newly formed Air Afrique in the early 1960s. Exploiting the opportunities offered by free travel, Cuxac traveled to New York and Havana as often as possible. Starting "cold," he gradually built up his contacts in record distribution and musician circles in both cities. Initially there was some suspicion of the West African, who was an unknown quantity with minimal financial resources. However, his charm, command of Spanish, and deep knowledge of Latin music gradually gained him entry into the Latin music world.[74] It helped as well that West Africa in the early 1960s represented an emerging market for the Latin music industry. Musicians and industry executives were willing to take a chance on the stranger from Dakar if it meant new performance opportunities and additional sources of profits. One label owner let Cuxac become a distributor of his records in West Africa without putting up any front money. It wasn't long before Senegalese promoters like Cuxac were convincing major figures in the Cuban music world in New York to embark on Senegalese concert tours. Building on his success in Dakar, Cuxac later migrated to Abidjan in the mid-1960s and went on to become one of the most important figures in the history of African show business.

A crucial factor in the success of enterprises like Cuxac's was the expansion of media in Dakar in the 1960s. Because of this growth, it became possible to widely publicize concerts in a variety of media that previously were unavailable. Advertising in newly founded newspapers became an effective way to reach an elite segment of Latin music listeners. Radio was especially useful in alerting those who were not literate in French of upcoming events. Promoters also had the advantage of extensive social networks like the record clubs that could mobilize students and their friends to attend a performance. Poster announcements on walls, kiosks, and lamp poles further disseminated information about Latin music shows. Through this intensive citywide advertising in a variety of media, the Latin music community became more aware of itself as a spatially unified public, a community "that transcended the limits of [their own] place in the world."[75] Partially as a result of this newfound unity, Afro-Cuban music concerts became workshops where the audience imagined and actualized a new model of cultural citizenship. What was once a private pursuit done in small, homogeneous groups in neighborhood settings became a public spectacle involving large, diverse crowds from every corner of Dakar.

These favorable conditions would have been irrelevant if US-based Latin musicians had been unwilling to travel to Africa. However, famous groups and singers from New York were surprisingly ready to pack their bags and fly to Senegal even without significant advances. Latin musicians of this generation were used to basic working conditions and traveling far distances to find work. Many of them had done tours of rural Latin America, where rudimentary facilities and unreliable concert promoters were part of the job. As immigrants or children of immigrants, they were inclined to be mobile, and a significant number relished the adventure of playing to unfamiliar audiences in what was for them an exotic part of the world. Many of them found the concert fees much higher than was the norm in the United States. Others were pleased to be dealing with an entertainment business that was not dominated by criminal elements, as was the case with the salsa industry in the United States at that time. African impresarios might have been amateurs and sometimes unreliable, but their zeal and sincerity were welcome changes for the jaded Latin musicians.

Once they had experienced the sophistication and fervor of African audiences, it was even easier to lure the musicians back, despite the fact that the expected financial rewards didn't always materialize. The great flutist and charanga bandleader Eddy Zervigón was astonished by his first trip to Africa in 1972.[76] Zervigón was used to playing as many as four gigs in one night in the United States to make ends meet. Outside of Hispanic nightclubs, he was unknown. Mainstream English-speaking society regarded his music as marginal and frivolous. Yet when Zervigón's plane landed at the Dakar airport, he was greeted by five thousand fans. Some of the most important figures in Senegalese society attended his concerts. Perhaps what he found most gratifying was that Senegalese audiences saw his music as "high culture" and appreciated the subtlety of his artistry. Zervigón returned to Senegal a number of times, despite unfulfilled promises of concert fees (eventually, however, he demanded to be paid in an internationally convertible currency before he left the airport to start a tour). Today, a huge framed poster announcing his first appearance in Dakar hangs in the entrance to his home in Queens, New York.

By the 1970s a solid circuit for Latin music had developed in Senegal. A Latin ensemble might play at four different types of events during a tour. Besides the stadium concerts, prominent Senegalese hired Latin musicians to play at their "society" weddings. In addition, it became almost a tradition for some government ministries to import Latin groups to provide dance music for their annual New Year's parties. As a network of elegant music clubs emerged in Dakar, some Latin groups played limited, special engagements at the larger clubs for higher admission fees.

It is likely that the Dominican flutist and bandleader Johnny Pacheco was the first major Latin musician to tour Senegal.[77] In the early 1960s he was one of the leading proponents of the pachanga music, which was immensely popular in Senegal and a particular favorite of the record clubs. By April 1964 he was already playing dates in Dakar and continued to be a regular visitor for years.[78] Like Pacheco, many visiting Latin musicians during this period were part of charanga ensembles like Orquesta Broadway and Típica Ideal. In 1976 Típica Ideal recorded an album entitled *Vámonos Pa'Senegal/Para Bailar y Gozar*, reflecting how important Senegal had become to US-based charanga orchestras.[79] While the style's popularity had subsided in the United States by the 1960s, its hold on the Senegalese public continued unabated until the 1980s, providing much-needed employment opportunities for US charanga ensembles.

Other types of musicians were also visiting Senegal during this period. From the 1950s onward it was common for countries like the United States to send musicians to play for free or a minimal fee for African audiences. The US government used these traveling performers as "Cold War ambassadors" to win the "hearts and minds" of African listeners. The State Department, for example, often sponsored tours by jazz musicians like Louis Armstrong, Dizzy Gillespie, and Randy Weston and blues performers like Buddy Guy and B. B. King (King gave a concert in Dakar in 1970). By giving such high official visibility to African American artists, the US government was trying to counter charges that US society was racist.[80] As far as the State Department's cultural commissars were concerned, Latin music was peripheral to this racial project. Moreover, until recently in US history, Latin music lacked the cultural prestige of jazz and blues. An even greater problem for US cultural bureaucrats was that Latin music performers sang in Spanish, the language of a colonized Puerto Rico and a communist Cuba. The State Department probably believed such controversies were better left off stage. The sum total of these "limitations" apparently made Latin musicians unsuitable candidates for government patronage.[81]

Communist Cuba initially made little effort to fill the vacuum created by US neglect in this area. However, once Africa became a centerpiece of Cuban foreign policy during the 1970s, the Castro regime became more interested in mounting African tours by Cuban popular music groups. The revered Cuban charanga ensemble Orquesta Aragón led the way. When Aragón played a concert in Paris in 1965, they were surprised to discover that they had legions of African fans and that their records sold faster there than almost anywhere else in the world. In 1972 they toured Africa for the first time, playing in Guinea and Mali.[82] Hundreds of Senegalese, some with very little money, made a pilgrimage to the concert in Conakry when they learned their own government was unwilling to let the group play in Senegal for political reasons. Upon their return, their glowing reports made the Senegalese public even more eager to see their idols in person. According to Héctor Ulloque Germán, Orquesta Aragón finally played in Senegal for the first time in 1979 toward the end of President Senghor's reign.[83]

The first Aragón appearances in the late 1970s and early 1980s created a sensation. By compressing thousands of miles of diasporic space into the confines of a Dakar stadium and distilling four centuries of black Atlantic history into a two-hour recital, the concerts unleashed a complicated set of feelings and reactions in their Senegalese audience. Given the well-known opposition of the Senegalese leader to the Castro state, attending the concerts was for some an understated gesture of resistance against the "soft" authoritarianism of the Senghorian state. For others in the audience, the concerts were a celebration of a cohort coming into its own. The students of the record clubs had by this point moved into positions of responsibility in the Senegalese bureaucratic, commercial, professional, and academic realms. For them, Latin music had become the "anthem" of their generation. Orquesta Aragón in their eyes was the epitome of the cosmopolitanism and refinement they hoped to champion in the years ahead. For the few local musicians fortunate enough to join Aragón on stage for a song or two, the concerts were an opportunity to enhance their legitimacy and prestige. These impromptu collaborations represented roots in reverse: Senegalese finding their cultural essence in the music of another nation from the other side of the Atlantic.

This chapter has traced how private realms of consumption (record collections, record clubs, clothes, and concerts) helped forge a certain class-based habitus in Senegal in the 1950s through the 1970s. Through imported Afro-Cuban music and portable phonographs, young Senegalese fashioned their own subjectivities and structures of knowledge and feeling, staking their claims to modernity.[84] Their habitus established a new notion of cultural citizenship for Senegal based on sociality, cosmopolitanism, and cultural refinement. Their version of cultural citizenship and modernity, however, would have had limited impact on their nation if it had only been enacted in the semisecluded world of the record clubs and the occasional concert by a US salsa orchestra. Further changes were necessary to stimulate the circulation of their model beyond their generation.

FOUR

From *Sabor* to *Sabar*

The Rise of Senegalese Afro-Cuban Orchestras, 1960s–1970s

The months before Senegal achieved independence from France on April 4, 1960, were a period of gaiety and optimism in Dakar. The city's entertainment venues were filled with revelers, especially in the Medina, one of the designated African quarters of the city. The demand for diversion and novelty was high. As Senegal prepared for the end of French rule, Dakar's nightclubs resounded with Afro-Cuban music. More than just a new country was coming of age; Senegalese Latin musicians also were entering an epoch with unprecedented opportunities for enhancing their prestige and enlarging their public. Within twenty years of independence, using Afro-Cuban music as an underpinning they created a distinctly Senegalese style of popular music. This achievement is especially remarkable in that it was accomplished with little or no government support. Unlike in Mali or Guinea during this period, where musicians received their salaries and instruments from the state and enjoyed high visibility as a result of official sponsorship, Senegalese musicians were on their own.

If government aid was minimal, however, numerous other factors converged to create a positive climate for Senegalese Afro-Cuban performers. For example, after independence the rate of rural migration to the capital increased. Many of these new migrants were drawn to Dakar's burgeoning music scene. To better cater to this reconstituted audience for Afro-Cuban music, Senegalese Latin ensembles began incorporating more indigenous musical elements into their style. These developments transformed the nation's notions of cultural citizenship in what Michael Denning called "a decolonization of the ear."[1] New patterns of consumption paralleled a repertoire of refined behaviors in determining cultural "belonging." Accordingly, Senegalese cultural citizenship became more class inclusive and less dependent on the acquisition of Western education.

The emergence of a network of racially integrated nightclubs in Dakar, like Ibra Kassé's The Miami, with its house ensemble, The Star Band, meant that young musicians interested in playing Afro-Cuban music had something resembling steady work and enthusiastic, knowledgeable audiences. The growth of Senegalese radio resulted in their work reaching new listeners far from the capital. Later, with the construction of the first recording studios, Senegalese Latin musicians were able to study and learn from recorded performances of their music for the first time and expand their following even more. Benefiting from this improved musical infrastructure, a number of new Latin bands emerged, increasingly featuring full-time professional musicians from a non-griot background. More work and higher expectations from their listeners encouraged Senegalese Afro-Cuban musicians to perfect their technique and experiment with new musical forms. By the 1970s they were producing work of superior quality and great originality.

This chapter looks at the role these Latin orchestras played in the process of decolonizing their nation and constructing an inclusive national culture. As groups like Ibra Kassé's Star Band shifted from a devotion to the Cuban tradition to a broader approach in the 1970s, they brought sounds from both sides of the Atlantic into musical dialogue with one another, culminating in the transatlantic career of Laba Sosseh. In the process they reconfigured Senegalese modernity and helped spark a debate about cultural authenticity and cosmopolitanism that dominated the 1980s.

THE STAR BAND: FOUNDATIONAL ANCESTORS

Whenever Senegalese aficionados of Afro-Cuban music gather and discuss the history of Latin music, they identify the Star Band as the "foundational" ensemble of Afro-Cuban music in Senegambia.[2] Musicians are particularly emphatic in recognizing this band as their stylistic ancestor. Present-day instrumentalists and singers regard the members of the Star Band as the first generation of Senegalese Afro-Cuban musicians, regardless of who performed before them, establishing the roots of an artistic lineage that first transformed Senegalese music at home and then made it world famous. The Star Band initially became famous for setting a higher standard for the "authentic" performance of Afro-Cuban music. As the band's personnel changed, its artistic mission evolved. By the late 1960s the ensemble had initiated the process of indigenizing Latin music by incorporating local elements into the band's sound, such as *sabar* drumming and singing in Wolof. The group's influence has been so persistent that the Star Band "brand" retains its charisma in contemporary Dakar.

The Star Band's success in the late 1950s and 1960s arose from an artistic alliance between the Senegalese musician, entertainment entrepreneur, and nightclub manager Ibra Kassé and the Nigerian saxophonist Dexter Johnson (1932–1981). Kassé brought to the partnership a love and knowledge of Afro-Cuban music and an ability to locate and nurture new talent. In addition, his tough managerial style kept his band playing at a high level. Johnson contributed his mastery of a number of brass instruments and his exacting musical standards to the collaboration. Together they put their mark on the Star Band and Senegalese popular music.[3]

The Star Band's Pan-African personnel made it unusual among major African orchestras of the period. Musical groups in Nigeria, Ghana, the Congo, and Guinea during this era mostly consisted of citizens from that one nation. In the Star Band, by contrast, the musicians came from Anglophone, Lusophone, and Francophone Africa and hailed from at least four countries. The two trumpeters, Bob Armstrong and Mac Kenzie, for example, were Liberians. Both had served in the Liberian military, where they had played in the armed forces band. The guitarist virtuoso José Ramos came from Cape Verde. The vocalist Amara Touré, who also played timbales, was from Guinea. Senegalese who heard him sing recall his mastery of the Cuban *son* style.[4] The saxophonist Mady Konaté, whom many considered as gifted as Dexter Johnson, was also a Guinean. Both Dexter Johnson and the bassist Harrison were Nigerian. One of the few nations not well represented in the group, at least at its inception, was Senegal, although the famous Senegalese percussionist Lynx Tall was part of the rhythm section. The relatively low level of Senegalese participation in the ensemble aroused little local controversy. The Dakarois from the start embraced the orchestra, in part for its multinational membership.

Johnson's personality molded the band. A phlegmatic individual, he was punctilious about his fellow musicians being in tune and in rhythm. Much like the New Orleans jazzman Sidney Bechet, he was merciless with instrumentalists who had imperfect technique, and musicians still speak of him with as much fear as respect. Senegalese audiences adored him, not only for his playing but also for his serious and stylish bearing. He epitomized for them everything a "modern" entertainer should be. Johnson was born in Ibadan, Nigeria, in 1932 and was active in the Lagos highlife scene during the 1950s, playing drums with the Samuel Akpabot Orchestra. He then circulated as a saxophonist between Monrovia, Liberia, where he played in an orchestra sponsored by Liberian president William V. S. Tubman, and Bamako in present-day Mali, where he met a number of Senegalese musicians. According to the late Senegalese musical historian Garang Coulibaly, in 1957 Johnson moved to Dakar and tried to win over audiences there to highlife music, which was then popular in Anglophone West Africa.[5] However, the Senegalese and French listening public was uninterested in this calypso- and jazz-influenced style, and his playing initially attracted little notice. Johnson then joined forces with the Guinean guitarist Papa Diabaté, first in Guinea Jazz and then in a group of their own. The Johnson/Diabaté collaboration, while artistically and commercially successful, was short lived. However, by this time the Senegalese regarded Johnson as the best "modern" instrumentalist in Dakar. When Kassé first heard Johnson play at the Moulin Rouge Club, he knew he had found the perfect chef d'orchestre for his Star Band. Johnson left the Star Band in 1964 to set up his own ensemble, but before long he migrated to Abidjan in Côte d'Ivoire. Later, with the Cameroonian Manu Dibango and the Nigerien/Malian Boncana Maïga, he helped organize the orchestra of the Ivorian television and radio broadcasting service.[6] When he died in 1981, his funeral was a national event.

Johnson as the de facto leader of the Star Band chose much of the music in consultation with Ibra Kassé and did almost all the arrangements. The two men ensured that the orchestra had a varied repertoire, albeit one with a Latin emphasis. The ensemble played sambas, tangos, beguines, waltzes, jazz, and rhumbas—what the Senegalese guitarist Mbaye Seck, who later played with them, called the *grandes classiques*.[7] Their facility in playing all these styles cemented their reputation as a "modern," international-class orchestra, capable of competing with equivalent European outfits. Over time, however, the Star Band's stylistic focus narrowed. Increasingly the group's performances featured accurate renditions of Afro-Cuban music. Part of this shift can be attributed to changing popular taste. The Senegalese public, having discovered Afro-Cuban music through radio and records, wanted to hear it played "live" for dancing.

The musicians themselves were fascinated by the project of reproducing Afro-Cuban music in Africa. One daunting aspect of playing it was singing in Spanish, a language not commonly spoken in Senegal and at that point only beginning to be taught in schools. Musicians practiced their Spanish by singing along with records and learning it phonetically. Their sung Spanish, though filled with errors of pronunciation and inflection, greatly impressed their audiences, who knew even less of the language than the performers. It is not clear whether the Star Band's singers were more fluent in Spanish than their contemporaries, but just the fact that they were singing Cuban lyrics in their original form struck the Dakar public as a great advance in the nation's cultural development.

Few, if any, firsthand accounts or visual evidence exist of the performing style of the Star Band in its early days. What is known is that French *variété* entertainers like Tino Rossi provided one model of public presentation.[8] Entertainers like Rossi dressed in the latest style and exuded charm, dignity, and affability when performing. On stage he stood relatively still, conveying emotion mostly through his voice. Even more influential as a performance "template" were the Cuban groups of the 1950s, especially the charanga ensembles like Orquesta Aragón. In the "classic" Cuban tradition, Cuban singers were stationary and economical in gesture. They stood close to the microphone and delivered their songs in a straightforward manner with a slight smile, sometimes trying to make eye contact with someone in the audience. There was a marked contrast between the intensity of the vocals of a singer like Miguelito Cuní and the physically understated way in which they were delivered.[9] Cuban instrumentalists were more theatrical, particularly the *bongueros* and congueros during their solos. Yet they were physically more restrained than US rhythm and blues and rock and roll performers of the same period. The most spectacular showmen in Cuba were an ensemble's dancers, if present. Sometimes the dancers were instrumentalists who doubled as dancers, while at other times they specialized in dance alone. They would come out during certain numbers to animate the crowd by demonstrating the latest steps and amaze audiences with their grace and athleticism.

The Star Band for the most part embraced this Cuban performing tradition. Celebrating Afro-Cuban culture was more important than glorifying individual artists. Kassé and Johnson's musicians had a formal manner of playing and dressing, which the Senegalese public equated with modernity and refinement. The band's vocalists didn't indulge in attention-grabbing antics. Mindful of their prestigious position and reverent toward Cuban culture, they emphasized their material over eccentric showmanship. The brass section and the bassist were marginally more physically active but still exhibited elegant self-possession. The entire band wore well-tailored uniforms and was always carefully groomed. Its musicians were gracious and "correcte" in their interactions with their public. The band was respected for its tight organization. In contrast to the loose, spontaneous style of the griot-based traditions, the orchestra was rehearsed, on time for performances, and in tune. Its musicians were salaried if not always full-time musicians, dedicated to becoming virtuosos on their instruments. While perhaps not as disciplined as the Congolese ensemble OK Jazz, fronted by the guitarist Franco (Luambo Makiadi), the Star Band impressed Dakar audiences with its artistic seriousness and show business savoir faire.[10] The band's mastery of a large "international" repertoire and faithful re-creations of Afro-Cuban music symbolized for its public the potential of a postcolonial Senegal to successfully manage a modernized economy and complex bureaucracy.[11] The Star Band achieved on a smaller stage what Senghor sought to accomplish on a large scale.

However, in two significant respects the Star Band's performances deviated from the Cuban model. The ensemble lacked both professional dancers and flamboyant percussionists. These two stylistic departures reveal some of the significant obstacles the Star Band encountered in transplanting Afro-Cuban music to its nation. Unlike an equivalent Cuban orchestra, the band hesitated to incorporate dance into its live performances. Even though many of the group members were expert dancers, they considered it out of character for them as modern entertainers to prance around on a stage.[12] Moreover, the bandstands on which the Star Band appeared usually were too small to allow for any energetic dance routines.[13] Show business economics were another consideration. The Star Band was a large unit with a minimum of seven or eight musicians, all of them salaried. Including dancers would have added to Kassé's payroll and reduced his profit. Dancers on the stage would have diverted attention from members of the public demonstrating their command of Afro-Cuban forms on the dance floor, which had been one of the highlights of Afro-Cuban music performances in Senegal since at least the 1950s. Indeed, the performance of the *audience* during this phase of Senegalese Afro-Cuban music was extremely important. Their dignified comportment demonstrated that Senegal's citoyens were up to the task of governing a modern, cosmopolitan country.

The cultural significance of percussionists has differed between Cuba and Senegal. In Cuba, a common if overly simplistic view is that twentieth-century Cuban popular music arose out of a synthesis of African rhythms and European melodies. Indeed, complex rhythmic layers have been one of the distinctive features of many types of Cuban music such as the son montuno. Bongos and especially conga drums came to signify this fusion of musical traditions. As a symbol in Cuba, congas have had religious, racial, and class dimensions.

Audiences have associated them with Afro-Cuban religious practices, Cubans of full African ancestry, and the urban poor. Cuban popular music has been filled with secularized Afro-Cuban religious rhythms since the 1920s, a fact well known to Cuban audiences. Indeed, until the 1950s this aspect of Cuban music aroused much controversy among middle-class Euro-Cubans, many of whom found such religious references to *santería* disreputable. Most Cuban congueros and bongueros have been and are Afro-Cubans. In the 1930s and for most of the 1940s they were the only musicians of color allowed to play in large Cuban orchestras. Middle-class Cubans have tended to associate all African-based percussion in their nation with street music (rumba) played by what they regard as a semicriminal element.[14] As a result, for many Cuban listeners Afro-Cuban percussion has a wild, dangerous ambience, laced with eroticism and violence. Many expect percussionists to play with physical abandon and project an exotic appeal. To further their careers, many percussionists, like Chano Pozo in the 1940s, were willing to oblige.[15]

In Senegal the public and the musical community tend to regard percussion as the preserve of griots linked to tradition and localism, the antithesis of the modernity and cosmopolitanism the Afro-Cuban ensembles have wanted to project. Within the context of Senegalese Afro-Cuban music, percussionists thus have had an ambiguous position, artistically essential but culturally disconcerting. Most Afro-Cuban percussionists in Senegalese bands have been griots and are paid less than other musicians in the ensemble. Musically, unlike in Cuba, they are relegated to the back of the stage, where they are supposed to remain subdued and visually inconspicuous.[16] The Star Band percussionists rarely were given solos. In the few opportunities they had to be in the spotlight, they chose to display their subtle understanding of Cuban rhythm rather than exhibit their drumming prowess. While the Cuban public has honored its master percussionists, such as Patato (Carlos Valdez) and Changuito (José Luis Quintana),[17] Senegalese audiences ignore their Afro-Cuban percussionists (but not their m'balax counterparts). Not surprisingly, when the Senegalese discuss the Star Band, they never mention its percussion section.

Though the Senegalese recording industry was in its infancy when the Star Band was established, the group was recorded from time to time in the 1960s, mostly for local radio broadcasts. Consequently, more information is available about the orchestra's sound than about its live performances. The received wisdom about early Senegalese Afro-Cuban groups like the Star Band usually has dismissed them as unimaginative copyists. Yet recordings such as "Gerrando" reveal a different story.[18] While manifesting a knowledge of the Cuban tradition, the band drew heavily on local precedent. Under Johnson's direction, for example, the musicians strove for a seamless ensemble sound instead of layering different instrumental lines, as a Cuban group would do. As was the case nearly everywhere in Africa (but rarely in Cuba), the guitarists drove the band. Although steeped in the Cuban tradition, they also manifested a rock influence in their phrasing. By contrast, the horn harmonies were obviously derived more from US jazz than from Cuban music. Vocals were emotional but restrained, managing to sound simultaneously Cuban and African. In both Cuba and Senegal, singers often favor an emotionally intense, high, nasal sound. In Cuba this type of vocal was especially valued among members of the *coro*, while in Senegal it became typical of solo singers. The Star Band's music was preeminently for dancing in a stylish nightclub, not for passive listening. It had a pronounced lilt, with bass and guitar providing the rhythmic impetus more than the percussion, which was employed for texture and color. The group's overall sound lacked the propulsive energy of the best Cuban groups but projected much of the same melodic charm.

As the band's membership changed, so did its repertoire and sound. Turnover was always high in Kassé's orchestra. He was a difficult person to work for, and stories abound of his disputes with musicians who found his authoritarian manner unacceptable. Often, after acquiring a following and a measure of fame, musicians departed to make more money and have greater artistic freedom. Johnson was one of the first to leave, in 1964, organizing a new band, Super Star of Dakar.[19] In 1976 another group of musicians, this time led by the guitarist Yahya Fall, rebelled against Kassé's dictatorial style and low salaries and formed an ensemble called Star Band 1. Kassé's successful efforts to hold onto the Star Band "name" led the secessionists to adopt the name Number One, which they then made famous. In 1977 another cluster of musicians, this time led by two young vocalists, El Hadji Faye and Youssou N'Dour, withdrew from Kassé's orchestra and organized Étoile de Dakar, cleverly translating the Star Band's name into French, which would make it immune from charges of "copyright infringement."

As the original multinational personnel positioned themselves as competitors to the Star Band or migrated to Abidjan and other burgeoning markets for Afro-Cuban music, Kassé usually replaced them with Senegalese musicians. One of the most important activities of the Star Band was to entice young Senegalese into the music world and immerse them in the nuances of the Afro-Cuban tradition. When the guitarist Mbaye Seck in the 1960s discovered Dexter Johnson's music, it had a major impact on his artistic development. "We were crazy about Johnson," Seck recalls, "everyone wanted to be close to him." As a student in Moscow in the early 1960s, Seck somehow arranged for Johnson to give a concert. There the two established a lasting musical friendship. Upon his return to Dakar Johnson encouraged Seck to play in nightclubs after his day job. Mady Konaté also mentored the young musician. When he wasn't available to play at one of the band's engagements, he would recommend that Seck take his place. Ultimately Johnson and Konaté's protégé became a fixture in the group. Before long a cadre of young Senegalese instrumentalists and vocalists had developed along the lines of Seck. Kassé now had a pool of skilled local artists to fill the gaps created by departing personnel.[20]

This indigenization of the ensemble allowed Kassé to cater to the Dakar public's growing interest in "modernized" versions of local musical genres. The Star Band always had a wide range, and "folkloric" material was part of the mix. Sabar drummers were incorporated into the band, and performers like Mar Seck, who were comfortable singing in both the Afro-Cuban and various regional traditions, were hired as vocalists. A typical Star Band performance during this period allowed its audience to simultaneously embrace cosmopolitanism and authenticity by dancing to both Afro-Cuban music and electrified arrangements of Wolof and other Senegalese music. However, the band presented the Senegalese music as an "interlude," not to be confused with their raison d'être: the re-rooting of Afro-Cuban music on Senegalese soil.

A second generation of Senegalese orchestras, most of them filled with Star Band alumni, reordered these priorities. By appropriating the still existing Star Band's name, these bands sought to inherit the ensemble's prestigious legacy. They produced a modern popular music tied to the creation of an inclusive national culture for the independent Senegalese state. Although Afro-Cuban music for them comprised the aesthetic foundations of a truly Senegalese sound, they further infused it with indigenous traditions. In so doing they reconfigured the Star Band's mix of authenticity and cosmopolitanism.[21]

Examining why the Star Band "brand" achieved such legendary influence and status reveals many of the ways the Senegalese linked Afro-Cuban music with their conception and practice of modernity and cultural citizenship. The group's Pan-African personnel, sophisticated repertoire, linguistic flair (they sang in at least four languages), elegant performance style, and technical prowess conformed to what the Senegalese in the 1960s defined as international standards. Simultaneously, however, it catered to local aesthetic preferences in its exploration of Caribbean rhythms and song forms. The Star Band's professionalism and artistic panache represented for many audience members a new stage in their nation's development. By surpassing the French models of sophisticated entertainment prevalent in Dakar during this period, the group promoted cultural decolonization. Moreover, the Star Band's disciplined professionalism was in tune with the bureaucratic orientation of the Senghorian state. The group's commitment to latinité, albeit one different in emphasis and expression from the dominant Senghorian version, also struck its Senegalese audience as the epitome of African-based modernity.

However, the Star Band's position as a "society band" limited how much it could develop this concept of cultural citizenship and promote cultural decolonization. While its fame was widespread, its impact, was for the most part restricted to musicians' circles and the "elite" Dakarois who frequented the exclusive and expensive nightclubs of the capital. The ensemble had few opportunities to record and tour. Senegal had yet to build the communications infrastructure that would allow a musical ensemble to have an extensive regional reach. A compact audience had formed for local Afro-Cuban music in the capital and in a number of provincial towns, but a large national public had yet to coalesce. However, a second generation of Senegalese Afro-Cuban ensembles soon emerged that were able to preserve and extend the Star Band's legacy until its influence was felt throughout Senegal. The band Xalam "un" was one of the first of these ensembles to widen the appeal of homegrown Afro-Cuban orchestras and bring the music to new audiences.

XALAM "UN": THE BOHEMIAN TRADITION

During the 1960s and 1970s in Africa, Western-educated groups frequently championed and patronized popular music. In Nigeria, Fela Ransome-Kuti had a sizable university following, especially in the western region.[22] In Zaire, Tabu Ley and Joseph "Grand Kallé" Kabasele's audience included many intellectuals, attracted to their modern sound.[23] In Ghana, when E. T. Mensah's orchestra and other highlife ensembles performed, it was common to see some of that nation's artistic and intellectual elite in the audience.[24] In Senegal until the 1980s, Western-educated groups weren't just part of the public for Afro-Cuban music. Perhaps uniquely for Africa, teachers, students, artists, and writers also organized and led some of the leading musical ensembles. Their participation demonstrates the significant role Afro-Cuban music played in imagining a cultural citizenship that emphasized Senegal's diasporic ties with Spanish-speaking peoples of African descent in the New World.

One of the first of these ensembles was Xalam (always called Xalam "un" in Senegal to distinguish it from a later famous group of the same name that specialized in jazz/soul fusion). It spearheaded the second generation of Afro-Cuban musicians in Senegal and reinterpreted the Afro-Cuban tradition in influential ways. For the generation of the Star Band, Afro-Cuban music was iconic of modernity and sophistication. Xalam built on this legacy by promoting Afro-Cuban music as a truly national music, unattached to any ethnic, regional, or religious agendas. Moreover, it championed Senegalese Afro-Cuban music as a transnational *tropical* music, owing more to its Caribbean and African roots than to European musical and performance practices.

Xalam "un" was the most famous of all the groups that emerged from the bohemian subculture of postindependence Dakar. Though little known outside of Senegal, its impact on Afro-Cuban musicians in Senegal has been marked.[25] Even more than the Star Band, it presented Latin music as something other than a stylish pastime for a Western-educated elite. For the group members and their public, Afro-Cuban music was the anthem of a rising generation. In addition, they brought a more relaxed attitude to the performance of Latin music, widening its appeal to include the young and the culturally marginalized. They performed for their peers as much as for those in power. The Star Band usually played for an audience of *functionaires*, politicians, and successful businessmen. The public of Xalam "un" was more diverse, recognizing that the appeal of Latin music in 1960s Senegal had expanded to include many different urban constituencies.

Coming together around 1964, Xalam "un" was comprised of the first generation of Senegalese to grow up primarily listening to Afro-Cuban music. The singers Charles Dieng and Tidiane Thiam both frequently heard Cuban music in their childhood homes. Dieng's mother, who was Cape Verdean, even encouraged him to learn Spanish and become a sonero, highly unusual advice from a Senegalese parent at that time.[26] Thiam remembers his parents in St.-Louis dancing to Cuban music and recollects that the city resounded with radios and phonographs playing Latin music during his childhood in the 1950s. Unlike Dieng, Thiam became a professional singer against his family's wishes. He found the lure of performing Afro-Cuban music too strong to resist, though he did complete his education and become a teacher.[27]

Xalam "un" was one of the first Senegalese bands to draw its members from the academic and artistic worlds. One alumnus of the group became a professor of mathematics and then the rector of a private university. Another of its singers, Magay, became a movie actor (and then a restaurant owner). While training to be a painter, Magay joined the music ensemble and also became active in the Dakar theater scene.[28] Eventually, through his roles in several productions, he got to know Djibril Diop Mambéty, already a noted actor and filmmaker. Mambéty, who was a Latin music enthusiast, eventually cast Magay as the lead in *Touki Bouki* (1973).[29] Magay kept up his double career, unusual in Africa, for a number of years. The presence of such individuals in the group illustrates how Afro-Cuban music along with jazz had become the music of avant-garde circles in 1960s Dakar.[30] Sophisticated public opinion in Senegal considered the music modern and in tune with the latest cultural and intellectual trends.

Xalam "un" made few recordings, and almost no documentary evidence exists of the band's performance style.[31] Reportedly the ensemble lacked the class and artistic self-control of the Star Band. The band preferred a more informal and emotive performance style. Its young audience admired the performers' skill as well as their devotion to the Afro-Cuban tradition. Xalam "un" failed to achieve the fame of other Senegalese Afro-Cuban orchestras, although the band went on regular national tours and played in other West African countries, including Guinea, Mali, Côte d'Ivoire, and Cameroon. While its popularity with the greater Senegalese public proved fleeting, the band's impact on Senegalese Latin musicians was profound. Two of its musicians, the guitarist Cheikh Tidiane Tall and the flutist and saxophonist Bassirou Lô, influenced Senegalese Afro-Cuban music into the twenty-first century. The group's name (the *xalam* is a four-stringed Senegalese traditional instrument associated with *gewel* culture) indicates that even by the 1960s the Senegalese were "localizing" Afro-Cuban music and laying the groundwork for a genuinely indigenous popular music of national scope. The bands No. 1 and Orchestre Baobab, which emerged in the 1970s, were to carry this process of fashioning a distinctly Senegalese music even further.

Senegal in the 1970s was a different society from the newly independent Senegal that had spawned the Star Band and Xalam "un." After ten years of independence the nation had substantially improved its mass communication infrastructure. The national broadcasting service had widened the range of its transmission, and the spread of transistor radios made its programming more accessible. The content of what was being transmitted changed as well. There was a greater emphasis on highlighting indigenous culture and playing Latin music, whether from Senegal or abroad. To facilitate more of the radio network's content being produced "in house," the broadcasting service built recording studios. This development made it possible for Senegalese bands to record in their own country. At first the sound quality of these recordings was undistinguished. However, the sound engineers and record producers gradually learned their craft. Musicians now could produce an album that would command respect both in Dakar and in the neighboring countries of Guinea and Mali.

A large public for popular culture coalesced during this period and constituted a potential market for these recordings. The nation's rural economy had begun to falter, and young people were migrating from the countryside to rapidly growing cities like the railroad hub Thiès, the market center Kaolack, and the capital Dakar. Moreover, the growth of Senegal's educational system at all levels resulted in large concentrations of students in towns and cities. These new urban populations were open to novel forms of leisure and consumption, like listening to and dancing to Afro-Cuban music and purchasing locally manufactured records. Both Orchestre Baobab and No. 1 emerged during this era and took advantage of Senegal's expanded communication infrastructure and enhanced commercial opportunities. In so doing, they fostered the creation of a Senegalese cultural citizenship underpinned by consumption of Afro-Cuban music.

Though both bands were responding to the same social and cultural conditions and both saw themselves as the guardians of the Star Band's cosmopolitan tradition, they followed significantly different artistic paths. Together, they represent two trends *within* Senegalese modernity in somewhat the same fashion as the band leaders Joseph "Grand Kallé" Kabasele and Luambo "Franco" Makiadi did in the Congo in the 1960s. There, Franco's OK Jazz emphasized a "folkloric" African approach, while Kabasele opted for a more diasporic one.[32] Orchestre Baobab had a sleek, streamlined sound and sought an intellectual and international following. No. 1 had a more rhythmically jagged style and appealed to a more locally oriented and streetwise audience. Their artistic trajectories in the 1970s trace the development of a decolonized Senegalese popular culture, national in scope and veering away from French influence.

ORCHESTRE BAOBAB: FOR THE RECORD

Formed in 1970 as an offshoot of the Star Band, Orchestre Baobab quickly became one of the most important groups in Senegalese musical history. It is renowned for a deceptively simple, languid ensemble sound, more reminiscent of the great Guinean bands to the south like Balla et Ses Balladins and Bembeya Jazz than of the usual tougher Dakar style. This section focuses on how improvements in music recording helped shape the group's sound. As the group became more experienced in the studio and the recording equipment available became more advanced, its music grew more technically assured and sophisticated.

Baobab was the first major band to emerge from the Casamance region of Southern Senegal. Separated by the country of Gambia from the rest of Senegal, Casamance has developed its own distinct regional culture. In at least three respects, Casamance is significantly different from the rest of Senegal. First, like Central Nigeria and northwestern Cameroon, it is a linguistic shatter zone, with many small language communities. The rest of Senegal is organized into sizable language communities like Wolof, Serer, and Pulaar/Tukolor. Casamance's physical environment also contrasts with the rest of Senegal. Whereas most of Senegal lies in semiarid ecological zones, Casamance is in a well-watered area, with thick tropical vegetation. Agriculturally, it has the best farmland in Senegal, yielding fruit, peanuts, rice, and palm products. Casamance is equally religiously diverse, with Senegal's largest concentration of Christians and practitioners of African religions. The cultural impact of Islam is far less in this region than elsewhere in Senegal.

These differences did not keep Casamance from sharing the rest of Senegal's infatuation with Afro-Cuban music. By the 1950s the regional capital of Ziguinchor had developed into one of the nation's most important centers of the Latin sound. Indeed, the founding of the area's UCAS Jazz Band (Union Culturelle et Artistique de Sédhiou), the oldest continuous Latin ensemble in Senegal, predates that of the Star Band.[33] Baobab's two founders, Balla Sidibé[34] and Radolphe "Rudy" Gomis,[35] both were products of this provincial Latin scene, before migrating to Dakar in the late 1960s.

In 1969 Ibra Kassé recruited both singers for the Star Band. Their stint with the ensemble did not last long. In 1970 they left to become the mainstays of the house orchestra at the newly opened Club Baobab in the Plateau, the European "quartier" of Dakar. The band they anchored, though firmly ensconced in the Afro-Cuban tradition, was the first Senegalese ensemble to explore and integrate the musical traditions of both northern and southern Senegal. The group also was one of the first in Senegal to excel at writing its own material. Gomis's compositions in particular were adept at expressing local concerns within a Latin context. Much of the band's repertoire had a pronounced Pan-African feel as well. Sidibé added to Baobab the same Mande musical elements that could be heard in the Guinean and Malian popular music of the era, while Gomis specialized in the rhythms and melodies of Guinea-Bissau. The Togolese lead guitarist Barthélémy

Attisso[36] even brought in a subtle highlife inflection from Ghana. The result was a bricolage of West African and Cuban elements that seemed to musically encompass much of the tropical worlds of the South Atlantic.

Baobab from its formation was an artistically ambitious ensemble, seeking to bridge cultural and social divides. The orchestra drew its musicians from three disparate groups: university students, professional musicians from a non-griot background, and griots. In addition to Gomis, two other members of the group had university training. Attisso was originally a law student at the University of Dakar who played music as a sideline.[37] Latfi Ben Geloune, the band's rhythm guitarist, moved at the highest levels of Senegalese society when he wasn't playing with the orchestra. His wife is a niece of Léopold Senghor, and Geloune has many friends in Dakar artistic and political circles.[38] From the pool of professional musicians in Dakar who were proficient in Afro-Cuban music the ensemble recruited the bassist Charlie N'Diaye, the saxophonist Issa Cissokho, and the celebrated singer of boleros and slow ballads, Medoune Diallo.[39]

One of the ensemble's most significant innovations was to feature Wolof gewel (griots). Unlike in neighboring Mali and Guinea, where Mande *jeli*[40] were crucial in the development of Cuban-based popular music, in Senegal until the formation of Baobab, gewel and "modern" musicians moved in separate spheres. The gewel participated in folkloric troupes based at the government-run Théâtre Daniel Sorano and played at functions like baptisms, marriages, and private parties throughout the Dakar region. However, it was rare to see them in a sophisticated club setting unless they were playing a modern style or a *boîte* was featuring a Senegalese culture night.

When Baobab selected the gewel Abdoulaye Laye M'Boup in 1970 as one of its lead singers, it was a major departure that was to have a significant impact on Senegalese music. Since 1964 M'Boup had been one of the stars of the Théâtre Sorano Company. Along with N'Diaga M'Baye, he was considered one of the greatest traditional Wolof vocalists of his generation. Baobab hired M'Boup precisely for his talent as a singer of traditional Wolof music, not in spite of it. He was expected to add a Senegalese tinge to the Baobab ensemble sound. When the irrepressible M'Boup proved too free a spirit for the ensemble, often showing up late for work or not at all, the Orchestra hired his protégé, Thione Seck, also a gewel, as a backup.[41] Seck, who was already singing for Ibra Kassé, had a formidable vocal instrument and a broad stylistic range. He was equally at home in Afro-Cuban music, Wolof praise singing, or the newer musical hybrids that Baobab was developing. The combination of M'Boup and Seck thrilled audiences, and Baobab became one of the most popular bands in Dakar. After M'Boup died in a car accident in 1974, Seck continued to gain in popularity. Eventually he went on to form his own group, Le Raam Daan, and became one of the major figures in Senegalese and African music. Mapenda Seck, his younger brother, temporarily took his place in Baobab, ensuring a continuing strong Wolof gewel musical presence in the group.

The diverse backgrounds of the band's personnel reveal its multifaceted cultural aspirations. Whether by design or not, the ensemble's team of singers represented the three major regions of Senegal. Sidibé and Gomis drew on their Casaçais roots, the Seck brothers and N'Diouga Dieng could sing "deep" Wolof, and Medoune Diallo was from the Tukolor area in northern Senegal. Being grounded in the Afro-Cuban tradition allowed the band to sample Senegal's varied musical traditions without being too closely identified with any particular ethnicity or region. The orchestra's repertoire could have a national reach without diluting the artistic integrity and intensity of the music.

The band similarly bridged Senegalese and European audiences in 1970s Dakar. In contrast to the Star Band, which played at the Miami in the African section of Dakar, Orchestre Baobab's headquarters, Club Baobab, was at 44 rue Jules Ferry in the Plateau, the most important business and residential neighborhood for Europeans in Dakar at that time. The ensemble usually played for a mixed audience, consisting of well-heeled Senegalese and expatriates from Dakar's large international community. Gomis always has had a sizable US following, consisting of Peace Corps volunteers, diplomats, development workers and consultants, academic researchers, and study abroad students. Through them he was exposed as a young musician to US folk and rock music and other aspects of North American popular culture. It is not clear whether Gomis and Sidibé wanted Baobab to cater to this expatriate audience in the 1970s and 1980s, but certainly the ensemble's sound, which strikes some Western ears as "psychedelic," has always appealed as much to foreign sensibilities as to Senegalese.[42] Indeed, it was this ability to seduce non-Senegalese listeners that led to the band's unexpected resurgence in the 1990s.

Orchestre Baobab was among the first Senegalese bands to respond to the aesthetic quandary created by touring Latin orchestras from the United States and Cuba. Starting in the 1960s, the Senegalese experienced in person musical styles they had previously only known from records. After hearing and seeing live artists like Johnny Pacheco from New York, the public's expectations of their own Afro-Cuban musicians' club performances rose. For many Senegalese, their homegrown Latin bands, with their staid arrangements, apolitical repertoire, and grave stage manner, began to sound more like colonial relics than harbingers of postcolonial cosmopolitanism and modernity.

For an ensemble like Baobab during this period, the challenge was to renovate its performing style without violating the decorum so prized by Senegalese audiences. Baobab resolved this conundrum by refashioning its appearance but not completely abandoning the dignified stage presence championed by the Star Band. One of the earliest photographs of the band in 1972 shows the musicians in the Baobab club with their gewel singer Laye M'Boup.[43] M'Boup is flanked on either side by three members of the group. Instead of the formal attire often favored by the Star Band, the group, with the exception of M'Boup, is dressed in dark casual trousers and light brown T-shirts with a red baobab tree and the name of the club printed in the center. In Cuban style, the T-shirts are not tucked into the trousers. The six musicians on either side of M'Boup also are wearing black European shoes. Their postures are relaxed and youthful. With outspread arms and big smiles, they gesture toward their lead singer in the middle of the group. M'Boup is dressed in a completely different style from the rest of the group. Where the others are hatless, he wears a red felt fez. Where the rest of the orchestra's clothes are tropical chic, M'Boup is wearing African clothes—a white *boubou* with huge blue polka dots and white Moroccan leather slippers. M'Boup appears to be singing a song, his uplifted arms indicating his passion and engagement. The image projects the same embrace of hybridity—Cuban, European, and African—that undergirds the band's music.

Another later candid photo of the group shows Attisso, Thione Seck, and Balla Sidibé during a live performance, probably in the mid-1970s.[44] Both Attisso and Sidibé are wearing tie-dyed tunics. Thione Seck is dressed in elegant European style with a sharply cut suit and a white shirt opened at the neck. In the photo, Attisso is playing guitar with an introspective look in his eyes. Seck, by contrast, is planting a kiss on Sidibé's cheek. The startled but grinning Sidibé is holding a *shekere* (a rhythmic gourd instrument). In its gestures, posture, clothes, and emotions, the image has a distinct African *feel*, suggesting that Baobab had progressed in developing a stage presence that was both modern *and* Senegalese.

In addition to its innovations in performance style, Orchestre Baobab was among the first Senegalese bands to record extensively. Access to recording technology and the larger publics it generated was a significant factor in the group's artistic growth. A number of scholars of African music have looked at how the spread of recording technology affected regional style, but researchers have paid less attention to how the recording process itself influenced African popular music ensembles.[45] In the case of Baobab, the band's recordings from 1970 to 1982 move from a casual sense of organization to polished performances. Interestingly, the group's recordings contradict the prevailing histories of Senegalese music, which argue that Senegalese bands progressed from imitations of Cuban music to a more culturally authentic African sound. Baobab did the opposite. Its first recordings in 1970 show an ensemble deeply embedded in local musical traditions.[46] By 1982 its music, in its commitment to tautly patterned song forms, layering of sound, and emphasis on a unified ensemble sound, had moved much closer to an Afro-Cuban model.

This stylistic evolution of the band contrasts with the history of other ensembles elsewhere in Africa, on whom the advent of new recording technologies had a different impact. In Nigeria and Zaire the advent of the long-playing record in the 1970s allowed rumba, *juju*, and *fuji* bands to explore rhythmic grooves that lasted for thirty minutes or more. Ensembles became less interested in structure and more concerned with producing an uninterrupted stream of music that could keep dancers on the floor for longer periods of time. Franco and OK Jazz, for example, started out in 1956 playing songs like "Merengue," which lasted just three minutes and four seconds, perfect for a 78 rpm record.[47] However, by 1986 they were recording songs like "La Vie des Hommes," which was longer than twenty minutes.[48] When performed in front of a live audience, such songs could be twice as long.

It was uncommon, however, for a Baobab song to last more than eight minutes. Solos stayed within the confines of a given song and reinforced rather than extended its structure. Local practice was one factor limiting song length. Audiences in Dakar and elsewhere have preferred to return to their seats after a song and mingle before flocking back to dance. Shorter songs have permitted this constant circulation between a club's tables and its dance floor. The musicians' and the public's continuing adherence to the aesthetics of Cuban music also was significant. Cuban songs until recently seldom lasted more than five minutes and usually adhered to a prescribed form.[49] In addition, the ensemble itself, especially Gomis, was fascinated by Cuban song forms like the son montuno and its harmonic and rhythmic possibilities.

While having the opportunity to record did not push Baobab to lengthen its music, it did allow the band to perfect its ensemble sound and adjust its sense of musical organization. The sound systems in most African clubs tend to blur and distort instrumental playing. Bad acoustics partially account for this poor live sound, as does the expense of importing high-quality amplification equipment. Few club owners have the capital to buy and maintain premium mixing boards and speakers; audiences do not seem overly concerned with perfect sound quality. Recording studios, however, enabled the musicians to hear themselves more clearly. Moreover, the band could hear a problematic section many times in succession. Continual aural exposure to their music allowed the musicians to rectify artistic shortcomings like inconsistent meters and off-key horn playing and to experiment with different vocal timbres. Their first recordings made in Club Baobab in the 1970s now sound murky and tinny. However, in the context of the time they represented a great advance and constituted a permanent record that could be listened to time and again. By 1978 the band had access to a Parisian recording studio with all its sonic sophistication. The impact of this improved technology on the band's sound was immediately audible.

As a consequence of its extensive recording experience during the 1970s, the band's sound became crisper. The balance improved among the band's various elements, such as solos by tenor sax and electric guitar as well as the rhythm section. In addition, the band began to layer its sound in the fashion of the Afro-Cuban groups that were its original inspiration. By 1982, when Baobab recorded its collection of songs, *Ken Dou Werente*,[50] the band's music had improved technically (more on key, improved accuracy, more complex harmonies, better vocal choruses) but at the sacrifice of its earlier wilder improvisational energy. A quest for technical proficiency had replaced the adventurousness of the band's early recordings.

Orchestre Baobab's first recordings in 1970–1971 were originally meant to be souvenirs sold during their live performances at the Club Baobab. They were recorded by Jules Sagna, an engineer with the Senegalese national radio station, who later produced some famous charanga recordings in New York for the African market.[51] Songs like "N'Diaye" show that from its inception, Baobab was seeking to play a tropical music reconnecting the African and diasporic musical worlds. Laye M'Boup's vocal, with its keening high tones and rhythmic thrusts, is rooted in the Wolof gewel culture, as are the backup vocals of Thione Seck and N'Diouga Dieng. Issa Cissokho's melodic sax solo is coming out of a jazz idiom. The rhythm section, while not playing in clave, obviously has been influenced by Cuban percussion. The way these individual approaches come together as an assemblage of diverse voices is more reminiscent of early New Orleans jazz (or Ornette Coleman) than of Afro-Cuban music.

In 1978 the band traveled to Paris to record for a Senegalese entrepreneur, Ledoux, and for a concert tour. Although this was an unhappy business experience for the ensemble, the French recordings represent one of the artistic high points of the Baobab oeuvre.[52] Released as an LP, *On Verra Ça*, the album shows a deepening engagement with Afro-Cuban music.[53] Three out of the ten songs are covers of Afro-Cuban classics. At least four other tracks manifest a marked Afro-Cuban influence. The album's title song, "On Verra Ça," illustrates how the band in the late 1970s was adhering much more closely to Afro-Cuban models than it did at its inception. The song begins with N'Diaye articulating the song's rhythm, and throughout he provides a rhythmic reference point for the other musicians (as well as for the dancers). Mountaga Kouyaté's drumming now has the timbre and pulse of a typical Cuban conguero. Even more emphatically, the guitar and tenor saxophone are much more clearly in the Cuban style. Barthélémy Attisso's guitar has toned down its rock influences. With its occasionally discordant harmonies, supple embellishments, and percussive attack, it now sounds like a piano in a charanga orchestra. Issa Cissoskho's tenor saxophone in these recordings functions somewhat like a violin in a danzón ensemble. When he is not soloing, he plays riffs on top of which other players can introduce their musical ideas. When he is soloing, his work is more restrained and in harmony with the rest of the group. Perhaps in response to the loss of two of its star singers, Thione Seck and Laye M'Boup, Baobab by 1978 had revamped the vocal section of its ensemble sound. In "On Verra Ça," the background coros became more musically significant than they were in the early 1970s, sung in classic Cuban style with the coro harmonizing and engaging in well-coordinated call and response interchanges with the lead singer. The lead singer, in this case Balla Sidibé, has replaced the passion of Laye M'Boup and Thione Seck with a cooler approach. The ensemble is better integrated. The result is one of the group's most artistically distinguished numbers.

By 1982, when the band recorded the cassette *Ken Dou Werente*, its style had matured. Each member of the group had become a virtuoso on his instrument. The musicians' playing is laconic. The music has a variety of moods and musical textures. The arrangements layer the group's sound. Balla Sidibé's timbale, Charlie N'Diaye's bass, and Mountaga Kouyaté's conga lay down a foundation with the rhythm guitars, and the coro provides the counterpoint riffing. All together, they create space for the vocalists, Issa Cissokho's tenor saxophone, and Barthélémy

Attisso's guitar to improvise. In the way that the group combines Cuban rhythmic ideas with African style singing and harmonies, it is clear that the orchestra has realized the essence of the Afro-Cuban tradition without sacrificing its Senegalese musical sensibility.

The band's suave ensemble approach is shown to its best advantage in the song "Utrus Horas" ("other hours").[54] Composed by Gomis, the number is a cross between a Cuban bolero and a Guinea-Bissau folk song. It also is reminiscent of Mande music in its minor key signature and full-throated vocals. An evocative song of loss and romantic betrayal, its elegiac tone invites listeners to read their own meanings into the lyrics, whether they understand the language they are sung in or not. Some hear the ballad as a lament for the neglect of Casamance by the postcolonial Senegalese state. Others believe that it is bemoaning the end of Afro-Cuban musical hegemony in 1980s Senegal. Still others argue that the song is really about the band's decline in popularity with the Senegalese public. Gomis himself stoutly maintains that the song is nothing more than a melancholy meditation on a failed love affair.[55]

"Utrus Horas" demonstrates Gomis's mastery of musical form. Gomis organizes the song into five sections, revealing his debt to Cuban music and the son montuno genre. His vocals are unadorned and direct, owing more to folk music than to the operatic bolero style. As Gomis sings of his romantic disillusionment, Attisso on guitar and Cissokho on tenor saxophone provide pithy commentary. All the while, Kouyaté's conga keeps the instrumental backing grounded in the Afro-Cuban tradition.

In addition to its coherent and taut form, the song is also distinguished by its subtle orchestration of dark and light instrumental textures. Attisso's guitar resonates with a slight reverb, perfect for a performance at a club with poor acoustics. Cissokho's hard-driving tenor saxophone highlights the music's melodramatic overtones. The sparse percussion stands in contrast to his assertive playing. Equally, the coro's relaxed interjections pungently pair with Gomis's vocals. The overall ensemble sound has a light and airy quality, redolent of the tropics.

Indeed, in its use of space and silence and its preference for harmonic exploration over heavy percussion, the group's music on the cassette *Ken Dou Werente* uncannily resembles the music being made in the 1960s and 1970s by the *bossa nova* and *Tropicália* musicians in Brazil, another "tropical" country. While there is no evidence that Brazilian music from this period had any overt impact on Senegalese Afro-Cuban artists, Gomis's Mandiack linguistic community, some of whom live in neighboring Guinea-Bissau, already had been exposed to centuries of Lusophone influence. He and his Brazilian counterparts during this period faced some of the same artistic predicaments and responded in roughly similar ways. Both were preoccupied with the place of folklore in modern popular music, and both wanted to create national music that was "an uninhibited collage drawn from universes that are isolated in space and time."[56] By incorporating Wolof gewels into the band, Orchestre Baobab was trying to dismantle the walls between indigenous cultural expression and "high" culture erected by the Senghorian state. In so doing it was broadening the scope of cultural citizenship. By assembling its music from a diverse array of sources ranging from Mande music to Guinea-Bissau folk songs to US rock and soul music and, most of all, Afro-Cuban music, the band was perpetuating and extending Senegalese cosmopolitanism by linking it to artistic developments elsewhere in the tropical world.

Paradoxically, though Baobab's music was in step with cultural trends in the South Atlantic, it was increasingly out of touch with social and cultural changes in Senegalese society. By the late 1970s, as the first generation of young people born after independence was coming into its own, negritude was losing its grip on the country's intellectuals. This new public, many migrants to Dakar, regarded "deep Wolof" not as a fast-vanishing, exotic tradition but as the living language of urban youth. Though still attached to Afro-Cuban music, this audience wanted a grittier sound. A new band, Number One (No. 1), formed in 1976, was more in tune with these cultural shifts than Orchestre Baobab.

NO. 1: FROM URBANITY TO URBANISM

No. 1 was the first major orchestra in Senegalese history to give voice to the emerging street culture of postcolonial Dakar. If Baobab's songs referenced the Dakar of the 1960s, a city of broad boulevards and stylish boîtes, No. 1's music depicted a bustling port, crowded with newly arrived immigrants from the interior. Baobab used Wolof, the lingua franca of 1970s Dakar, as an evocation of Senegal's precolonial past. No. 1 approached Wolof from a different angle. For this band, Wolof was the sound of the present and the language of the future. Baobab positioned Senegalese musical traditions within the Afro-Cuban tradition, linking the local with the global. No. 1 resituated Afro-Cuban music within a Wolof cultural context, connecting the global with the local. In the process, it ensured that Afro-Cuban music would remain one of the foundations of a decolonized Senegalese national music and that Wolof would assert its place in Senegal as a language of modern artistic expression.

While No. 1, like Orchestre Baobab, was a musical cooperative, two individuals—the singer Pape Seck (1946–1995)[57] and the guitarist Yahya Fall[58]—dominate its history. Each greatly contributed to the rapprochement between Afro-Cuban music and Wolof culture. If Seck was not the first Senegalese to sing Latin music in Wolof (there were other vocalists in No. 1, such as Mar Seck and Doudou Sow, who also were pioneers in adapting Wolof to Afro-Cuban music), he excelled at reconciling Wolof speech patterns with Afro-Cuban phrasing. Fall was equally adroit in fashioning a bricolage of Wolof and Afro-Cuban musical elements. His guitar playing, though ensconced in the Cuban tradition, is reminiscent of the staccato attack of the traditional Wolof instrument xalam, and his arrangements brought Wolof and Cuban rhythms into close alignment. Together, Seck and Fall demonstrated the compatibility of Senegalese and Cuban musical practice within a modern popular music.[59]

Up until the early 1970s, Senegalese popular musicians largely neglected the commercial aspects of music making. Few expected to make much money as performers. Most entered the profession for the public recognition it granted and because they loved the music they were playing. As a rule, musicians were uninformed about music industry dealings like recording contracts and copyright. This naïveté evolved into a more sophisticated business sense. As Senegalese musicians saw such Congolese orchestra leaders as Luambo "Franco" Makiadi and Tabu Ley in Kinshasa become wealthy and observed the profits being made in Dakar by club owners, their inexperience gave way to a savvier business sense. This growing awareness was especially acute among Afro-Cuban musicians. They usually had a higher level of formal Western education than other musicians in Dakar and were less inclined to enter into the patron-client relationships characteristic of performers with a griot background. Moreover, their espousal of modernity and cosmopolitanism primed them for new ways of organizing their work lives.

Given this increasing awareness of the business side of entertainment among Senegal's Latin musicians, it is not surprising that many Afro-Cuban artists, Pape Seck among them, were active in the formation of L'Association des Musiciens du Sénégal in 1975. Since its founding, the association has fought with mixed success to improve working conditions for Senegal's musicians and negotiate better copyright protection for songwriters. Ironically, it was Pape Seck's participation in this organization along with many of his friends that led to the formation of No. 1. At its inception, Dakar club owners and Senegal's nascent recording industry sought to undermine the association in any way they could. In 1976 AMS staged a heavily publicized fund-raising concert at the Iba Mar stadium that attracted many of the most prestigious bands in Dakar. Ibra Kassé's Star Band with Pape Seck was among them. Kassé was upset that so many of "his" musicians were AMS activists. Not long after the concert, the personnel of the Star Band and Kassé clashed and the musicians under Pape Seck's leadership stalked off to form their own group, independent of Kassé's control. The new ensemble initially called itself Star Band Number 1. Kassé, though, believed that the "brand name" Star Band was his property. He used his influence with the Ministry of the Interior to ensure that the renegade band had to come up with a new title. The musicians dropped the label Star Band and called themselves Orchestre Number One.

During his time with No. 1, Pape Seck sought to reappropriate Afro-Cuban music and establish it as an integral component of postcolonial Senegalese culture. For him, that meant overlaying Cuban music with a Senegalese sense of melody and harmonies. In a Pape Seck song, a listener was as likely to encounter a figure from Senegalese history as a Cuban *caballero*; similarly, the rhythms come from both sides of the Atlantic. His accentuation of the African elements in Afro-Cuban music resembles what his counterparts in the Congo, such as Joseph "Grand Kallé" Kabasele and Victor "Vicky" Longomba, were striving for in the 1950s and 1960s. However, unlike the Congolese originators of rumba, Seck stopped short of attempting to convert Afro-Cuban music into a new African popular music. He always remained true to the Afro-Cuban tradition in spirit and often in form.

Seck was well suited for the project of indigenizing Afro-Cuban music and making it a cornerstone of Senegalese modernity. He was one of the first Senegalese musicians to construct an identity as a professional entertainer independent of both the griot and French music hall traditions. A lively figure, celebrated for his humor, he brought a theatrical flair to Senegalese Afro-Cuban music. Perhaps because his wife, Isseu Niang, was a famous stage and television actress, he moved easily between the theatrical and musical worlds. This artistic versatility, along with his technical proficiency, enabled him to mold Afro-Cuban music to Senegalese aesthetic preferences, ensuring its survival in the post-Senghorian era.

Seck used his voice in a horn-like manner that attractively accentuated the "heft of his timbre."[60] Midway through his career, like most Senegalese singers, he developed vocal problems. In order to continue as a performer, he had to learn to sing from a different part of his throat. The result was a gruff, raspy voice that reminds many listeners of Louis Armstrong. He employed it in the rapid, percussive fashion of traditional Wolof singers, most famously in his many renditions of "Yaye Boy" or in "Nongui, Nongui" (recorded in 1978).[61] He was just as comfortable with melodic ballads like "Walo."[62] He was particularly effective in slow Afro-Cuban influenced songs like "Macakki," one of his big successes in the 1970s with the band No. 1.[63] Whatever style he was undertaking, he brought to the ensemble the vivacity of an *animateur*, the inventiveness of a jazz singer, and the refinement of an aficionado.

Yahya Fall demonstrated that it was possible to incorporate global musical influences into a Wolof-based style that still sounded Senegalese and modern. In Fall's playing for No. 1, a listener can hear all the music echoing in the neighborhoods of 1970s Dakar—sabar drumming, Jimi Hendrix-type wah-wah pedaling, Carlos Santana Latino-rock harmonies, charanga violin riffs, 1960s rhythm and blues chording, Sufi Islamic chanting, and traditional xalam playing. It is a style so rooted in a specific time and place that it is common for non-Senegalese to be deaf to its complexities. While Fall's contemporary, Barthélémy Attisso of Orchestre Baobab, has achieved international fame, Fall remains obscure outside of his native Senegal, even within Africa.[64]

In the 1970s Fall embarked on an artistic project to devise a way of playing electric guitar that was distinctly Senegalese but still based on the Afro-Cuban style. By incorporating several innovations into his playing, he was able to superimpose a dense Senegalese layer on No. 1's Afro-Cuban foundation and enable No. 1 to realize a fuller Latin sound. By the time Fall joined the group, he was keenly aware of other postcolonial national guitar styles that had developed elsewhere in Africa. In the Congo, guitarists like Luambo "Franco" Makiadi, Nicolas "Dr. Nico" Kasanda, and Nedule "Papa Noël" Montswet had devised a rippling sound reminiscent of the Congolese thumb piano *likembe.* In Mali and Guinea, a rolling guitar style had emerged that reflected the prominence of the kora, the twenty-one-string African harp in twentieth-century Mande music. Fall based his guitar playing on the xalam, a four-string instrument especially important in Wolof music.[65] From the xalam tradition he borrowed fragmented, driving rhythms, conveyed through rapid chording. He also was drawn to finding the equivalent of the crackling sabar drum in his playing. Fall experimented with using the new technology of the wah-wah pedal to approximate the snap of a stick hitting a drumhead. For Fall, these stylistic advances were not at odds with Afro-Cuban music. His reliance on chording made his guitar sound as much like a tres, a Cuban stringed instrument, as a xalam (thirty-five years later Fall took up the tres with great artistic success). Using his guitar percussively to evoke the sabar had the added advantage of hinting at the sound of bongos in his ensemble mix, an instrument that is rarely played in Senegalese Latin orchestras but is an integral part of Cuban music.

Seck and Fall's artistic experiments with No. 1 reached their creative fruition in songs like "Diongoma," a piece still heard on Senegalese radio nearly forty years after its release. While this number doesn't feature Pape Seck, it highlights two other No. 1 vocalists who also excelled at bringing a Wolof feel to Afro-Cuban material: Mar Seck and Doudou Sow.[66] A showcase for the band's virtuosi, the song balances Wolof and Cuban musical elements. It pleased No. 1's older listeners, attached to Afro-Cuban tradition with its *típico* trumpet solos, and attracted droves of younger ones who responded to its inclusion of Wolof-derived rhythms and harmonies. Structurally, "Diongoma" significantly departed from the Cuban model by dispensing with an opening melody statement before moving into the montuno. Instead, the band fused the song's melodic and rhythmic dimensions to intensify its propulsive properties. Most likely the musicians' decision to eliminate a leisurely melodic introduction was dictated by the needs of the dance floor, increasingly dominated in the 1970s by younger couples.[67] Ultimately this generational shift in taste and in public demand had fateful consequences for Afro-Cuban music in Senegal.

Fueled by the success of songs like "Diongoma," No. 1 reputedly became the first act in Senegalese history to play in stadiums. Previously, only touring acts from the United States and Cuba like Johnny Pacheco and Orquesta Broadway had played these venues on a regular basis. The large potential live audience for No. 1 meant that entrance fees for its public appearances were lower, thus expanding its audience. Perhaps because it had such a demanding performance schedule, No. 1 doesn't seem to have paid as much attention to its recordings as did Orchestre Baobab. Whereas Orchestre Baobab sought a cool technical perfection in the recording studio, No. 1's recordings have a spontaneous ambience with occasional missed notes and imprecise ensemble playing. They sound more like souvenirs of live performances than studied exercises in mastering new audio technology. However, this rough recording quality might have been an advantage in the transistor and car radio era that was just under way in 1970s Senegal. The fidelity of both types of radios was limited, and No.1's pulsating sound was ideally suited to the aural limitations of both music transmitters.

The primary appeal of No. 1 lay in its club dates and concerts. Senegalese fondly remember the band's performances. The orchestra's appearances generated tremendous excitement from those present, in contrast to the detachment characteristic of Senegalese Afro-Cuban audiences from the café society era of the 1950s and early 1960s. Live performances proved a lucrative proposition for the band. Allegedly they were the first ensemble in Senegalese music history to all have Mercedes Benzes.[68] The band's members recall the 1970s as the most prosperous period of their careers, when they had extensive wardrobes and frenetic personal lives.[69] They were the toast of the nation: played on the radio, written about in the popular press, and celebrated in markets and kiosks and wherever Senegalese gathered.

The popularity of No. 1 was symptomatic of significant changes in Senegal's public sphere. During the 1970s a national public for popular culture crystallized around the demand for Afro-Cuban music. As this public formed, an alternative version of cultural citizenship developed that differed from the official Senghorian model of the lettered citoyen. Multicentric in practice, it was less devoted to cultural exchange between two civilizations than to the flow of sounds, images, and ideas through circuits that bypassed the economically dominant regions of the world. Where the Senghorian model drew on Western European "high" culture and the "treasure house" of the French language, this counterhegemonic cultural citizenship looked to the Caribbean and the untapped potential of Wolof as vehicles for modernity. Where Senghor's cultural citizenship rested on a command of the written word and the visual image, this alternative cultural citizenship linked to the Afro-Cuban bands had its basis in an embodied aural modernity, based on the centrality of dance and the consumption of Afro-Cuban music performances and recordings. Where Senghor's cultural citizenship was international in scope, encouraging the infiltration of French cultural concepts into Senegalese indigenous cultures and hopefully the reverse, the new generation's cultural citizenship transcended national boundaries. Until the twenty-first century these two models of cultural citizenship influenced Senegalese debates on a host of issues ranging from what constituted cultural authenticity to what comprised a usable past. In all these discussions, Afro-Cuban music reverberated.

THE TRANSNATIONALIZATION OF SENEGALESE AFRO-CUBAN MUSIC: THE CAREER OF LABA SOSSEH

The Afro-Cuban bands of Senegal's belle epoque embraced the diasporic currents that linked Senegal to the Hispanic Caribbean to formulate a type of cultural identity largely free of European dominance. Initially this new way of belonging and behaving, with its emphasis on modernity and cosmopolitanism, was confined within their nation's borders. However, this situation changed with the life of the Senegambian sonero Laba Sosseh (1943–2009). Sosseh used his music to export this concept of cultural identity to the rest of Francophone West Africa. In the process he became, along with the Congolese rumba orchestras, one of Africa's first transnational music stars.

Sosseh devoted his career to expanding musical exchanges between West Africa and the Caribbean, both developing regions, by skirting the usual international circuits of cultural exchange. Initially he championed a more authentically Cuban style of performing Afro-Cuban music in Africa. Later he reversed direction by spearheading the spread of an Africanized salsa to the United States and the Caribbean. In the years before his death he attempted to introduce his style of Cuban music to communist Cuba itself. His work demonstrates, as does the entire history of Afro-Cuban music in Senegal, that globalization doesn't inherently produce cultural homogeneity. Instead, non-Western communities in nations like Senegal can deploy communication technologies (records, cassettes, radio) to create new varieties of counterglobalization and new transnational forms of cultural citizenship.

Sosseh was born March 12, 1943, in the "half died" section of Banjul (then Bathurst), the capital of the Gambia, into a notable griot family.[70] Growing up, he remembers hearing Cuban music all around him.[71] He was especially attracted to such early son groups as Septeto Habanero and Septeto Nacional. Like many of his generation, he learned to sing Afro-Cuban music (and Spanish) by singing along with 78 rpm discs as an adolescent. By the time he was age twenty he had become a professional musician, performing with a number of local bands like the Harlem Jazz Band and Rock a Mambo. Demand for these bands increased as the Gambia prepared for its independence celebrations in 1965.

As part of these celebrations, the Dakar impresario Ibra Kassé and the Nigerian saxophonist and bandleader Dexter Johnson, then resident in Dakar, came to Banjul. When Kassé and Johnson heard reports of an extraordinarily gifted young Gambian singer, it was no surprise that they tried to recruit him for their ensemble, the Star Band.[72] Sosseh accepted the offer to relocate to Dakar and soon was rehearsing six days a week with Johnson. The two quickly established a musical rapport. Sosseh remembers him as an agreeable person who was uncompromising only about achieving technical precision in music.[73]

Sosseh helped reorient the Star Band toward a more típico, traditionally Cuban sound. Until Sosseh joined the Star Band, the songbook of Senegalese groups reflected an orientation toward what the Senegalese call variété: a potpourri of Latin, French popular music, calypso, and even rhythm and blues. A standard set randomly jumped from genre to genre with little alteration in style. Once Sosseh joined the Star Band, the orchestra distilled this mélange down to essentially its Latin pieces. Simultaneously, the group abandoned the easy listening approach associated with much of the hotel music of this period.[74] Its new sound was more kinetic, the Senegalese equivalent of the Cuban conjuntos of Arsenio Rodríguez, Chappotin, and Cheo Marquetti. Sosseh's vocals, while retaining their traditional Senegambian grace, adhered more scrupulously to clave than other Senegalese singers had done up until that point, a preoccupation that remains important in Senegalese Afro-Cuban music performances today. By emulating the slightly nasal tone characteristic of many Cuban singers, he also brought Senegalese Afro-Cuban music into closer stylistic alignment with Cuban practice.[75]

Aided by the spread of government radio stations to rural areas with programming that stressed salsa, these modifications ushered in a new era in Senegalese music when a Cuban sound dominated popular taste, both among the Western-educated elites in Dakar and St.-Louis and young students in the countryside.[76] Sosseh soon became one of the most sought after singers in Dakar. Before long, through broadcasts and touring, his reputation began to spread throughout Francophone West Africa.

Despite his burgeoning fame, Sosseh would have remained just a notable performer in a small West African country if other changes in the 1960s hadn't altered the popular culture landscape in Africa. His rise coincided with the emergence of an African show business that was regionally rather than locally based. The growth of this new economic and cultural phenomenon was fueled by the advent of an African-based recording industry and the emergence of transnational entertainment entrepreneurs like Daniel Cuxac and Aboudou Lassissi, who recruited talent from all over the continent and marketed their products without regard to postcolonial national boundaries. These impresarios saw in Sosseh and his Africanized Cuban music a cultural commodity whose appeal could transcend ethnic, religious, and national divisions and even compete with imports from abroad like US soul and rock music. His promoters urged him to migrate to Abidjan in the Ivory Coast, which by the late 1960s, along with Kinshasa in the Congo and Johannesburg in South Africa, had become one of the three commercial centers of the African entertainment industry.[77]

Sosseh needed little convincing. Abidjan during this period was one of the most cosmopolitan cities in Africa, with a rapidly growing entertainment sector. He was aware of the success his colleague, Dexter Johnson, had been enjoying there since 1968. When Johnson, wanting to take advantage of his spreading renown, left Dakar and relocated to the booming capital of the Ivory Coast, his arrival caused a stir. Almost immediately he was recognized by some of the most important figures in Ivorian society, including the president, Félix Houphouët-Boigny. Johnson's band played at some of the most exclusive venues in the country, and both money and fame quickly came his way. By the end of the year Sosseh had decamped to Abidjan and plunged into the Ivorian music scene. He organized an ensemble, the Super International Band of Dakar, and like Johnson rapidly became a celebrity. He was to move in the highest echelons of the Ivorian entertainment world, becoming one of West Africa's first recording stars until he departed for the United States in the 1980s.

The African entrepreneurs who made Abidjan a show business hub initially made their fortunes by distributing records, mainly Latin music, to the rapidly expanding West African market, gradually pushing aside the Lebanese merchants who previously had controlled this lucrative sideline. They invested the profits from this activity in artist promotion and management and in staging ever-larger concerts.[78] However, they soon realized that with many more Africans owning phonographs, there was a huge untapped domestic market for records geared specifically toward African tastes. By the 1970s two enterprising Africans, the Senegalese Daniel Cuxac and the Nigerian/Ivorian Aboudou Lassissi, had established record companies. Cuxac's DC Productions concentrated on compiling erudite collections of classic Cuban music that were distributed both regionally and globally. Lassissi's Sacodisc International, in contrast, specialized in recordings of musicians from all over West Africa, with an emphasis on the region's Afro-Cuban music. Sosseh already knew Cuxac from Dakar and eventually became a featured artist with Lassissi's record label.[79]

Initially Ivorian recordings were made and pressed in Paris. However, by 1974 a sophisticated recording studio had been set up in Abidjan. The lower costs of recording at home stimulated the growth of Lassissi's company. In 1977 Sosseh made his first album for Sacodisc, *Lassissi presente le Formidable Laba Sosseh—Special Liwanza Band*. The record was an artistic and commercial triumph and made Sosseh a star throughout West Africa and beyond. For reasons that are not clear, Sosseh was slow to capitalize on his success and return to the recording studio. For the next three years he performed frequently in Abidjan and elsewhere, maintaining his status as a champion of a típico style of Cuban music.

Given the favorable conditions for performers there, musicians flocked from all over Africa to play in Abidjan's clubs and record in its state-of-the-art studios. Live music of many types was performed everywhere, but Latin music was especially prevalent. Wealthy Ivoirians were great aficionados of Cuban music and sponsored local tours of their favorite New York Latin artists. They paid these musicians well and treated them with more respect than they were accorded in the United States.[80] As a result, it became common for US Afro-Cuban music performers to spend extended periods of time in Abidjan.

The Cuban singer and bandleader Monguito (Ramón Quián; 1925–2006), who eventually incorporated Laba Sosseh into his orchestra, found the atmosphere in Abidjan particularly welcoming. Born in Cuba, Monguito played with the Conjunto Modelo before migrating to New York after the Cuban Revolution. In New York between 1962 and 1966, he worked with Orquesta Broadway and Johnny Pacheco's pachanga band, two celebrated Latin ensembles. In 1967 he branched out as a soloist, part of the famous Fania roster. By the mid-1970s, when his career had declined somewhat in the United States, he began to commute regularly between New York and Abidjan, where he was revered. Given the high status and popularity that both he and Sosseh enjoyed in Abidjan Afro-Cuban music circles, it was inevitable that the two would meet. Proximity alone, though, doesn't explain the bond the two established. Monguito's contemporaries regarded him as the "blackest" of all Afro-Cuban/salsa vocalists in the United States. Sergio George, who produced one of his records in the late 1980s, said: "If salsa had black music, Monguito was it. . . . I mean 'black' as in its simplest, most raw form, just focusing on the Afro-Cuban percussive element. . . . It was similar to Africando in a way, but, of course, before that record was done."[81]

Playing with Sosseh provided Monguito with an opportunity to situate his "blackness" in an explicitly African context and locate his music within a larger black Atlantic world. While a number of jazz artists like Randy Weston were involved in similar enterprises of racial redefinition during the same period,[82] it was path-breaking for a Latin musician to do so.[83] For his part, Sosseh was eager to use Afro-Cuban music as a tool for simultaneously being African and modern in a culturally globalized world. The two projects intersected in a variety of ways, and in the late 1970s Monguito and Sosseh began to perform together. The artistic partnership worked so well that Sosseh became an ad hoc member of Monguito's band. Lassissi saw a rare business opportunity in this ensemble that straddled both sides of the Atlantic. He agreed to finance a recording session in New York with Sosseh and Monguito's band. Sosseh was eager to make the trip. Ivorian musical taste was beginning to change, and Latin music was losing some of its popularity in Abidjan.[84]

In 1980 Sosseh left Abidjan for the United States. He knew that with his fluent

English and mastery of Spanish, he was well prepared linguistically to adjust to US society and take advantage of the commercial opportunities for an Afro-Cuban musician in New York.[85] The city had a music industry infrastructure, with recording studios, record companies, radio stations, and a network of salsa clubs that was unparalleled in Africa. With its pan-Hispanic community of Latin musicians and audiences, the city offered him the chance to expand his vision of Afro-Cuban music beyond what was possible in Senegal or the Ivory Coast. Sosseh immediately felt at home in New York, reveling in the city's size and ethnic diversity. He was to stay there for eight years, one of the most productive periods of his career.[86]

During his stay in the United States Sosseh endeavored to bring African and Caribbean music back into collaboration. He and Monguito recorded four LPs together. The first of these, *Salsa Africana, Vol. 1: Monguito El Unico and Laba Sosseh in U.S.A.*, made in 1980, has been the most influential.[87] The music reveals that a four-century conversation has been taking place across the Southern Atlantic, not just a one-way transmission of artistic influence. The recording recognizes and celebrates the artistic differences between the Cuban Monguito and the Gambian Sosseh, arising out of their distinct historical experiences. Their music together is a "stream laden with . . . many colliding temporalities" that powerfully evokes the continuities and disjunctures of the black Atlantic.[88] It charts an alternative model of globalization, powerfully analyzed by Paul Gilroy in *The Black Atlantic*, that takes the tropical societies of the South as its reference points and largely bypasses the industrialized powers of Europe and North America.[89]

According to Sosseh, he and the Cuban American and Puerto Rican musicians he recorded with faced few obstacles in discovering a common musical language, a tribute to his mastery of Afro-Cuban musical forms and the other musicians' openness to new ideas.[90] Under Sosseh's tutelage, the Caribbean American Afro-Cuban music instrumentalists on the recordings were able to achieve an African lilt in their playing. Sosseh was never overly articulate about his working methods. However, it is likely that he interacted with Monguito and his musicians in the same way that he instructed young Senegalese Latin musicians in the period before he died. During rehearsals, when Sosseh heard something that didn't sound right to his ears, he would stop the band. A master of every instrument in an Afro-Cuban ensemble, he would precisely demonstrate to the offending musician what sound he was looking for, sometimes waving his walking stick for emphasis. His approach was both stern and humorous.[91]

The records that came out of this transatlantic encounter are a convincing intermingling of "Fania"-style salsa brass arrangements, Cuban percussion, and Senegambian melodies. Despite its uniqueness and cultural significance, the project went unnoticed by the musical and academic worlds in the United States and the Caribbean, although it was well received in Latin music circles and given extensive radio airplay. African audiences and connoisseurs were quick to recognize its import, especially in Senegal and the Ivory Coast, where it had significant impact. The sales were impressive, and the record supposedly attained "Disque d'Or" status.[92]

Sosseh's next recordings during this period further intensified his Africanization of Afro-Cuban music. Not long after his collaborations with Monguito, Sosseh signed a contract with the SAR music company of Miami, run by the Cuban American singer Roberto Torres. He recorded two albums for the label, one in 1981 and the other in 1982.[93] On one of the record covers Sosseh poses in a beautifully embroidered African gown on the Brooklyn Bridge, a perfect visual summary of what he was trying to achieve with his work on Torres's label. Working with the Cuban American SAR session musicians, who had no previous experience of African music, Sosseh made albums for the US Latin music market that sounded as if they could have been made in Abidjan or Dakar.[94] He wrote nine of the twelve songs and ensured that the material had African tempos and musical textures. The music is in 4/4 time like most salsa, but the rhythm is much more like an African "shuffle" or a Colombian *cumbia* than a Cuban *guaracha*. The records were a minor commercial success in the Latin music market and circulated widely around the Caribbean basin. They especially appealed to Colombians; so much so that in 1987 Joe Arroyo, one of Colombia's most famous singers and band leaders, "covered" one of Sosseh's songs, "Diamoule Mawo," which he retitled "Yamulemao."[95]

Sosseh's later ventures furthered these diasporic explorations. In the mid-1980s he had a recording session with Orquesta Aragón, done with an African public in mind.[96] The rumor that Aragón had consented to record with an African sonero caused a furor in West Africa. Africans in Latin music circles regarded this session as evidence that Senegambian salsa had come of age and that their brand of Afro-Cuban music was ready to be exported back to its point of origin. It was as if Senegalese musicians, after passing through a long period of musical apprenticeship, had finally mastered the Cuban sound.

Both Sosseh and Orquesta Aragón have fond memories of the collaboration that was aimed more at African listeners than Cuban or US audiences.[97] Sosseh found the charangueros of Aragón professional and sympathetic and basked in their acceptance of him as a master of the Cuban idiom. These Cuban musicians who had repeatedly toured Africa since the Cuban Revolution were grateful that their music, which had gone out of fashion in Cuba, was still commercially viable and aesthetically prestigious in Africa.[98] Indeed, the recording session marked the start of Orquesta Aragón's marketing itself as a world music act, with more audiences in Europe and Africa than in its home country. Though widely discussed in West Africa, these sessions were completely overlooked in Cuba (and in the United States). Neither the Cuban public nor the government's cultural bureaucracy showed much interest in the project's diasporic dimensions. When Sosseh was next to have contact with Cuba, nearly twenty years later, he was to find the situation little changed.

The combination of the merengue craze and the rise of *salsa romántica* in New York In the late 1980s left little room for Sosseh's style in the United States.[99] As a result, Sosseh returned to Dakar and Banjul. In addition, a new generation of Afro-Cuban musicians whom Sosseh wanted to mentor, like Pape Fall, was emerging in Senegal.[100] With a minor Latin music boom in Dakar, there was much more work available for Afro-Cuban musicians in the city's nightclubs. Also, the resort hotels of the Petite-Côte, a tourist zone about two hours from Dakar that caters to Europeans, offered lucrative employment. While his fame was not as extensive as it once had been, Sosseh still commanded great respect in West Africa. He was welcomed home as the one Senegambian musician who had played with some of the "immortals" like Monguito and Orquesta Aragón. Without missing a beat, he took his place as the returning prodigal son of an Africanized Afro-Cuban music.

Not long after his homecoming, Sosseh was able to accomplish two of the goals of his career that had so far eluded him. Despite his travels around the Atlantic world, this performer so dedicated to faithful renditions of Afro-Cuban music had yet to undertake a tour of Cuba itself. Through a fortuitous series of events, he was to find himself and his Senegalese colleagues playing with their Cuban counterparts in the sacred precincts of Havana's Hotel Nacional in July 2001. Although this tour failed to meet the African musicians' expectations, Sosseh and his colleagues had fond memories of Cuba itself and were proud to have performed there.

In 2002, after his tour of Cuba, Sosseh released his last important recording—*El Maestro: 40 Años de Salsa*—which sought to further Cubanize the Senegalese Afro-Cuban style.[101] With this album Sosseh had come full circle, playing his

Afro-Cuban repertoire from the 1960s and using only local arrangers and musicians. It received extensive airplay in Senegal, particularly during the media celebrations of Senegal's soccer triumphs in the 2002 FIFA World Cup competition. However, without any advertising or publicity, the album attracted little attention abroad. Its emphatic Latin sound underscores the Afro-Cuban foundations of much of modern Senegalese urban dance music and demonstrates its continued vitality. When Laba Sosseh died on September 20, 2007, his protégé, Pape Fall, announced his death on RTS, the official Senegalese radio and television service. Senegal's press treated Sosseh's passing as a major event and recognized his key contributions to the cultural history of Senegal. In Gambia celebrations of his career took place. Similarly, the Latin music press in the United States mourned his demise. In death, as in life, he remained a transnational and international figure.

Laba Sosseh's career is replete with irony.[102] He began as an agent of globalization in his own society, but in the latter part of his life he initiated a process of roots in reverse. An individual of great fame in West Africa, he mostly labored in obscurity in the United States, on the periphery of the Hispanic Caribbean communities. It is unlikely that many who heard his music over the radio in New York and Miami knew he was Gambian. Even fewer realized that his work constituted a daring intervention into the complicated terrain of diasporic cultural politics, creating "world music" before that term had been invented. For many, living "on the hyphen" induces psychological anxiety and cultural confusion, with troubling feelings of marginality. Sosseh was able to avoid this "nervous condition" by living *in* the hyphen. For him, living in the hyphen engendered groundbreaking music and a deeper sense of his Africanité. Rather than being caught between two cultures, his artistic modus operandi was to be African in a Cuban context and Cuban in an African context.

Sosseh's early and middle career coincided with the high point of Afro-Cuban music in Senegal. However, in the early 1980s young Senegalese increasingly were drawn to homegrown music like m'balax, at the expense of Latin music's popularity. For a brief period Afro-Cuban music faded into obscurity, and many of the major groups disbanded. However, this eclipse proved to be only temporary. Afro-Cuban music had put down deep roots in Senegal, and before long prominent individuals, still devoted to the music of their youth, sowed the seeds of a revival.

FIVE

Re*SON*ances Senegalaises

Authenticity, Cosmopolitanism, and the Rise of *Salsa M'balax*, 1980s–1990s

An air of crisis prevailed in Senegal during the 1980s. The country had to contend with multiple predicaments, including a faltering rural economy, chronic urban unemployment, and the determination of the ruling Socialist Party to hold onto power despite its diminishing popularity. Faced with economic contraction and political stagnation, many Senegalese became increasingly anxious about what constituted their national heritage.[1]

This anxiety found expression in the differing conceptions of what comprised authenticity and cosmopolitanism in a Senegalese context. Was authenticity anchored in local Islamic traditions and Africanité, or did it have its roots in a more secular, diasporic cultural nationalism? Was cosmopolitanism solely the preserve of the lettered classes, or was there another type of cosmopolitanism "from below,"[2] informed by the experiences of small-scale merchants who participated in global trading networks? As the country struggled to reverse its economic decline and come to grips with these cultural issues, a nostalgic yearning for a simpler, less contested world pervaded Senegal's public sphere. This nostalgia took different forms. Some evoked the dynamic communes, small kingdoms, and chieftaincies of Senegal's precolonial era, while others craved a return to the worldly society of negritude's heyday. The rise of television and cassette tapes expanded the scope of this debate about which of Senegal's many pasts should be the focus of the nation's nostalgic longing. Previously, consideration of such questions had been restricted, for the most part, to salons, newspapers, and books.[3] However, now, new media allowed previously silenced or marginalized groups to actively participate in the dialogue.

These "shifting cultural hierarchies" had an impact on the musical taste of the Senegalese public.[4] Many in the rising younger generation regarded Senegalese Afro-Cuban music as culturally inauthentic, an uncomfortable relic of a colonial past and a neocolonial present. Others saw Senegalese Latin music as stale and formulaic, creatively inert. Still others viewed it as merely a sound track for elitist pastimes, disengaged from a rapidly changing Dakar. Large segments of the Senegalese public lost interest in Afro-Cuban bands like No. 1 and Orchestre Baobab and gravitated toward the ensembles that recycled traditional Wolof rhythms through electric guitars. In some respects these bands had the same cultural objectives as the Afro-Cuban orchestras. However, their spatial and temporal orientation represented a radical departure from the Latin tradition. New artists like Youssou N'Dour and Omar Pene sought to shift the Senegalese musical focus from the Hispanic Atlantic world of the 1950s to the Anglophone Atlantic world of the 1970s and 1980s, a zone in which new musical influences like funk, reggae, and rock held sway. To many ears this new geographical orientation sounded revolutionary. These groups soon garnered much of Senegalese media attention, and their recordings dominated sales at market stalls and roadside vendors.

Left with few club dates and even fewer recording opportunities, Afro-Cuban orchestras disbanded. For much of the 1980s it appeared that Senegal was following the lead of many other African countries like the Congo and relegating Afro-Cuban music to the ash heap of history. However, by the late 1980s Afro-Cuban music arose, phoenix-like, from obscurity. This chapter traces the societal conditions that brought about its temporary eclipse and uncovers the cultural dynamics and institutions behind its renaissance at the decade's end.

AUTHENTICITY AND COSMOPOLITANISM IN 1980S SENEGAL

In the 1980s ideas of authenticity and cosmopolitanism shaped the audiences for popular music in Senegal. Globally, authenticity as a concept has had a long and labyrinthine history. The term has varying meanings in different parts of the world, and even within a society the concept can be used in contrasting ways.[5] In Europe since the age of romanticism, authenticity has been an important preoccupation of literature and philosophy.[6] In Africa it became significant in the twentieth century with the rise of independence movements and with the project of creating postcolonial national cultures. Given how music has become so intertwined with the creation of cultural identities, it is a term with particular relevance to the categorization and evaluation of music making around the world. In the United States the public will view as "authentic" a musician who, on the surface, resists meeting the demands of the marketplace and supposedly refuses to "sell out" to the agents of commercialization. Within the community of musicians the word often denotes someone who is faithful to a particular style, such as hard bop in jazz or honky-tonk in country music. When European and US audiences and scholars seek to understand African popular music (or any world music), authenticity acquires a third meaning of being primal, associated with origins and timelessness (one of the first world music labels in the United States called itself "Original Music"). Western observers working from this perspective contrast the supposed genuineness of African music with the perceived artificiality of most Western popular music.

Africans by contrast have situated authenticity within their quest for modernity. Authenticity, however it has been defined, has been a way of being modern without the reimposition of European cultural hegemony. It has entailed an objectification of different aspects of African cultures, validating the local through a "rearticulation of tradition."[7] Often a search for and celebration of what is authentic has been an integral part of cultural nationalism. This search can take paradoxical turns. In the 1970s, for example, in Anglophone West Africa, many musicians like the Sierra Leonean Geraldo Pino (Gerald Pine) and the Nigerian Fela Ransome-Kuti proclaimed their Africanness by playing rhythm and blues and funk music from the United States, rather than folkloric music from their home communities.[8] Although Western observers frequently are unaware of how African intellectuals and audiences have conceptualized authenticity, Africans have paid close attention to the history of the concept in the West. Indeed, Western notions of authenticity influenced the cultural debates surrounding the resurgence of Latin music in Senegal in the late 1980s.

There have been contrasting notions of cosmopolitanism inside and outside of Africa.[9] As a rule, Western scholars have conceptualized authenticity and cosmopolitanism as polar opposites. In this zero-sum model, an increased accent on one diminishes the other. From this vantage point, incorporating too many external musical influences dilutes authenticity and results in artistic mediocrity. The Senegalese, however, have not seen these two concepts as being in opposition to one another. They have exploited both authenticity and cosmopolitanism in their quest to become modern. If authenticity has meant celebrating the local in the face of competition from the global, cosmopolitanism has been a means of *linking* the local to the global to better appreciate the local's aesthetic and cultural worth. In Senghor's negritude ideology, for example, cosmopolitanism *was* authenticity.

As has been the case elsewhere in Africa, the Senegalese have continually reformulated their conceptions of authenticity and cosmopolitanism since independence. The decade of the 1980s was a particularly fertile period for this cultural reexamination. A new wave of globalization hit Senegal, and the nation experienced a wrenching social and cultural transition to a more market-driven society.[10] During this decade population mobility once again roiled Senegal. Displaced individuals flocked to the nation's cities or increasingly left for uncertain opportunities abroad. These internal and international migrations resulted in a splintering of the society's once cohesive understanding of what was meant by cosmopolitanism.

By mid-decade at least three varieties of cosmopolitanism were in play. The first was an elite cosmopolitanism articulated almost entirely in rarified artistic and intellectual circles in Dakar and St.-Louis. This cosmopolitanism, in the words of Achille Mbembe, involved the "emergence of a modern and de-territorialized self . . . linked to an emergence of a private sphere."[11] Obviously influenced by the work of the French cultural theorists Gilles Deleuze and Félix Guattari, Mbembe implicitly postulates that "late capitalism" with its economic and cultural dislocations has forced numerous Africans to master many other languages beyond their own.[12] In the process of becoming multilingual, according to this argument, they transform their identity and become unmoored. This model of cosmopolitanism, though, has only limited applicability to Senegal. For centuries before "late capitalism," large numbers of Senegalese have spoken more than one African language. Moreover, a substantial proportion also have spoken either French (or Portuguese) or one of the creolized trading languages that developed along the Senegambian coast. Dakar and other Senegalese cities and towns bear only a superficial resemblance to Kafka's Prague. While these communities historically were multiethnic and multilingual, the stress and alienation of managing multiple identities was less than in Mitteleuropa. The closest the Senegalese came to the ethnic conundrums of Central Europe were Senegalese Muslims having to reconcile the different temporalities of global Islam and French universalism.[13] However, this Senegalese project of cultural mediation should not be construed as an aftershock of the incorporation of Senegal into a New World economic order.

Far more significant in Senegal than this "elite cosmopolitanism" was the increasing visibility in the 1980s of a homegrown "vernacular cosmopolitanism."[14] This phenomenon was connected to the national and international economic and political growth of the Murid *confrérie* and posed a threat to the cosmopolitanism connected with Senegalese Afro-Cuban music. Travel, adventure, and experiencing the cultural diversity of the world are intrinsic features of Muridism. Its expansion has involved ever-widening circulations of people, goods, and images. Amadou Bamba, the founder of the confrérie, had extensive dealings with the French. Wary of his power, they exiled him to Gabon for a number of years. Significantly, Bamba performed some of the many miracles attributed to him, such as praying suspended over the sea, outside the borders of Senegal. As is well know in scholarly literature, the Murids have not been hostile to global capitalism.[15] Instead, they have bent it to their own ends, producing peanuts for export and importing consumer goods from Europe, the United States, and Asia.

Although the Murid confrérie includes Senegalese from all walks of life, including university professors and multinational executives, the classic Murid archetype is the itinerant peddler, known for his entrepreneurial energy. Salvation in Murid theology is linked to ceaseless labor. Sparked by this work ethic, Murid small-scale merchants crisscross political and cultural boundaries in search of worldly success without loosening their attachment to a locally anchored cultural and religious identity.

Typical of these petty traders is Pap Khouma, the author of the autobiographical *I Was an Elephant Salesman*.[16] As a young man Khouma migrated to Europe because of the lack of economic opportunities in Senegal. There he faced privation and constant police harassment. He ultimately created a life for himself in Italy, where outside of his business activities, he still largely moved in a Senegalese mental universe. Khouma's cosmopolitanism was not concerned with obtaining cultural citizenship or resuscitating diasporic ties, although he engaged in political organization to secure his economic rights. The struggle for economic security superseded all else. Negotiating the world outside of Senegal rather than strengthening a culturally autonomous self heightened his Senegalese identity. This process of adaptation solidified cultural boundaries as opposed to expanding them.

In the first half of the 1980s the growing influence of "elite" and "vernacular" cosmopolitanisms eclipsed the third variety of cosmopolitanism linked to Afro-Cuban music. This cosmopolitanism resembles the approach championed by the Anglo-Ghanaian philosopher Kwame Appiah: "universal concern and respect for legitimate difference."[17] The events of the 1980s undermined this position's dominance in Senegal. However, neither of the two other competing cosmopolitanisms could effectively address all the pressing issues facing Senegal during this turbulent decade. How was Senegal to manage the challenges of religious, ethnic, and political heterogeneity and the maintenance of a polyvocal polity? How was Senegal to repair frayed national and diasporic ties? The failure of "elite" and "vernacular" cosmopolitanisms to provide satisfying answers to these questions left a void, allowing for the revival of "salsa cosmopolitanism" at the decade's end.

"WE ALL DIED FOR SALSA": THE DECLINE OF SENEGALESE AFRO-CUBAN MUSIC IN THE 1980S

By the late 1970s Senegalese Latin music had been the dominant music in Senegalese clubs, recording studios, and radio stations for a generation. Dakar's boîtes were filled with patrons whose appetite for Cuban dance music was insatiable. Senegalese groups like Orchestre Baobab and No. 1 produced Latin-infused recordings of artistic distinction. Senegalese radio regularly broadcast the music of such Cuban ensembles as Orquesta Aragón and Orquesta Broadway. Senegal had become an obligatory stop on the touring itineraries of New York–based Latin music ensembles, and Senegalese and Ivorian impresarios even traveled to the United States to record Afro-Cuban music for the Senegalese market. Though ignored by the Senegalese government, Latin music's hold on the popular imagination seemed secure.

Within five years, however, the rise of what came to be known as m'balax ensembles almost completely eclipsed Afro-Cuban music.[18] These new bands relegated Afro-Cuban rhythms, melodies, and harmonies to the background in favor of mostly Wolof drumming and singing traditions. The gentle sway of the cha-cha-chá was replaced by the gyrations of new dance styles. Wolof "folkloric" musical forms long had been part of many bands' repertoires. Numerous recordings exist of m'balax-tinged music from the 1970s by the Star Band and No. 1. Even Orchestre Baobab, despite its Casamance orientation, performed some Wolof material (as did the Super Eagles band of neighboring Gambia, whose work greatly influenced N'Dour).[19] Other bands, such as Diamono, emphasized m'balax rhythms and sabar drumming more than the Afro-Cuban bands.[20] *Ndaga* and traditional ensembles went even further in their explorations of local musical traditions and attracted sizable audiences. While to many listeners outside of Senegal, local Latin music and m'balax sound similar, to Senegalese ears the two genres of music are separate and distinct. Sometimes their meters overlap, but the arrangements distinguish one from the other. M'balax is more percussive and often is played at a rapid clip. Afro-Cuban bands by contrast aim for fluidity and restraint. The bass lines are especially different. Senegalese Afro-Cuban bass players lay down a beat heavily indebted to the clave, while m'balax bassists instead are influenced by jazz and rock.[21]

When m'balax rose to prominence in the 1980s, it was the culmination of a gradual process through which ensembles had adjusted their song lists to reflect the new preferences of their publics. Even more important, what sometimes has been presented in African musical studies as a debate about modernity was actually a conversation *within* Senegalese modernity that involved changes in government policies, economic and social crises, competing generations, and the development of a local entertainment "business." While this process of redefinition in the 1980s was dramatic, it was part of a long conversation about authenticity and cosmopolitanism in Senegal that began before the ascent of m'balax and still continues today.

In 1981, after twenty-one years in office, Senegal's first president, Léopold Sédar Senghor retired and was replaced by Abdou Diouf, a leading member of his Socialist Party.[22] While the handing over of power was designed to ensure continuity, the beginning years of the Diouf presidency saw two major departures from the Senghorian legacy. Under Senghor, the doctrine of negritude structured Senegalese cultural expression. Artists who subscribed to this ideology enjoyed state economic support and had easy access to government-controlled exhibition and performing spaces.[23] The Senghorian state, however, largely excluded musicians from its patronage system. State sponsorship was sporadic and limited compared to the lavish support given to visual artists. Practice space was at a premium, and salaries paid to the musicians who were employed in government ensembles was minimal.[24]

Though Senghor opposed Afro-Cuban music on political grounds (he abhorred Fidel Castro and refused to establish diplomatic relations with communist Cuba), many Senegalese found Afro-Cuban music in tune with the aesthetic priorities of Senghor's ideology. One of Diouf's early initiatives was to progressively distance himself and the Senegalese state from negritude. While Senegalese Afro-Cuban performers had had little interest in Senghor's philosophical and literary systems, the Senegalese public nonetheless associated Cuban music with negritude. As negritude gave way to new notions of authenticity, the Senegalese Latin musical community found itself out of step with the new intellectual fashion. M'balax much better suited the cultural mood of the first half of Diouf's presidency than did the tropical cosmopolitanism of No. 1 and Orchestre Baobab.[25]

Almost immediately after assuming office, Diouf had to contend with a serious economic downturn. France and international lending agencies put pressure on Senegal to revamp its economy in the early 1980s. With few options open to him, Diouf put a severe structural adjustment program into effect. The Senegalese state ended all agricultural subsidies, throwing an already troubled agrarian sector into crisis. The cost of living in Senegal, already burdensome for a poor nation, skyrocketed. Simultaneously, years of environmentally destructive practices began to sharply cut into agricultural productivity. The rate of migration from rural areas, already high, soared, especially among the young. Dakar's overtaxed and neglected infrastructure was ill equipped to absorb the new migrants.[26]

Senegalese Latin music seemed out of touch with such economically troubled times. Bands like Étoile de Dakar, with their spiky rhythms and their evocations of a "traditional" Wolof world in their lyrics, appealed to the new urban populations[27] in much the same way that bugaloo and salsa had comforted migrant Puerto Rican populations in the US Northeast after World War II.[28] When Youssou N'Dour sang of heroic Wolof kings from ages past, in a song like "Njaajan Njaay,"[29] he reassured Senegal's new Dakarois. Melancholy songs extolling the beauty of the Cuban countryside had little relevance for 1980s youth, struggling to survive in a shrinking economy.[30]

The installation of Abdou Diouf in 1981 ushered in a new generation. Competition between generations for dominance and competition within generations for leadership was a conspicuous feature of Senegalese life in the twentieth century. Senegalese were keenly conscious of what generation they belonged to and its agenda. In many respects, generations functioned as age grades, training cadets, designating elders, and inducing solidarity. Generations could be writ small or large. The close-knit Afro-Cuban music community, centered in Dakar, saw itself as organized into four generations. Other generational groupings, mainly political, were nationwide in scope.

In Senegal, much like elsewhere, each generation chooses a particular type of music as its anthem. For the first postcolonial generation, Afro-Cuban music filled this role. When the Diouf generation came into power, it gravitated toward another style of music to clearly demarcate its intellectual and political boundaries. The members of this generation, as so often is the case, were looking for a music that could differentiate them from their elders and give them an aural identity. The new style of m'balax, with its heightened ethnic awareness, its youthfulness, and its greater openness to the propagation of Islamic values, suited their purposes exactly.

Changes in the organization of the Senegalese entertainment world also favored the rise of m'balax. With the possible exception of No. 1, Senegalese Afro-Cuban musicians up until the 1980s were known for their free and easy bohemian lifestyle. There often was an air of high amateurism to their music. Those who played in the Cuban style rarely expected to make a full-time living from it. It was a labor of love and cultural self-recognition. Few musicians invested the money they earned. None had skilled management; in fact, most had no management at all. Most musicians and their entourages had little concept of publicity and only vague ideas of intellectual property. The m'balax star Youssou N'Dour, in contrast, approached music as a business (although it must be said that other m'balax musicians did not). N'Dour knew how to maximize profit, protect copyright, and create and manipulate his public image. For the ambitious youth of the Diouf era, m'balax stars such as N'Dour and Omar Pene had shed the remnants of Senegal's griot past (though many, like N'Dour and Thione Seck, were from griot families) and had the panache and discipline of North American and Congolese performers. Their public considered them both more modern and more authentic than their Afro-Cuban counterparts.

The m'balax stars were especially proficient at adapting their music to the new technology of the cassette revolution. In the 1970s, long-playing records and the phonographs to play them on were expensive commodities in Senegal. A sizable record collection was a sign of prestige, indicating that one had financial resources and international contacts. Recorded Latin music flourished in such a climate, its prestige enhanced by its scarcity. The relatively low cost of cassette players and tapes enabled musicians to record for much larger and broader markets than before.[31] The m'balax bands as a result were able to cater to the large pool of recent arrivals to Dakar. Their music eased the transition to urban life and spoke to these listeners in an artistic language they could understand. It allowed this population for the first time to participate, at least as consumers, indirectly, in the debates in Senegal on authenticity, cosmopolitanism, and development. The rapid, percussive m'balax style also sounded better acoustically on poorly manufactured cassettes than the more languid, melody driven Afro-Cuban music. As cheaply produced tapes are played they stretch, and the sound quality quickly deteriorates. Music that emphasizes drumming, like m'balax with its crackling sabar and tama drums and its repetitive chord progressions, is less affected than layered music like Senegalese Afro-Cuban music.[32] Perhaps realizing the aesthetic challenges of the cassette revolution, m'balax stars like N'Dour soon mastered the recording studio and refined their sound to take advantage of the possibilities offered by improved audio technology. Afro-Cuban musicians, tied to a tradition emphasizing live performance and dance over recording, lagged significantly behind in this area, with the notable exception of Orchestre Baobab.

Another important difference between the Afro-Cuban ensembles and the m'balax bands was how they situated themselves in transnational culture flows. The Senegalese Afro-Cuban musicians focused on Havana and Hispanic New York in a diasporic gaze. They aspired to one day play with the Caribbean masters, whom they revered as Laba Sosseh had done. The m'balax stars by contrast looked farther north to the United Kingdom and the United States, to rock and funk. While Laba Sosseh was laboring in relative obscurity in the small, commercially limited world of Afro-Cuban music, Youssou N'Dour was able to market himself as one of the first world music stars, championed by British rock personalities like Peter Gabriel and influential elements of the British music press. His international visibility lent him great status at home, a common tendency in societies that regard themselves as peripheral.

The triumph of m'balax music in the 1980s devastated the Afro-Cuban music community in Senegal. Some performers, such as the singer Nicholas Menheim, who performed with Youssou N'Dour and the guitarist Yahya Fall, adjusted to the new realities. Others retreated into silence or played small neighborhood clubs in Dakar's suburbs. All remember the 1980s as a difficult period during which they struggled to keep the Senegalese Afro-Cuban tradition alive and vital. As Mar Seck said: "We all died for salsa."[33] The 1990s were to show that they succeeded in this objective far beyond their expectations.

DANCE MATTERS: THE CULTURAL POLITICS OF MUSIC REVIVAL IN SENEGAL

> People always make a parallel between what
> they're dancing and who they are.
>
> *Patrick Nancy*[34]

After nearly disappearing from Senegal, Afro-Cuban music gradually began to engage the public's imagination again in the late 1980s. Its resuscitation reveals how cultural institutions in Senegal mold public taste. It also illuminates how strong the link between Afro-Cuban music and Senegalese cosmopolitanism remained during the first thirty years of Senegalese independence. For many influential figures in Senegal, the death of Senegalese Afro-Cuban music would have represented a blow to the tropical cosmopolitanism they long had advocated. Just as seriously, they felt it would undermine the ideals and practice of socialbility and cultural refinement that had become cornerstones of the national identity they were propagating. Their persistence in perpetuating the Latin tinge in Senegalese music gave a second life to Afro-Cuban music in the nation and initiated a new phase in its artistic development.

Tastemakers, broadcasters, academicians, club owners, and cassette producers and distributors pooled their power and influence to restore Afro-Cuban music to a high level of cultural prominence. They saw the revitalization of Latin music in Senegal as defending a vision of modernity that eschews ethnic particularism and decries postcolonial institutional decay. Though they played different roles in Senegalese society, these individuals, some of whom had grown up together in Dakar's Latin record clubs, knew and liked one another. They had a highly developed sense of generational mission, nurtured by shared cultural interests and frequent collaborations on various projects. Rescuing Afro-Cuban music was one way they had of flexing their political muscle. As one professor at Université Cheikh Anta Diop stated, referring to his generation's hold on power: "We still are in charge and as long as we are, Afro-Cuban music never will die here."[35]

A key figure among the tastemakers committed to keeping the Latin tradition alive was Garang Coulibaly, a retired civil servant. A famous athlete in his youth and a participant in Dakar's Latin record clubs, Coulibaly had a distinguished career as a sports administrator.[36] Upon his retirement, Coulibaly devoted his energies to ensuring that Afro-Cuban music would continue to be performed in Senegal. He undertook extensive original research to preserve the rich history of this music and disseminated the results in Senegalese newspapers, in seminars, and on radio and television.[37]

Though not a wealthy individual, Coulibaly helped and encouraged musicians. Such open patronage, while common elsewhere in Africa, has been rare in Senegal. One way Coulibaly assisted Senegal's Latin artists was by sponsoring the formation of the ensemble World Melody Makers, which was dedicated to keeping alive the repertoire and performance style of the original Star Band. Coulibaly served as artistic adviser to the group and let the musicians practice in the courtyard of his home in the middle-class HLM quartier. When possible he helped the band financially by buying and maintaining their instruments.

He frequently used his prestige and personal connections to secure work for the orchestra at some of the better hotels and clubs in Dakar.[38]

Coulibaly's most ambitious project was to set up a nonprofit music institute to train the next generation of Senegalese Afro-Cuban musicians. He deliberately kept tuition low to attract talented newcomers. The faculty included such individuals as the guitarist Yahya Fall. Coulibaly turned his house over to the school, and his home became a gathering place for Afro-Cuban musicians, both old and young. The bassist David Ndione, one of the better younger bassists in Senegal, is a product of this school, and several promising drummers are graduates as well.

Even more important than Coulibaly in keeping Latin music alive in Senegal in the 1990s were key figures in broadcasting. These individuals ensured that programming formats on radio and television always included Cuban music, both locally produced and imported, regardless of the vacillations in public taste. Djibril Gaby Gaye was representative of this group.[39] After returning from finishing his higher education in the former Soviet Union in the 1960s, Gaye became one of the most vivid media personalities in Senegal, recognizable by his bright blue eyes, stylish hats, and eloquent spoken French. Gaye's knowledge of Latin music was immense, and he was resourceful at putting that knowledge to use promoting Senegalese Afro-Cuban music. His Sunday night radio show on RTS exhaustively mined the Afro-Cuban tradition, alternating classic recordings with commentary and interviews with major figures from Senegal and abroad. Another one of his weekly slots on RTS's schedule showcased new talent and new releases in Senegal and frequently featured musicians from the local Afro-Cuban musical community. Gaye also was involved in a widely circulated documentary on the career of Laba Sosseh and the "first" generation of Afro-Cuban musicians in Senegal.[40] By keeping Latin music so much in the public eye, he and other broadcasters, such as Mas Diallo and Pierre Gomis, opened up a space for the development of salsa m'balax in the 1990s.[41]

Spanish departments in Senegalese universities also participated in the re-emergence of Afro-Cuban music. Spanish has been widely spoken by secondary school and university educated Senegalese since the early days of Senghor's presidency.[42] Senghor's education policy stipulated that university educated Senegalese had to speak a second European language other than French. Many students chose Spanish because of their enthusiasm for Afro-Cuban music. Indeed, many of the Spanish faculty in Senegal's universities were initially drawn to study Spanish by their desire to comprehend the lyrics of the Cuban music they loved so much.[43] Since the 1980s these faculty members have increasingly emphasized the Hispanic Caribbean in their teaching and research. The former chair of the Spanish and Portuguese Department at Université Cheikh Anta Diop, the late Dr. Amadou Ndoye, for example, was a connoisseur of Latin music. His colleague, Anna Gueye, is a respected scholar of Afro-Cuban religion. The seminars these academic leaders organized on Cuban culture sometimes focused on music, and from time to time they collaborated with public figures such as Garang Coulibaly to publicize the activities of Senegalese Afro-Cuban musicians. Behind the scenes, through constant advocacy they also helped make Afro-Cuban music intellectually legitimate in Senegal.

Many foreign visitors to Dakar in the 1990s were surprised that so much Afro-Cuban music was being performed there. On a typical weekend, five different Latin bands might be appearing at some of the capital's most notable clubs. This continual showcasing of Afro-Cuban ensembles highlights the role club owners played in supporting the salsa revival in the 1990s. Since the early days of Senegalese music, club owners and managers have been a force in the music world. During the 1990s and at the turn of the millennium, they nurtured new Latin music talent. Three of them—Alhassan Ngom of The Ravine, Abdoulahi Fall of Fouquet's, and Ibru Iba of Chez Iba—provided venues at which Afro-Cuban bands could reclaim their once wide audience and get enough work to make a living.[44]

These club owners had complex reasons for their commitment to Senegalese Afro-Cuban music. One factor was their genuine love for the music. At least in the case of Ngom and Iba, both successful businessmen, they could have invested their money in more financially rewarding ventures. However, they were interested in more than just profits. Each told me that he felt that by booking Afro-Cuban bands, he was adding to the prestige of his nightclub. Iba also indicated that he felt that Senegalese Afro-Cuban musicians were more reliable than their m'balax counterparts, a significant change from what was the case in the 1980s. Ngom added that Afro-Cuban bands had extremely loyal if not always large followings, and they could be counted on to fill a small- to medium-sized club whenever they played. These followings tended to be well heeled and well connected. They usually ordered lots of refreshments, a perennial source of profits for clubs, and stayed out of fights. With the exception of Youssou N'Dour's fans, most m'balax audiences were less interested in purchasing drinks and were more prone to public fracases. If the public for Latin music was smaller than the audience for m'balax music in the 1990s, in many respects from a club owner's perspective, it still was more lucrative and manageable.

The Afro-Cuban music community in the early 1990s found another ally in the late Ibrahima Sylla, one of the major distributors and producers of popular music cassettes in Senegal. Sylla, who came from a prominent Senegalese marabout family, had loved Afro-Cuban music since his youth.[45] Over the years he had amassed a collection of Puerto Rican and Cuban music, which he estimated at more than six thousand records. Despite his love of Latin music, Sylla's commercial activities until the early 1990s had not involved promoting Cuban music. He had produced a recording session for Youssou N'Dour and had successfully marketed m'balax cassettes. In 1990, perhaps sensing a change in Senegalese musical taste, Sylla resolved to financially back and publicize Africando, a group comprised of Senegalese soneros (Pape Seck, Medoune Diallo, and Nicolas Menheim) and New York Latin session musicians (see chapter 6).

What especially united these tastemakers, broadcasters, and academicians was a feeling that the ascent of m'balax was an assault on Senegalese modernity and sociality. In Senegal, since at least the 1940s, the public performance of modernity had entailed dancing to Afro-Cuban music in public or attending academic congresses and private salons. For the defenders of Afro-Cuban music, the vitality of these cultural institutions was essential if a tradition of tolerance and sophistication was to continue to flourish in Senegal.

Dancing Latin music in the proper fashion is at the core of the Senegalese version of the soirée that crystallized after independence in the 1960s and still retains its cultural significance into the twenty-first century. According to the actress Isseu Niang, the late widow of the famous salsero Pape Seck, dancing at a soirée is like a ceremony that has three equally important parts: the approach, the dance, and the exit.[46] The ceremony commences with a properly attired man (pressed trousers and ironed shirt, jacket, shined shoes) walking over to a woman to inquire if she would like to dance. The question is delivered respectfully with a half-bow. The woman also must be fashionably but modestly dressed, wearing either "up and down" African cloth or a European style gown. Most women wear high heels and have mastered the difficult art of dancing in them.

The second part of the ceremony is the dance itself. The couple on the dance floor must conform to a rigorous, if subtly evolving, set of aesthetic rules. Senegalese Latin dancing draws primarily from the Cuban tradition. Other Latin American dancing "schools" from Puerto Rico and Colombia have had little impact in Senegal. There is a consensus in the country that the pachanga, an outgrowth of Cuban cha-cha-chá, has provided the template for how the Senegalese should dance to Latin music.[47] Djibril Gaby Gaye also maintains that

Dominican merengue influenced Senegalese dance styles, though its influence is difficult to detect.[48] More persuasively, the Antillean Patrick Nancy, a leading Latin dance instructor in Dakar, argues that the Senegalese combined pachanga with European ballroom "rumba" dancing.[49] If Nancy is correct, that would account, in part, for the reserved style of Senegalese Latin dancers.

On the Senegalese Latin dance floor, the man leads and dominates, leaving little room for autonomous physical expression on the part of his female partner. The dancers' steps make a circle as they hold each other at what locally is considered an appropriate distance from one another. Only during a slow "bolero" is sustained physical contact permissible. The Latin dance public in Senegal frowns on flamboyant "moves." The ideal is a measured pace that will allow couples of any age to last through an evening of constant dancing without becoming exhausted.

Over time the Senegalese have inadvertently created their own distinctive national style. Many today believe they are dancing in a típico traditional Cuban manner. In reality, they have "Africanized" pachanga, first dancing to a 3 beat and often now to a 2 beat (elsewhere, pachanga is danced in 4/4 time to 8 beats). Dancers start their steps on the first beat, unlike salsa dancing in New York, which prefers to begin on the second beat to encourage more individuality on the part of the dancers. While the Senegalese dancers' stately way of moving is graceful to watch, it would not strike Caribbean observers as especially Cuban or Hispanic.

After a dance number is over, the ceremony concludes with a man escorting his partner over to a table or chaise, where they will sit and chat quietly with one another or with other couples until they are ready to dance again. This ceremony embodies many values that the "Afro-Cuban generation" held dear, such as urbanity and civility. The rise of m'balax trampled these values and did violence to this generation's notion of a cosmopolitan public sphere. In their eyes, m'balax dancing is loutish and socially divisive. It is danced best by the young, usually in short bursts of wild energy to 12/8 time.[50] Frequently, m'balax dancers lack partners and engage in dances like the *ventilateur* that involve exaggerated hip rotations and frenzied movements. Some Senegalese linked m'balax music with aggressive behavior more appropriate to the marketplace (*feyda*) than a modern decorous social life. The roots of this decorum lie both in twentieth-century French pedagogical notions and in indigenous concepts of correct comportment. Colonial French schooling in Senegal stressed carrying oneself well, with dignity, grace, and élan. This emphasis coincided with the Senegalese concepts of *kersa* and *teggin*.[51] Kersa involves modesty and discretion, while teggin refers to respect and deference. M'balax for the Senegalese of the Afro-Cuban generation

Mapathé “James” Gadiaga outside of Chez Iba, Dakar, Senegal.
Photo by Djibril Sy

Pape Fall playing maracas, Dakar, Senegal. Photo by Djibril Sy

Alias Diallo performing at Chez Iba, Dakar, Senegal. Photo by Djibril Sy

Yahya Fall playing guitar at Chez Iba, Dakar, Senegal. Photo by Djibril Sy

Camou Yandé singing and playing congas at The American Club, Dakar, Senegal. Photo by Djibril Sy

Mar Seck singing at Chez Iba, Dakar, Senegal. Photo by Djibril Sy

Laba Sosseh, CD cover from 1981. Photo by Rafael Llerena

Africando, *Trovador* CD cover from 1993 Stern's Music

represented the invasion of market values into previously sacrosanct arenas of social life. It compromised the need to be "correcte" at all times and challenged the cultural assumptions underlying the Senegalese Afro-Cuban generation's practice of sociability. For this generation, their Afro-Cuban music, with its emphasis on elegance, a gender-integrated social life, and a ritualized respect for women, was a crucial dimension of modernity. Dance for this group was more than just movement. Properly dancing the cha-cha-chá was not merely keeping up with the latest trends. It was laying the foundation for a viable postcolonial national culture, rooted in the cosmopolitanism of the diaspora.[52]

For the Latin music public, the m'balax dance style meant a societal abandonment of the inner discipline they so prized. It is difficult to convey how troubled they were in the 1980s by the public displays of eroticism, especially by women, in nightclubs featuring m'balax music.[53] Nightclubs in the 1960s and 1970s had been laboratories where new forms of sociability could take hold. The advent of the m'balax era turned these nightclubs into cultural battlegrounds on which two generations mixed uneasily. The older patrons felt the first casualty of this clash was the loss of the distinguished ambience of Dakar's musical establishments. Dancing their precise Afro-Cuban style next to the flashier m'balax moves made them feel embarrassed and estranged in spaces they had previously controlled. Moreover, the rougher atmosphere in the m'balax clubs made them increasingly disreputable places to visit. Few high-ranking public officials, intellectuals, or successful businesspeople felt they could risk being seen in them without diminishing their status. Distressed, they withdrew from Dakar's nightlife to their lovingly preserved Afro-Cuban LP collections. Increasingly this generation demonstrated its power by segregating itself from the rest of Senegalese society. The tall barriers surrounding their homes concealed them from the rest of society. In contrast to elsewhere in Africa, such as Nigeria, where well-known figures conspicuously and perpetually circulate, the Senegalese governing class began to move in spatially constricted realms after working hours (in residences, receptions, and private parties), consciously retreating from the public sphere.

Along with dance, etiquette, and proper comportment, another issue provoking opposition to m'balax was that an important segment of the Senegalese public began to link m'balax's ascendancy to increased Wolof political and economic dominance.[54] Almost all m'balax is sung in Wolof, rather than French or another Senegalese language; and several leaders of m'balax ensembles have been active in the Murid confrérie, associated by some Senegalese with Wolof economic power.[55] For those worried about m'balax's supposed Wolof orientation, Senegalese salsa represented a culturally viable alternative. Afro-Cuban musicians in Senegal always have been an ethnically diverse group, with a particularly large contingent from Casamance (Balla Sidibé, Rudy Gomis, Camou Yandé, and Alias Diallo, to name just a few). Within the Afro-Cuban music community, artists have minimized ethnic and regional differences in the interest of sustaining an inclusive cosmopolitanism.[56]

Some Senegalese also perceived m'balax as being part of a disturbing trend of the further Islamization of Senegalese society. In their eyes, the rise of m'balax undermined Senegal's secular traditions.[57] M'balax bands sang much more about religious topics than did Afro-Cuban ensembles. Their personnel rarely included Christian musicians, not because m'balax bandleaders were discriminatory, but because Christian musicians tended to gravitate toward Afro-Cuban orchestras, which were more religiously pluralistic in their make-up. Some m'balax musicians, like Youssou N'Dour, also have been very open about their deep attachment to Islam. While a number of Afro-Cuban musicians are strict Muslims, their religiosity has no place in their public personae. Indeed, Senegalese salsa is conspicuous in its lack of interest in any type of religious expression, whether Muslim, Christian, or Afro-Cuban.

MUSICAL PAS(T)TIMES: THE CULTURAL POLITICS OF NOSTALGIA IN SENEGAL

The same cultural, economic, and political changes that helped bring m'balax to the fore also contributed to a ubiquitous sense of unease in 1980s Senegal. As the web of arrangements that had held the Senghorian state together began to unravel, many Senegalese began to long for a return to a belle epoque when supposedly there were full employment, myriad educational opportunities, and less corruption. Nostalgia became widespread among all social classes. Since throughout history music frequently has served as a vehicle for nostalgia, not surprisingly it especially figured in the competition between m'balax and Senegalese Afro-Cuban music.

As the literary critic Svetlana Boym has observed, nostalgia is a complicated cultural phenomenon. She identifies two major varieties: restorative nostalgia and reflective nostalgia.[58] Both have considerable relevance for discussing Senegal in the 1980s and early 1990s. Restorative nostalgia often has been connected with authenticity movements. Those engaged in restorative nostalgia dream of rebuilding a lost homeland, obliterated by conquest and/or capitalist development. They view embracing the past as a pathway to a better future. Because of this orientation toward the future, they don't see themselves as nostalgic. The sense of permanent loss, of the past being a foreign country, is largely absent. Those indulging in reflective nostalgia, on the other hand, dream of other eras and places but recognize the impossibility of re-creating what has been lost. Instead, their nostalgia induces a melancholy consciousness of time and history, and they savor the bittersweet interplay of remembering and forgetting.

In Senegal, however, restorative nostalgia communities dwell on a glorious precolonial past, regarding with suspicion, or even hostility, cultural developments like Afro-Cuban music associated with the colonial period. M'balax music has numerous examples of praise songs for notable Wolof political and spiritual figures from the period before the French colonial occupation, remarking on their bravery, integrity, wisdom, and cultural authenticity.[59] While m'balax's first practitioners regarded themselves as innovators and pioneers, they simultaneously thought of themselves as "electronic griots," deeply attached to a Wolof traditional culture that they believed had an important place in a modern Senegal. Nostalgia in this context contrasts a troubled present with a heroic past to promise a better future.

Reflective nostalgia in Senegal focuses on the struggle to ensure that a tolerant tropical cosmopolitanism remains the foundation of postcolonial Senegalese identity. This type of nostalgia celebrates the sensations of pleasure and intellectual discovery that accompanied the rooting of Afro-Cuban music in Senegal. In Senegalese such as the late El Hadj Amadou Ndoye, it manifested itself in casual conversations with others and in attending private Afro-Cuban parties in secluded locations. A shared sensibility and a commitment to a form of cultural participation and citizenship, not based on ethnicity and religion, permeate this form of nostalgia. In this respect, reflective nostalgia reformulates the cultural citizenship associated with Dakar's record clubs of the 1950s. Where before cultural citizenship had emphasized consumption, it now centered on secularity and ethnic equality. Those recalling their formative years from this perspective implicitly were taking a political position, though one not tied to any particular party platform.

Because this sensibility is so tied to the experience of youth, there is no possibility of returning to the past, only a wry appreciation of discerning the contours of one's early self from the perspective of late adulthood. In a sense, this nostalgia doubles on itself, since Afro-Cuban music tends to be highly nostalgic. An individual such as the late author and librarian Cheikh "Charles" Sow would become nostalgic about feeling nostalgia, an emotion linked in his mind with civility and sophistication. This variety of experience promises no escape from the unpleasant realities of the present, and it rarely leads to pondering the future. Instead, in Boym's words, it leads to "the exploration of other potentialities and unfulfilled promises of modern happiness."[60]

The contest in the 1980s between Senegalese Afro-Cuban music and what came to be known as m'balax constituted an arena in which Senegalese could discuss the proper relationship between an individual's inner life and external conduct. In their different preoccupations with the unfulfilled promises of the present, both forms of nostalgia in Senegal "pose complex and lively questions about public life at a popular level."[61] Tastes in music and styles of dancing were not just matters of personal preference. They were intertwined with a national culture in the process of coalescing. Because these debates were couched in a musical language, many Senegalese, whether literate or not, felt confident weighing in on these issues. During the 1980s the Senegalese Latin music community, musicians and tastemakers alike, spoke a beautiful but increasingly archaic form of this "language," disconnected from the general music public. As a result, they found themselves relegated to the cultural margins. In order to reengage with these debates about personhood and nation, they had to master a new musical dialect, one more in tune with the shifting realities and priorities of their country. The creation of a new musical form, salsa m'balax, grew out of this challenge to address a new generation on its own terms without abandoning the commitment to refinement and tolerance that had characterized the Afro-Cuban music community since its emergence in Senegal.

URBANE RENEWAL: THE RISE OF *SALSA M'BALAX*

Two developments in particular sparked the renaissance of Afro-Cuban music in the 1990s. The first was the Africando recording project initiated by Ibrahima Sylla. Africando found a significant multigenerational listenership in Senegal but, more important, it was a critical success internationally. In Senegal, as elsewhere in Africa, fame abroad often translates into prestige and recognition at home. Africando's global visibility helped bring Senegalese Afro-Cuban groups out of the shadows. In the same way that the worldwide sensation of "El manisero" helped implant modern Afro-Cuban music in Africa in the 1930s, the attention that Africando received in North America and Europe in the 1990s sowed the seeds for the revival of Afro-Cuban music in Senegal, albeit on a more modest scale.

The rise of salsa m'balax, a combination of salsa and m'balax, resuscitated Senegalese Afro-Cuban music. This new musical form addressed problems that were limiting the popularity of Afro-Cuban music in Senegal: the perceptions that it was culturally inauthentic and socially irrelevant. The Afro-Cuban groups of the early 1980s had difficulty coming to terms with their nation's new way of defining authenticity. Senegalese salsa's claim to cultural legitimacy was rooted in its celebration of the country's diasporic ties with the societies of the Caribbean, especially Cuba. Many Senegalese began to regard Latin music as passé in the 1980s, when Senegal's conception of authenticity became more locally oriented. During this era it was commonly thought that those in the Latin music community saw their music "as a higher, more civilized form of music than our [Senegal's] own."[62] When artists such as the guitarist and arranger Yahya Fall incorporated m'balax rhythms into their work, that brought Afro-Cuban music back to street level and liberated the music from the misconception that it was reserved exclusively for a Western-educated elite. Around the same period, new definitions of authenticity influenced by thinking in the United States began to circulate in Senegal. A growing emphasis on artistic integrity led to a deeper appreciation of the fidelity of Senegalese Afro-Cuban artists to a musical tradition and repertoire that had temporarily gone out of style. A new generation regarded with more respect musicians such as the singer Nicolas Menheim, who easily could have had a successful career as an m'balax star but chose to perform Afro-Cuban music, with all the sacrifices that that decision entailed.[63] The transformation of the m'balax star Youssou N'Dour into a major figure in world music who routinely gave concerts in Paris, London, and New York destabilized the contrast between Afro-Cuban music and m'balax. Paradoxically, m'balax was becoming more international just as Afro-Cuban music veered toward the local. This stylistic reversal made room for Senegalese salsa to rebuild and expand its public.

Many Senegalese listeners found Afro-Cuban music bound by an imported aesthetic, uncompromising in its adherence to a set tradition. By contrast, salsa m'balax for Senegalese audiences was refreshing in its willingness to depart from accepted musical norms. "Salsa-mbalax is more alive," said Pierrot Ndour, an accountant interviewed by the *New York Times* in 1999, "because of course it doesn't have to follow the rules."[64] Many of the young generation of musicians who pioneered salsa m'balax, such as "James" Gadiaga of Super Cayor, were as brash as their m'balax counterparts, as comfortable in Sandaga, Dakar's central market, as in a posh club.[65] They demonstrated that the Afro-Cuban musical traditions that flourished in the impoverished barrios of Havana and Santiago in the first half of the twentieth century could equally be at home in the *quartiers populaires* (the working class neighborhoods) of 1990s Dakar. Once the perception gained ground in Senegalese society that salsa m'balax reached broader social classes than just functionaires and wealthy entrepreneurs, its public began to grow and diversify.

Salsa m'balax changed the form, instrumentation, personnel, and repertoire of Latin music in Senegal. Its structure follows Cuban son or Congolese rumba. A salsa m'balax song begins with an extended melodic statement of a theme. However, instead of a montuno or a *sebene*, the Senegalese artists often shift into 12/8 m'balax rhythms without missing a beat. At the song's conclusion, they frequently return to their Cuban theme. Super Cayor's "Xamsa Bopp" and Pape Fall's "Teungeth" are two typical examples of this style.[66] "Xamsa Bopp," which is about knowing yourself well so that you can be sincere in your dealings with others, starts off with a piano playing Afro-Cuban *tumbaos*. After a timbale solo midway through the song, the ensemble seamlessly shifts into a rhythm more typical of m'balax. Pape Fall's "Teungeth," arranged by Cheikh Tidiane Tall, explores a number of rhythms, ranging from the clave to reggae to m'balax. Halfway through the piece, where the montuno section would be in an Afro-Cuban song, Fall engages in a duet with his male coro, and rhythms characteristic of m'balax start to dominate. As in "Xamsa Bopp," the differentiation between Afro-Cuban music and m'balax is subtle.

Both songs demonstrate that salsa m'balax ensembles are more percussively oriented than the first two generations of Senegalese Latin bands. Usually in salsa m'balax ensembles, a band will have a drummer playing a modern drum set, another drummer playing local versions of congas, and a third drummer and sometimes a fourth on the sabar and *tama*. The personnel of salsa m'balax bands are younger than those in the more traditionally oriented son groups, incorporating a new generation of musicians. A further significant departure is that the salsa m'balax bands are less apolitical than the earlier Afro-Cuban ensembles. Like their m'balax counterparts, they occasionally opine on the pressing issues of the day.[67]

Salsa m'balax changed the public for Afro-Cuban music. The audience now included as many women as men. When m'balax first cut into the popularity of Senegalese Afro-Cuban music, one of the first groups it attracted was women. They were drawn by the performers' youthfulness and charisma and perhaps the possibility for greater physical expressiveness by women on the dance floor. However, the furious pace of m'balax left little room for elegance or romance. Ultimately, the promise that the new music would provide a more prominent role for women went unfulfilled. While men could flaunt their male prowess with acrobatic exhibitions, women engaged in erotic displays that objectified their bodies and cheapened their reputations. Many performers, such as Fallou Dieng, incorporated women dancers in their performances who would engage in public exhibitions of sexuality that are rarely seen in Senegal. Even mainstream vocalists such as Coumba Gawlo had dancers of this type in their stage shows.[68]

As mentioned previously, some Senegalese considered clubs that featured m'balax to be uncouth, with an atmosphere that many women in particular found intimidating. For these women alienated by the earthiness of m'balax, salsa m'balax represented a viable alternative. This was especially true for middle-aged women who had their own legitimate income and were secure enough in their status to be with other women for "nights out on the town." Women from this group flocked to the clubs where salsa m'balax ensembles played. There they found the respect and decorum lacking in the m'balax nightspots. Even better, there they could meet men who were fashionably dressed and polite and who, more often than not, had good jobs. The salsa m'balax bands responded to these women's presence by incorporating more slow ballads and boleros into their playbooks. They softened their sound by turning down the volume and emphasizing songs from their Afro-Cuban and Wolof repertoire that had dreamy, sentimental lyrics. Even the fast numbers required much less feverish effort than the typical m'balax song. The music created an ambience that was relaxed—lively but not wild, contemporary but not controversial.

The salsa m'balax bands positioned themselves on a stylistic continuum ranging from an attempt to re-create a "pure" Cuban style to a harder m'balax sound.[69] Although competition between these bands was intense, there was much mutual recognition and appreciation. In the Afro-Cuban musical community, stylistic choices reflected personal preferences and musical strengths. The great Cuban roots band from 1997 to 2003 was Nicolas Menheim's Super Sabador. Menheim, whose maternal grandmother was from the Canary Islands, sang in impeccable Spanish, a rarity for contemporary Senegalese Latin vocalists. His style and repertoire revealed influences unusual for Senegal, such as Beny Moré and the *nueva canción* movement. Super Sabador was unique in other respects as well. It had the only woman Senegalese Latin singer of note, Maguette Dione, who modeled her singing and personal appearance after the late Celia Cruz.[70] Unfortunately Menheim developed vocal problems in the years immediately following the new millennium, and his band is now inactive.[71]

Pape Fall's African Salsa, the Chez Iba House band, and Super Cayor all veered more toward m'balax. African salsa, which was still active as of 2018, strikes a balance between son music and m'balax, managing to be faithful to both.[72] Pape Fall's arrangements strive for a conjunto effect, with two trumpeters and a key role given to the pianist, Safirou Dieng. As a protégé of Laba Sosseh, his singing keeps alive the Cuban tradition championed by the great Gambian sonero. His ensemble aims for a tonier public than the other salsa m'balax bands and often plays at elegant soirées and government-sponsored functions.[73] Yahya Fall's Chez Iba group was the continuation of No. 1 under a new name. The band was a specialist in all styles, ranging from twangy surfing music to lounge music to Latin music. The arrangements hinged on Fall's impressive guitar playing. In 2004 Fall obtained a tres and became extraordinarily skilled at playing it. Super Cayor was the most m'balax-influenced of the 1990s bands. It had a more improvised sound than the other Senegalese salsa ensembles. Its songs also were more topical and streetwise. Because of its close ties with the German record company Popular African Music, Super Cayor had more opportunities to tour outside Senegal than the other salsa m'balax ensembles.[74]

While the revitalization of Senegalese salsa led to more employment opportunities for these local Afro-Cuban musicians, recording opportunities for them remained rare. From the 1990s onward Afro-Cuban music survived in Senegal by being an integral part of a ritualized affirmation of a generation's ideals of sociality. It also served to preserve and propagate this cohort's concept of cultural citizenship. Both these roles involved public performance more than recording. The music became caught up in a contradiction regarding this age group's ambivalence about participating too visibly in Senegal's civic and cultural life. Though this generation may have had a restricted presence in the public sphere, they were aware that they partially derived their status from their capacity to appear distinguished when in the midst of their fellow citoyens and enjoyed wielding power behind the scenes. In their youth many had made their mark by participating in Dakar's "café society," in which their ability to dance well and to exhibit their connoisseur's appreciation of Afro-Cuban music were social and political assets.[75] The refined behaviors they championed still served as models for how to conduct oneself properly in public. Hence these behaviors had a performative dimension and needed an arena for their actualization. The closing of the Afro-Cuban music clubs in the 1980s was a minor crisis for this generation because no other public stage served their social purposes as well as a genteel dance floor with live Afro-Cuban music. They now had to negotiate the shifting boundaries between public displays and private "structures of feeling."[76]

The decline in the mass popularity of Latin music was not a grave problem for this group because in certain respects mass popularity, in their eyes, detracted from the music's prestige. However, the disappearance or decline of clubs like the Baobab and the Miami was a more serious matter. New establishments like Chez Iba that flourished in the first decade after the millennium couldn't fill the void left by the shuttering of the old soigné nightspots. They lacked the atmosphere of exclusivity that had made the clubs of the immediate postindependence period feel like the workshops of a secular republic. However, these establishments still provided an opportunity for a grand entrance during special celebrations or a vehicle for showcasing one's air of distinction. Even if this generation rarely visited these "temples of salsa," they knew that the less refined public that now frequented these clubs would keenly note their absence. Their invisibility was one more sign of their lingering influence.

SIX

"Music Has No Borders"

The Global Marketing of a Local Musical Tradition, 1990s–2006

Importing music from societies far beyond their own borders has always been part of Senegalese Latin musicians' cultural practice. This openness to external influences has not meant distancing themselves from their African identity. Instead, Senegalese have incorporated musical traditions from Cuba to become more themselves, to enter modernity on terms that allow them to preserve what they highly value in their own culture. They borrowed from the world not to dilute their traditions in hope of foreign commercial success but to create for domestic consumption a national music that promotes elegance and cosmopolitanism.

However, even if they had wanted to export their product, there would have been few ways to do so before the 1980s. The entertainment industry infrastructure did not exist for Africans to profitably market their music to wealthy countries abroad. In the 1980s, however, a market for music from around the globe, including Africa, developed in Western Europe, Japan, and North America. Record companies formed and distributors emerged to document and market music from nearly everywhere to nearly everyone. As the creators of a global music, Senegalese Latin musicians hoped to exploit these favorable conditions to achieve more financial security, travel overseas more frequently, and amass more cultural capital at home. This chapter examines the various strategies they and their promoters used to make a place for themselves in the world music scene.

The phrase "world music" originally arose in the 1980s as a promotional tool, used to establish a space for non-Western music in "first world" record/CD stores.[1] Over time the term entered academic discourse as an indicator of global culture flows. Researchers who use the phrase often argue that twentieth-century communication technologies like records and radios have promoted the global dissemination of "Western" music. This dissemination stimulates the creation of new musical forms. Some of this "exotic" music finds its way to the industrial West, where various media transform it into a consumer good to be sold both locally and internationally. Deborah Pacini Hernandez makes a further useful distinction between world music and world beat: world music refers "to all that was not necessarily Western (linked, then, to roots music), whereas world beat refers to more modern products that took into account the cross-fertilization of styles between the first and third worlds."[2]

One of the problems faced by Senegal's Latin musicians in selling themselves as world artists was that their music didn't fit neatly into any of these cultural categories. They didn't conform to Western paradigms of "roots music," and the cross-fertilization that shaped their music almost entirely bypassed the "first world." As a result they sometimes confounded Western audiences, who were nonplussed by encountering Afro-Cuban music sung in an African language. In spite of these obstacles, a number of Senegalese groups found paths into the world music spotlight.

This chapter traces three of these journeys. It first looks at how a British record label owner "discovered" Orchestre Baobab and, without altering its music, succeeded in making it a major world music act. The chapter then relates how an African impresario, Ibrahima Sylla, took three Senegalese singers to record with Latin musicians in New York and managed simultaneously to make a mark in three dissimilar markets: world music, Latin music in the Americas, and African popular music. The cultural ramifications of Sylla's project continue to resound around the black Atlantic, even after his death in 2013. The chapter concludes by looking at "roots in reverse": the homecoming of Senegalese Afro-Cuban music to Cuba. Cultural exchanges have often propelled musicians into international careers. In the case of the Senegalese musicians who toured Cuba in 2001, unfortunately, this has not been the case. Derailed by byzantine political maneuvering in both their country and Cuba, their tour slowly became a minor catastrophe. Though their cultural "return" to Cuba was historic, their voyage left only a light footprint on the black Atlantic. The range of experiences these Senegalese Latin musicians had in the global cultural marketplace illustrates the complexity of the world music phenomenon and the limits of treating it as a monolithic entity. As

Senegalese Afro-Cuban music has echoed across the ocean, it has taken root in unexpected places, fashioning new meanings and blazing new routes for further transatlantic musical conversations.

TROPE TROPIQUE: ORCHESTRE BAOBAB'S REINCARNATION AS WORLD MUSIC STARS

The ascent of Orchestre Baobab to world music prominence in Europe and North America during the fin-de-siècle period is one of the more improbable stories in recent global cultural history. Most world music performers, such as Salif Keita from Mali and Oliver Mtukudzi from Zimbabwe, progress from achieving fame in their own countries to having an international breakthrough. Orchestre Baobab turned this model on its head. Though unable as a group to land club engagements in Senegal in the 1990s, it was filling prestigious midsized concert halls abroad by 2004. Ignored by Senegalese youth at home, two popular "jam" bands—the Dave Matthews Band and Phish—championed the group's music abroad and helped it attract college-aged fans.[3] Though there was no interest in recording the band's music at home, its recordings on a world music label based in the United Kingdom beginning in 1988 have sold well internationally and have been praised by both the mainstream press and specialized music magazines. Indeed, only after the musicians became world music celebrities in the United Kingdom and the United States did they enjoy a mild revival of interest in their music back in Senegal.

Orchestre Baobab's transformation into an important world music act demonstrates how a web of cultural misunderstandings ensnares contemporary African musical performers and their Western audiences. These misinterpretations often enhance the commercial viability of these ensembles and increase their cultural capital, both abroad and back home. Largely because Orchestre Baobab has been marketed globally, nearly all of its foreign listeners are unaware of the cultural and historical contexts that have shaped the band's artistic development, and few would consider themselves enthusiasts of Afro-Cuban music. Only a handful would equate Baobab's music with a tradition of elegance and cosmopolitanism. Overseas publics don't perceive the ensemble as an exemplar of Africanité. Many instead associate the band with tropical fantasies, unanchored to any particular place or time, mistakenly assuming that the suppliers of these alluring reveries are cultural naïfs, living in a state of primordial artistic innocence.

When one examines the multinational character of Orchestre Baobab's membership, the group's international success appears less surprising and almost inevitable. Just as the group profited in the 1970s from the ethnic diversity of its personnel, its international composition helped it break into the world music market thirty years later. The ensemble has especially benefited from the presence of two of its non-Senegalese members, the Togolese guitarist Barthélémy Attisso and the Guinea-Bissau / Senegalese singer and songwriter Rudy Gomis.[4] Attisso's spacey solos strike foreign listeners as psychedelic and have made him a figure of cult adoration.[5] Indeed, his guitar style shows traces of many musical influences, a number of them familiar to Western listeners. Attisso grew up in postwar Togo, which was a music crossroad. He remembers hearing as a young student many types of non-African music: jazz, Afro-Cuban, US rhythm and blues. When he relocated in Dakar in 1966 to attend law school at the Université de Dakar, he heard the music of Jimi Hendrix and Carlos Santana, which also made a deep impression on him.[6] These elements in Attisso's playing give Western audiences a sonic core around which they can orient themselves to the band's complex sound. His guitar work simultaneously thrills and reassures these listeners.

In addition to his songwriting talents, Rudy Gomis brings to the group a profound knowledge of Western popular music and the ability to bring an evocative Lusophone tinge to the band's sound. Because of Gomis, the band has had a coterie of devoted Western listeners (and patrons) since its formation in the early 1970s. While Gomis was a student in Dakar in the 1960s, he had the opportunity to interact with many US Peace Corps volunteers. He and the young Americans would often swap songs and musical ideas. Through these friends and their record collections, he was exposed to Western rock and folk music. Later Gomis served for many years as a Wolof and French instructor at the Centre Baobab in Dakar.[7] The center, run by two Americans, catered to study abroad students and foreign scholars in need of language training. Gomis on many occasions organized music for the center's receptions and parties, and many of the students studying at the center attended Gomis's musical engagements at various Dakar clubs. As a result of his teaching, Gomis was able to keep his finger on the pulse of popular music taste in the United States. This knowledge was to prove invaluable to Orchestre Baobab when it launched its international career.

Even more important, Gomis brought a quality of *saudade* to Baobab's music. Saudade is an untranslatable Portuguese word for a melancholy, nostalgic longing: for family, homeland, or a romantic partner. Musically, it is an important mood throughout the Portuguese speaking world, but it has played an especially significant role in Lusophone music in Africa—whether from Angola, Cape

Verde, or Guinea-Bissau—because of the dislocations brought about by the independence struggle, postcolonial political turmoil, and stagnant economies.[8] It permeates Gomis's masterpiece "Utru Horas" ("Other Hours"), first recorded in 1982. A disappointed lover sings the song, which may have a deeper allegorical subtext. The song was featured on the group's first release in the West in 1989, *Pirates Choice: The Legendary 1982 Session*.[9] Its elegiac tone, combined with its aural portraits of a languid world, proved seductive for the Western listeners who discovered the band in the early 1990s. Perhaps it was this tropical saudade that attracted Nick Gold, the proprietor of the World Circuit CD label, to the group's music in the 1980s. At the turn of the millennium this aural soundscape provided the central concept for World Circuit's successful promotional campaign for the group.

THE ART OF MAKING RUINS: THE BUENA VISTA SOCIAL CLUB AND ORCHESTRE BAOBAB

One of Orchestre Baobab's strokes of commercial good fortune was to attract Gold's attention in the 1980s.[10] Without his marketing savvy, it is doubtful that the band, despite all its talent, would have been able to launch an international career. Gold excels in repackaging African and Caribbean acts for global consumption. Shrewdly, he leaves their music relatively unchanged but encapsulates it within exotic narratives that tap into Western desires. His handling of Baobab is replete with irony. For example, it was reputedly his exposure to Baobab's music in the 1980s that sparked his interest in prerevolutionary Cuban music, an interest that was to culminate in his Buena Vista Social Club venture in 1997.[11] This CD, which brought together the US guitarist Ry Cooder and old Cuban musicians from the 1950s (and earlier), was an international triumph, selling millions of units. It made Nick Gold an important force in the global entertainment industry but only minimally and indirectly benefited Orchestre Baobab, whose music inspired the project in the first place.

In 2001 Gold helped "revive" and reinvent Orchestre Baobab as a combination of a tropical "jam" band and a West African equivalent of the Buena Vista Social Club. The image of Africa that emerges from Nick Gold's reformulation of Baobab is diasporic, without a trace of cultural nationalism. While the group's music in Senegal is linked to a reflective nostalgia tied to conversations about national identity and cosmopolitanism, its world music reception is based on catering to an ersatz nostalgia divorced from any sense of history or lived experience. In Gold's hands, Orchestre Baobab became a tree without any roots.

Nick Gold comes from an unusual background for a major figure in the music business. After graduating from the University of Sussex with a degree in African history, he became involved with Britain's burgeoning world music scene in the 1980s. Two world music promoters, Ann Hunt and Mary Farquharson, seeing that concerts by touring African musicians had created a demand for their recordings in the United Kingdom, set up an independent label, World Circuit Music, to cater to this new, if still small, market.[12] They hired Gold to manage the label, even though he had scant experience in the music industry. However, he had several attributes that were to ensure his success in his new career. He was a discerning listener of musical traditions other than his own, and his taste was close to infallible. He was equally gifted at recording and packaging his musical product. Working closely with the recording engineer Jerry Boys (from 1993 on), he was able to produce very clear recordings of African instruments, like the kora, that presented thorny technical problems. His sense of graphic design was as impeccable as his ear. His stylishly designed CD packages stood out in a CD bin, luring the casual buyer. But perhaps Gold's most useful talent was his ability to spin mythic narratives about his performers that resonated deeply with fin-de-siècle European and North American zeitgeists.

Gold has become celebrated for two types of musical projects. He initially gained renown for his staging of unlikely encounters between US and African musicians. In 1993 he brought together the US rock and folk guitarist Ry Cooder and the Malian Tamashek musician Ali Farka Touré. The matchup was a fortuitous one. Cooder often plays in a bluesy bottleneck guitar style, while Touré's music sounds like an ancient variant of the blues to many overseas listeners. Although the musicians failed to achieve any meaningful personal rapport, their CD, *Talking Timbuktu*, received favorable reviews and sold a quarter of a million copies.[13] It launched Ali Farka Touré's career as a luminary of the world music scene and made Gold a force to be reckoned with in the music industry.

Gold's other project resulted in even more commercial and critical triumphs. Following *Talking Timbuktu*, he roamed the black Atlantic to rediscover once famous musicians from the tropical world who now were old and obscure but still spry and spirited. In the early 1990s he came up with the idea of uniting Cubans and West Africans in a "diasporic" reunion CD. However, his new venture focused on bringing Malian, not Senegalese, musicians to Cuba to record with

Cuban son musicians such as Eliades Ochoa from Cuarteto Patria. Gold included Cooder in the mix to make the undertaking even more global in scope.[14] For various reasons the project went awry, and the Malians never arrived for the recording session.[15] Having already rented studio space and paid both a recording engineer and Cooder, Gold decided to salvage his investment by producing a different sort of album. With the help of a young Cuban musician, Juan de Marcos González, from the son revival group Sierra Maestra, with whom he already had a business relationship, he brought a crew of mostly retired Cuban musicians to make an album with Cooder of Cuban son "standards": *The Buena Vista Social Club*.[16]

The album was an immediate artistic and commercial hit.[17] What made it especially noteworthy was that its sales continued to rise after its initial rapid success. A major factor in the album's staying power was the marketing campaign that accompanied its release, especially in the United States. The campaign marked the beginning of an alliance between Nick Gold's small British company and the US media giant Time Warner, owner of the Nonesuch music label. This association provided Gold with the capital and media access he required to disseminate his music to a larger transatlantic public and the muscle he needed to book his acts into some of the world's major music venues, such as Carnegie Hall in New York. This promotional effort employed narrative strategies and images that Gold later deployed on behalf of Orchestre Baobab. It offers a picturesque vision of an urban tropical landscape in ruins, largely populated by older men and women. In this world in terminal decline, state and society disregard formerly illustrious musicians, who now survive in genteel poverty, their talent undiminished by the ravages of time and neglect. The musicians artistically and financially rehabilitate themselves by endearing themselves to US, Canadian, and Western European audiences. Their redemption stands in stark contrast to the decaying tropical cities that serve as a romantic setting for their fairy-tale metamorphosis.

An integral part of the Buena Vista Social Club's success was a 1999 documentary on their rise from obscurity to fame by the renowned German filmmaker Wim Wenders.[18] The film received international acclaim and had a respectable run in movie theaters. It was even more commercially viable as a DVD, still in circulation a decade after its release. It was Cooder, not Gold, who recruited Wenders to make the film. Cooder wrote the music for a sound track for one of Wenders's productions. While they were collaborating, the guitarist played the director the tapes from the Buena Vista Social Club sessions. Wenders was entranced, and when Cooder suggested that he make a film about the 1998 recording of an album by one of the Buena Vista Social Club's stars, the sonero Ibrahim Ferrer, the German cinéaste seized the opportunity.

The film has some hokey footage of the hipster Cooder riding around the streets of Havana (he is listed as the movie's producer) and some stirring scenes of the Buena Vista Social Club performing live in New York and Amsterdam. However, its most powerful images depict the disparities between a crumbling but enchanting Havana, where the musicians walk the streets largely unrecognized, and a shimmering and prosperous New York, where the musicians are awed by the view from the Empire State building. Whether by design or not, the film inspires conflicting reactions. On the one hand, it makes viewers revel in the overdue international recognition of a coterie of previously underacknowledged musicians.[19] On the other hand, it induces nostalgia for a collapsing Havana that very few of the viewers have experienced firsthand. This Western longing for a dilapidated tropics played a significant role in the "second" career of Orchestre Baobab as a major world music ensemble. With the marketing of Buena Vista Social Club, this first world "tropical nostalgia" was an unanticipated development. However, it was a calculated strategy on the part of Gold and his staff in the relaunching of Orchestre Baobab in 2001.

This ersatz nostalgia differs from the reflective and restorative varieties of nostalgia discussed in chapter 5, in that it relates more to fantasy than memory. It is an example of what Mikhail Bakhtin called "historic inversion": "[T]he idea that is *not* being lived now is projected into the past."[20] With this "imagined nostalgia," individuals experience a sense of longing for things that never were and feel a sense of loss for what they never have suffered.[21] These projects select which moments of the past to memorialize, to forget, to distort, and to concoct, and then to sanitize and decontextualize, distancing spectators from both their history and the history of others.[22] In the case of Cuba and Senegal, the "tropical nostalgia" connected with the marketing of Buena Vista Social Club and post-2001 Orchestre Baobab edits out slavery, racism, Castroism, and French colonialism from its visual and aural narrative. What remains is a touristic tableau of weather-battered buildings in ruins, the worn but sweet faces of musicians, and music divorced from the historical conditions and audiences that originally shaped it.[23]

"MYSTIC CHORDS OF MEMORY": DESIGNING ERSATZ NOSTALGIA

If you want to sell something, you have to create a myth.

Juan de Marcos González[24]

Orchestre Baobab had long ceased to exist as a working unit by 2001, when Gold "rediscovered" the group through the efforts of Jenny Cathcart, a British music journalist who became the band's manager for two years.[25] However, the musicians from the group still maintained close ties with one another. Some former members of the ensemble played club dates together, and Gomis, in an attempt to revive the group, recorded several cassettes with some of his erstwhile colleagues, including the vocalist Balla Sidibé, the bassist Charley N'Diaye, and the guitarist Barthélémy Attisso.[26] Gold began to design a marketing campaign to raise the international profile of the reassembled group by presenting it as a symbol of African modernity gone to seed in a ramshackle developing world

His strategy, which has served as a template for the revival of other belle epoque African bands as world music acts, involved three phases. First, Gold and Cathcart arranged for the group to give a concert at London's prestigious Barbican Hall in May 2001. In that same year World Circuit released for a second time *Pirate's Choice*, this time with heavy promotion.[27] Finally, Gold's plan culminated in the group's recording a new album for World Circuit in London's Livingston Studios. The CD, entitled *Specialist in All Styles*, was released in 2002 and was both a critical and a commercial coup.[28] The album was a careful re-creation of the group's 1970s sound. It avoided incorporating any innovations from the 1990s salsa m'balax or newer Afro-Cuban and salsa styles. If Baobab's musicians had been semiretired septuagenarians like the Buena Vista Social Club artists, such a "retro" take on popular music would have sounded delightfully "authentic" and "traditional." However, that wasn't the case with the members of Baobab. Almost all of them were middle-aged, working musicians who had kept abreast of developments in Senegalese music. Gold didn't try to change their music, with the exception of inviting "big name" musicians such as Ibrahim Ferrer and Youssou N'Dour to participate in a re-recording of "Utru Horas."[29] Instead, he encouraged the ensemble to "time-capsule" its repertoire.[30] The result had numerous subtle touches but lacked the originality and willingness to experiment that always had been a hallmark of the group. The exigencies of tropical nostalgia trumped artistic ambition.

Gold boosted his crusade to refurbish Orchestre Baobab with a publicity campaign and graphic design branding that mythologized the lives of the ensemble's members, converting them into conduits for tropical nostalgia. Strikingly, he superimposed the Buena Vista Social Club narrative of neglect, rediscovery, and redemption on the more complicated history of Baobab. Apparently with Barthélémy Attisso's cooperation, Gold equated his musical biography with that of the pianist Rubén González of Buena Vista Social Club. Supposedly Attisso had given up the guitar for years, just as González had given up the piano (after he retired as a musician when he was in his seventies). Both, according to the publicity for the two projects, took up their instruments again because they were inspired by the intervention of a British world music impresario. Attisso, however, had not stopped playing the guitar, though he was working full time as a lawyer in Togo. As mentioned previously, he had recorded a cassette with Gomis a few years before Orchestre Baobab officially regrouped. That is why when he was asked to rejoin the group in 2001, he immediately accepted. There was no need for him to remaster his instrument; he had never put it down.

Gold spun another myth that the musicians were living in anonymity in Dakar and that it was only through the Herculean efforts of Youssou N'Dour that Gold was able to relocate them.[31] This imaginary situation mimicked the "rediscovery" of the Buena Vista Social Club artists. However, many of the Baobab musicians, including Balla Sidibé and Issa Cissokho, were still leading figures in the Dakar music scene; others, including Rudy Gomis and Lafti Benjeloun, moved in elite circles in Senegal. Any traveler to Senegal would have had little trouble contacting them. Gold's make-believe story allows audiences outside of Africa to feel the frisson of "rescuing" these purportedly starving artists from their squalor without leaving the comfort of their armchairs. Here, nostalgia for the tropics blends with paternalism and a quest for exotic experiences to produce a potent mix of music and myth.

The album art for the three World Circuit Orchestre Baobab releases since 2001 invites consumers to savor disintegrating tropical urban scapes. The creators of the artwork weave three ideas through their visual designs: the patina of half-recollected memories, urban vernacular art including graffiti, and Harmattan-eroded urban spaces. Each reinforces an ersatz mood of tropical nostalgia. A pastel palette of tans, greens, and oranges in the booklets accompanying *Specialist in All Styles* (2002) and *Made in Dakar* (2008) induces melancholy remembrances of things past. The insert for *Made in Dakar* uses a scrapbook as its organizing visual concept, contrasting the Baobab musicians in their prime as rambunctious youths with their later more sedate, prosperous, postrediscovery selves. For *Specialist in All Styles*, stylized, graffiti-like markings signify cultural authenticity and up-from-the-roots musical credibility. However, Orchestre Baobab never claimed to speak for the youth in Dakar's quartiers populaires and lacked the street aggressiveness that later typified hip-hop. The iconic painted barbershop illustrations of African hairstyles that are strewn throughout the booklet are similarly misleading. They are meant to provide a smattering of tropical exoticism along with a visual pun, comparing the capacity of Orchestre Baobab to play a varied repertoire with the ability of a master barber to cater to all tastes. However, these homages to African folk art do violence to the image of a band whose historic mission was to encourage stylishness and cosmopolitanism among its public. Culturally, its music is as far removed from a plein air haircutter as a car dealer's repair service would be from a roadside mechanic.

The publicity for the band and the illustrations in the booklets for the CD focus on shabby urban streetscapes. The inserts for *Specialist in All Styles* and *Made in Dakar* visually highlight poorly maintained, pockmarked stucco walls. Once again, the scruffy imagery serves to disassociate the band from its identity as an exemplar of elegance and sophistication in favor of its New World music identity as a purveyor of nostalgia for decaying tropical paradises. World Circuit's decision about which photograph of the band should dominate its Web site further demonstrates that this revamping of the band's cultural identity was an integral part of the record label's marketing strategy. The Web site buries one photograph of the band dressed in well-tailored European-style suits in order to showcase another peculiar portrait. In this featured image, the group poses around one of Dakar's famous blue-and-yellow *car rapide* buses on a Senegalese beach (Yoff or Ngor), a few of the members standing while others are seated in the vehicle.[32] The majority are wearing African garments; only a few are in European clothes. The outfits are subdued, with the exception of saxophonist Issa Cissokho's brightly colorful attire. In the distance a small child gazes at the group, his face invisible. A tropical sunset serves as an incongruous backdrop to this strange scene. The lighting is an unsettling mix of natural and artificial light. The composition of the photo delineates dualities: African clothes versus European fashion, the rural (the undeveloped beach) versus the urban (the car rapide), adult versus child, nature versus the machine. These interlocking dichotomies imply that the musicians in the band are interstitial figures, mediating among the realms of the ancestors, the divinities, and humankind. While it is true that some popular music artists in Africa have performed this spiritual function, including some in the Congo and the electronic griots of the Mande cultural complex that includes part of Senegal, it is an odd and inappropriate role for the members of Orchestre Baobab. The band always has been secular and urbane. However, in Gold's business plan, this imposed fabricated identity is the secret to success. Historical veracity would only get in the way. His manufactured image envelops the band in a mythic aura compatible with its supposed legendary status. Positioned by the photograph between tradition and contemporaneity, the ensemble seems to offer non-African audiences a palatable taste of both worlds: cultural authenticity along with an exotic musical modernity.

Gold's graphic designers' most startling aesthetic decision was to populate the insert accompanying the 2001 re-release of *Pirates Choice* with a large number of photographs from the great Malian photographer Malick Sidibé. Sidibé was renowned for his candid images in the 1960s of Bamako's youth entering modernity through embracing foreign popular culture and new patterns of consuming leisure time. The new youth culture they embodied would not have been out of place in 1950s Dakar, with its record clubs. However, it has little to do with the genteel precincts Orchestre Baobab inhabited in the 1970s. Sidibé's photographs in this context serve to dehistoricize and deterritorialize the ensemble. This unmooring of the band from a particular epoch and location makes it a suitable subject for a tropical nostalgia based on secondhand feelings about imaginary places. It simultaneously renders them both alien and familiar to audiences abroad, the visual equivalent of one of Attisso's guitar solos.

A final irony for Orchestre Baobab is that its success in the world music market led to new opportunities at home. The band began to play on a regular basis in some of Dakar's most prestigious clubs, such as Just4U in Point E, that catered to well-to-do Senegalese and the city's large expatriate and diplomatic community. The ensemble's career had now come full circle. In the early 1970s, after its formation, the group played for such a public at the Baobab Club. Forty years later, after surviving and to some degree bypassing the vicissitudes of the music business in Senegal, after performing in many of the major concert halls in Europe and North America, and after being repackaged internationally as an African version of the Buena Vista Social Club, the band at last returned to its roots.

Gold's marketing of Orchestre Baobab obviously came out of an appreciation for its music and a desire to disseminate that music to a large international public. However, by locking Baobab into a classic 1970s style, he reinforced the impression in Senegal and abroad that Dakar's Latin musicians are stuck in a time warp.[33] Nothing could be further from the truth. Though loyal to the Afro-Cuban tradition, Dakar's salsa artists have embraced innovation when it is in tune with their musical values. No development illustrates this openness to change more than Ibrahima Sylla's Africando project.

FROM AFRO-CUBAN TO AFRICAN/CUBAN: BECOMING AFRICANDO

The history of Africando demonstrates that the creation of world music was not always an exclusively "Western" project. Originally conceived as a project to resuscitate Latin music in Senegal, Africando's cassettes, CDs, and concert DVDs became artistic successes in New York, London, and Paris as well as in Dakar, Conakry, and Bamako. Even more remarkable is that a remix of one of the group's songs was a number one hit on New York's Mega Latin charts for six weeks and became a hit as well throughout the Caribbean basin.

From its inception, Africando was a transnational project in every respect. However, it took a divergent approach to breaking into the world music market from the World Circuit/Orchestre Baobab juggernaut. It had much more slender resources at its disposal and targeted different global audiences. Its significance in Africa was dissimilar as well. Orchestre Baobab's revival depended on luring white audiences in Western Europe and North America. As a result, its impact in Africa was relatively muted. Africando sought to reinforce and reinvigorate the cultural ties between Afro-Cuban and African popular music. It simultaneously tried to appeal to contemporary African listeners, a Latino audience in North America, and a world music public seeking novel experiences. Remarkably, it was able to achieve all these objectives to some degree in one of the most culturally noteworthy careers in the brief history of world music.

In large part, these differences occurred because an African entrepreneur, rather than a European or US producer, was the animating force behind Africando. The musical project was the creation of the Senegalese musical impresario Ibrahima Sylla (1956–2013), one of the most important figures in contemporary African show business. Sylla was born into a prominent Guinean/Senegalese marabout family and discovered Afro-Cuban music as a child when it was played in his parents' house. By the mid-1970s he had become a record producer, working with Orchestre Baobab. From there he branched out to produce Congolese and Cape Verdean music aimed at a Pan-African market. When the cassette revolution transformed the marketing of African music in 1978–1979, Sylla eventually became one of the major distributors of cassettes in Senegal and elsewhere in West Africa. Though Sylla's first love remained Afro-Cuban music, he was cautious about recording it because its popularity was on the wane in the 1980s. However, as he amassed his fortune he increasingly wanted to sponsor a renaissance of Latin music, both in his native Senegal and in Africa at large. Though he was hesitant to admit it publicly, the work of other African record producers had a significant impact on Sylla. Especially influential were the series of records produced by the Nigerian/Ivorian producer Aboudou Lassissi in the early 1980s with the Gambian sonero Laba Sosseh and the Cuban singer and bandleader Monguito and the Latin music produced by Sylla's former employer, Daniel Cuxac.[34] These recordings featured a balancing of African and Caribbean musical elements and embraced the concept of a black Atlantic.

By 1992 Sylla was ready to pursue his ambition of sparking a resurgence of Afro-Cuban music in Senegal. To implement his creative vision, he turned to his friend, the Malian/Nigerien flutist and arranger Boncana Maïga. Maïga has had one of the most transnational careers of any African musician in recent years. As a young man he formed a band to play Afro-Cuban music in the small towns of western Niger and eastern Mali. One night after an engagement in a Malian community in the early 1960s, some Malian officials approached Maïga and offered him a music scholarship to study in Cuba. Fidel Castro had given Modibo Keita's government a number of scholarships for players of specific instruments. According to Maïga, the government officials couldn't find another suitable flutist, so they pressed him into service. In Havana Maïga studied classical music at a conservatory during the day and played with leading Afro-Cuban musicians in Havana's nightclubs at night. Before long, in 1965, Maïga formed a band with other Malians resident in Cuba, Las Maravillas de Mali, which enjoyed some success in Cuba and caused a stir in Mali.[35] Maïga returned to Bamako just as Keita was driven from power. The new military regime looked askance at his Cuban training, and Maïga moved to Abidjan, where the Ivorian government was more welcoming. Maïga became the first staff arranger on Ivorian television and from there went on to become a leading large group arranger in Africa, in demand in Paris, Kinshasa, Dakar, and Bamako.[36] By the 1990s Maïga had already worked on a number of projects with Sylla, who respected his knowledge of Cuban musical traditions and his mastery of nearly every major African popular music style. He was the perfect creative partner for the producer.

The concept of Africando, on the surface, was simple: gather three of the best Afro-Cuban singers in Dakar and take them to New York to record with the best

Latin session musicians. However, this surface simplicity masked many cultural complexities. The Senegalese public for the previous three generations had embraced a form of Cuban music played by charanga ensembles. Many Senegalese Latin bands since the 1960s have played an Africanized version of charangas with synthesizers taking the flute part and with horns or guitars simulating the charanga violin riffs. However, even though assembling an excellent charanga ensemble would have been an easy proposition in 1990s New York, Sylla and Maïga, aside from a few obligatory charanga numbers, mostly opted for a brassy, percussion-driven salsa sound, based on the work the flutist and arranger Johnny Pacheco had created for Fania records in the 1960s. Sylla deliberately wanted a departure from the typical Senegalese way of playing Latin music. He wanted to do more than just revive Afro-Cuban music in Senegal; his ambition was to modernize the Senegalese manner of performing it, replacing the 1950s Cuban model with the 1970s and 1980s New York and Puerto Rico style.[37] He hoped the new grittier sound would attract a younger generation and garner cultural prestige with its intricate arrangements.

To symbolize his abandonment of the classic Senegalese Afro-Cuban style, Sylla opted not to include Laba Sosseh on his recording.[38] Instead he chose a gifted but relatively unknown singer, Nicolas Menheim; the ballad singer, Medoune Diallo, formerly of Orchestre Baobab; and the gravel-voiced veteran Pape Seck, previously with No. 1, one of the first Senegalese to sing Cuban music in Wolof. The choice of personnel showed that Sylla intended for the group to encompass the past, present, and future of Afro-Cuban music in Senegal. Seck represented the foundational generation of the 1960s who had pioneered faithful renditions of Afro-Cuban classics. Diallo was a member of Orchestre Baobab during the 1970s. These men and Menheim came together with Sylla to bring Senegalese Afro-Cuban music into the 1990s.

The group's name, Africando, devised by Sylla, signified that it was exploring new creative territory. A witty example of wordplay in two languages, Wolof and Spanish, that evokes intertextuality more than méttisage or hybridity, Africando simultaneously means, "an African Group" in Wolof (with "ando" being the Wolof word for "ensemble") and "becoming African" in Spanish ("and" being the suffix for the present participle). In Sylla's eyes, by privileging the salsa tradition of Latin music over the charanga sound, he was further decolonizing Afro-Cuban music in Senegal and making it more typically Caribbean.

To obtain the level of musicianship that he needed, Sylla knew he was going to have to outlay significant funds. In addition to flying the Senegalese singers to

New York and providing for their food and lodging, he also had to rent expensive New York recording studios and pay the high fees of much sought-after Latin session men. Not willing to shoulder the burden by himself, Sylla sought an overseas partner. He turned to a British/American record company with whom he often had done business in the past, Sterns. The executives at Sterns initially didn't have much confidence in the project. They felt Sylla's commercial instincts were off and that the music he wanted to produce was too old fashioned.[39] Ultimately they agreed to invest a considerable amount of money in Sylla's scheme because he had a history of consistent success as a producer, especially with the 1987 album *Soro* by the Malian singer Salif Keïta.[40] Partnerships distributing his music outside Africa had been profitable for the company, and the executives valued his commercial acumen. In the end, with misgivings, they decided to give him everything he requested up front in exchange for holding the licenses for Africando's product for the world outside of France and Africa.

The recording of the first Africando albums went smoothly and produced enough quality material to fill two CDs, but the experience was somewhat unsettling for the Senegalese musicians involved. Sylla unwittingly lodged them at a rat-infested Times Square hotel, where the rodents scurrying around after dark kept them up at night.[41] The only Latin musician with whom they had any sustained contact was the half Puerto Rican, half Cuban singer Ronnie Baro, who is Maïga's brother-in-law. The Latin session instrumentalists, all no-nonsense professionals, came in, recorded their parts, and then immediately left for other musical engagements. Though friendly enough, they showed minimal interest in socially interacting with the visiting African singers, only one of whom, Nicolas Menheim, could speak English or Spanish and whose music, in any event, was unfamiliar to most of them. A dispute with Sylla over his payment of their fees also might have led to the New York session men ignoring the Senegalese visitors. Moreover, Sylla, as always working with a tight budget, scheduled such long work days that there was little time for tourism or participating in after-hours *descargas* at Latin clubs. After a postrecording party hosted by Sterns, the singers returned to Dakar to await the reception of their album.

For Sylla, Africando obviously was a labor of love. He has stated that for him recording Afro-Cuban music was "a passion. Even if there are difficulties, I don't even notice them, I love the music so much. When I record Afro-Cuban music, I don't even notice the time passing."[42] He had realistic expectations for his project. He hoped it would stimulate a minor revival of Latin music in Senegal. If he realized a small profit and kept Afro-Cuban music alive in his native country, he would be satisfied. However, Africando succeeded commercially and culturally far beyond what he and his partners at Sterns Music anticipated. It briefly became a cause célèbre in Senegal; a critical success with the Latin and world music press in North America and the United Kingdom; and a hit with listeners in Francophone Africa, the Hispanic United States, and the Caribbean.

Sylla released the first Africando cassette in Senegal in the fall of 1992, and Sterns released the first CD, *Trovador*, internationally in 1993.[43] The cassettes quickly found favor with Senegalese music consumers, who found the revamping of their Latin music tradition refreshing. Its release particularly gratified Senegalese in their forties and fifties. This was the generation that had grown up with Afro-Cuban music and now was in power. One such fan turned out to be Abdou Diouf, the president of Senegal. He so enjoyed the cassette, he ordered the Senegalese television network, RTS, to book Africando for a live performance on New Year's Eve, one of the most important holidays in Senegal. The band's performance created a sensation, but not the kind that either Sylla or Diouf expected or wanted. Medoune Diallo showed up at the television studio inebriated; during the live broadcast he was obviously drunk and almost unable to perform. Diouf was displeased and Sylla disappointed, but Diallo's antics only served to increase the group's popularity with the Senegalese public.[44] Soon the Africando ensemble embarked on a lucrative West African tour, and the sales of the cassette continued to increase.

The release of the CD in the United States in 1993 led four years later to the band's traveling to New York to participate in Lincoln Center's Summer Festival as part of a series entitled *Expresiones Latinas*, with the Béninois sonero Gnonnas Pedro replacing Pape Seck. The group performed on July 25, sharing the bill with the revered Cuban bassist Cachao and his ensemble. The largely Hispanic audience, who had turned out to see Cachao, were bewildered by the West Africans, who came out dressed in loud green suits and moved stiffly to the music in typical West African performing fashion. Though the Africando vocalists sang with brio, they clearly would have benefited from having more rehearsal time with their New York Latin sidemen. Despite these drawbacks, a number of audience members at Lincoln Center thought that Africando had outshone the maestro himself, Cachao. Its performance was animated and charming. Regrettably, the group was unable to capitalize on its auspicious debut in New York. The New York media either ignored the concert or treated it as an ethnomusicological curiosity. The cost of touring North America with a large ensemble of first-rate Latin sidemen (at least twelve were needed) turned out to be prohibitive. The situation in Europe was more promising. The band's concerts in Paris, which drew many émigré Africans, became major cultural events. Subsidies from European government cultural ministries, combined with lower costs in Europe for backup musicians, made it possible for the group to undertake a European tour.

Ultimately, however, Africando remained more a recording group and never really emerged as a working ensemble.[45] The Senegalese musicians in the project were unable to capitalize on its success. Pape Seck died of liver cancer on February 2, 1995. Medoune Diallo's alcoholism impaired his ability to perform, and he played little part in the remarkable revival of Orchestre Baobab in the 1990s. Menheim hoped that Africando's success would enable him to have a global career like Youssou N'Dour's and Baaba Maal's. However, after the triumphs of *Trovador* and *Tierra Tradicional*, Sylla enlarged the concept of Africando to include all of Africa and its musicians, not just Senegal.[46] As subsequent recordings started to feature famous vocalists from around the continent, legendary singers like the Congolese Tabu Ley overshadowed the gifted but lesser known Menheim. When it became evident that Africando was not going to make him into an international star, Menheim formed one of the most artistically distinguished of all Senegalese Afro-Cuban groups, Super Sabor.

One of the reasons that the vocalists benefited so little from Africando is that Sylla and Sterns's marketing strategy increasingly promoted the diasporic concept behind the project more heavily than the group's members. Sylla and Sterns's approach to publicity had a different tone from the campaign for Orchestre Baobab. Since its founding Sterns has specialized in dignified, well-informed presentations of African popular musicians. Its design for Africando's albums was squarely within that tradition. The cover art for the first Africando album is a photograph of the three Senegalese frontline singers Medoune Diallo, Pape Seck, and Nicholas Menheim. The trio is stylishly dressed in European clothes, with Diallo and Seck wearing white sports coats and Menheim a herringbone jacket, black vest, and elegant tie. The art deco style artwork behind them is in pulsating orange and reds, a sunrise in opposition to the publicity photo of Orchestre Baobab posing in front of a sunset. There is nothing reminiscent of the past in the cover or the erudite accompanying album notes. Africando is very much of the present. The theme of an up-to-date band addressing a forward-looking public continued through the group's first four CDs. When the ensemble evolved into a Pan-African Latin project, the artwork shifted into more self-consciously African images (a male figure dressed in a suit wearing a masquerade on *Mandali*; a woman of color wearing a man's hat and smoking a cigar on *Martina*; a woman of color in a bikini playing a *djembe* drum on *Ketukuba*), still avoiding any nostalgic nods to a vanished golden age.

Africando, like the salsa m'balax bands, sought to update the Senegalese Latin style. Where salsa m'balax turned inward for its contemporaneity, Africando primarily drew its inspiration from external sources. Rather than incorporate m'balax rhythms, it chose instead to stress lyrics in Wolof and Boncana Maïga's modern Latin arrangements. Senegalese Afro-Cuban groups often featured vocal duets but rarely employed a coro in the Cuban manner that is such a conspicuous feature of Cuban and Puerto Rican popular music. Africando made heavy use of coros on its initial albums. In addition, Maïga played these Cuban vocal tropes off against the Senegalese timbre of the three soloists, Diallo, Seck, and Menheim, in a musical bricolage of the global and the local. The result could have proven distracting, but Maïga downplayed such contrasts by emphasizing the bass and percussion in his mix, favoring dance beats over explorations of cultural difference. Not surprisingly, this approach ultimately appealed to African and Hispanic listeners more than to the world music public. As Juan de Marcos, one of the two individuals behind Buena Vista Social Club, observed, world music is essentially concert driven.[47] It is for armchair travelers, not dance floor warriors. Orchestre Baobab resolved to attract this audience of audio anthropologists. Africando followed another path, revitalizing the south-south cultural dialogue that had marked the implanting of Afro-Cuban music in Senegal in the 1930s.

ROOTS IN REVERSE: LOS AFRO-SALSEROS IN HAVANA

For many Senegalese, the fame of Africando overseas, while gratifying, was somewhat beside the point. Senegalese audiences and musicians appreciated New York Latin music, especially Orchestra Broadway and Johnny Pacheco, but not even Sylla's creative and commercial achievements could shake their belief that what really mattered was artistic acceptance in Cuba, the home for them of musical refinement and cultural modernity. Before 2001 this acceptance was elusive. Senegal and Cuba had never established diplomatic relations. Occasionally ensembles like Orquesta Aragón toured Senegal, but it was politically impossible for a Senegalese group to play in Cuba, given the two nations' lack of formal relations. Moreover, the Cuban public was uninterested in African music of any type, preferring in addition to their own music US jazz and soul music and Brazilian bossa nova. In the 1980s Laba Sosseh had recorded with Orquesta Aragón in Havana, but this session was never released as a recording commercially. Outside of a few professional musicians, Cubans were unaware of the popularity of their music in Africa and the important role that the appropriation of Cuban culture played in the creation of African modernities in West and Central Africa in the twentieth century.

The Cold War played a significant role in impeding official cultural interaction between the two countries. Leopold Senghor abhorred Fidel Castro and, publicly at least, had little interest in Afro-Cuban music. Senghor was an admirer of Hispanic civilization, but his promotion of latinité stopped short of embracing the Cuban revolution and Cuban music. Though the Senegalese public's love of Cuban music almost entirely lacked an ideological dimension, Senghor largely prohibited Afro-Cuban music from being performed at the first FESMAN (Festival Mondial des Arts Nègres) in 1966 on political grounds. When Abdou Diouf succeeded Senghor, he felt it prudent to continue Senghor's anti-Castro policies, although bowing to public pressure, he did let Orquesta Aragón tour Senegal numerous times.

When Abdoulaye Wade became president of Senegal in 2000 and his party won a majority of seats in Senegal's legislative branch in 2001, he looked for ways to inaugurate what he called a new era in Senegalese politics. Establishing diplomatic relations with Cuba was one way he could do so without arousing debate. In 2001 the first Cuban ambassador arrived in Dakar. He immediately established contact with the Senegalese-Cuban Friendship Association, a surprisingly large and active organization with an influential membership. In their effort to orient the diplomat to Senegalese culture, some of the association members took the ambassador to one of Dakar's Afro-Cuban nightclubs. The ambassador was astonished to learn that his country's music had taken root in Africa and resolved that having a Senegalese salsa group tour Cuba would be a dramatic way to inaugurate a series of cultural exchanges between the two nations. His ministry back in Havana agreed, and the financing of the trip was arranged.

If the journey now was politically uncontroversial from the Senegalese side, it turned out to be culturally complicated from the Cuban side. It stirred up at least two hornets' nests in the Cuban government. The Cuban Revolution from its inception has been deeply committed to creating what the scholar of Cuban music Robin Moore calls a "raceless society."[48] The official line is that racism was endemic in the old regime but has no place in the revolutionary state. Hence, to recognize and privilege Afro-Cuban culture would counter some of the revolution's most deeply held beliefs. However, the Cuban state does recognize that the vast majority of Cuba's poor are of African descent. To force them to deny their cultural heritage would link the Cuban state with prerevolutionary racist policies. As a result, the Cuban state has a profound ambivalence about Afro-Cuban culture.[49] This ambivalence paralyzed several government ministries involved in planning the Senegalese visit. A second even greater problem is the Cuban state's suspicion of Afro-Cuban popular dance music. Fidel Castro considered such music irrevocably tied to the hedonistic excesses of the Batista regime he had overthrown. In the period after the revolution came to power, the Cuban state sponsored the Nueva trova movement with its militant folk songs. The Nueva trova troubadours produced music that became popular throughout Latin America in the 1960s and 1970s. However, the movement's music failed to catch on with the Cuban public, who preferred music they could dance to without being politically indoctrinated. In the 1980s the Cuban government permitted modern Afro-Cuban music to have a higher profile domestically as long as the groups were seen as supporters of the Cuban Revolution.[50] Still, few officials in the government wanted to be seen as encouraging a music that had been branded as decadent, even if non-Cuban Africans were playing it. As a result, these officials planned few public appearances for the Senegalese.

The Senegalese in Dakar were unaware of these contradictions and ambivalences. Excitement grew over the projected tour, which was seen as culturally prestigious and politically advantageous. Several power struggles ensued in the Foreign Ministry over who was to organize the delegation and who was to be included in it. Within the highly competitive Senegalese salsa community, maneuvering also commenced over who was to lead and play in the touring ensemble. The situation became even more heated with the arrival of Günter Gretz, the owner of a tiny, if artistically distinguished, German record label, Popular African Music. Obviously inspired by Africando, Gretz saw the Cuban trip as an opportunity to unite the black Atlantic musically. Using the lure of a recording contract, Gretz established clientage ties with several important Senegalese salsa musicians, who had no idea of the commercial insignificance of Gretz's record label. The infighting became so intense that no faction was able to prevail. The group that finally went to Cuba was based on a series of uneasy compromises. As a result of these rivalries, the Senegalese delegation was as paralyzed in its own way as its Cuban hosts.

The Senegalese were expecting a hero's welcome when they arrived in Havana but were instead met with administrative passivity and public indifference. The musicians waited for days for the promised tour to materialize, but nothing happened. Frustrated and bored, several of the musicians, including Laba Sosseh, began to drink heavily, becoming unmanageable. After a long delay the Senegalese finally learned that they were to play at the legendary Hotel Nacional with an all-star collection of Cuban musicians. The musicians arrived at the hotel, expecting an audience of Cuban aficionados. Instead, they encountered a horde of bored and bewildered Canadian and Japanese tourists who were not in the mood to hear Latin musicians from Africa play old-fashioned Cuban music.[51] The few encounters that the Senegalese group ultimately had with the Cuban public were equally unsatisfying. The Cubans found the Senegalese interpretation of Cuban music odd and unsettling. They took offense at the bad Spanish of some of the Senegalese singers and found it weird when the Senegalese sang in Wolof. The fact that the Senegalese appeared ignorant of how Cuban music had changed since the 1950s also alienated Cuban spectators. They felt little kinship with what they considered to be strange visitors from overseas. The Senegalese musicians fortunately had more positive interactions with their Cuban musical counterparts. Some of the Buena Vista stars, including Rubén González, played some descargas with them, and the musicians had opportunities to play with other Cuban artists of similar stature.[52]

Before they departed for home, the Senegalese recorded a session at Cuba's state-owned Egrem studio, the same studio where the Buena Vista Social Club put together its album. This experience was as troubled as the rest of their trip. Gretz was unable to secure Cuban musicians for this session, either because they were unavailable or because he was undermined by some of his detractors in the Senegalese delegation. Once in the studio, Gretz clashed repeatedly with the guitarist and arranger Yahya Fall over the creative direction the project should take. Fall wanted the music to have a rough edge like one would hear in a Dakar club. Gretz, thinking of his international public, wanted a smoother sound. Ultimately, Gretz prevailed. The Cuban engineering staff in the studio clearly were unimpressed with what they heard. They repeatedly interrupted takes to correct the Spanish of the Senegalese singers. One of the singers grew so annoyed, he declared he would only sing in Wolof for the rest of the recording session. Despite these difficulties, the resulting CD features strong vocals and excellent arrangements. Unfortunately Gretz's label had an extremely small budget for promotion, even less than Sterns's. The project's release, *los afro-salseros de senegal en la habana*,[53] received minimal attention from the international press, and its sales to date have been insignificant. The musicians involved hoped it would launch their careers globally. Like the stars of Africando, they have been frustrated that nothing of lasting importance for them has come out of their time in Cuba. By and large, though, they have good memories of their trip and particularly favorable impressions of the Cuban health-care system and social life.

Although these ventures in reforging diasporic ties may have been disappointing for the Senegalese participants, the cultural significance of what they accomplished looms larger every year. Cuba's invitation to the Senegalese is only one of several that the Cuban government has initiated. Since the turn of the century at least one delegation from Calabar, Nigeria, has traveled to Havana. Perhaps learning from their mistakes with the Senegalese salsa musicians, the Cubans gave the Nigerians a rousing welcome.[54] However, it is unlikely that a Senegalese Latin group will tour Cuba any time in the foreseeable future despite the improved diplomatic relations between the two nations. Apparently the propitious moment for such cultural exchanges has passed.

However, if direct cultural exchanges between Cuba and Senegal are likely to remain sporadic until the end of Raúl Castro's regime in Cuba (Fidel Castro died in 2016), Senegal's cultural dialogue with many other Hispanic cultures in the Caribbean basin, such as Colombia and Puerto Rico, has intensified in recent years. As societies in the Caribbean have been more exposed to Senegalese Latin music through academic conferences, radio, and the Internet, receptivity to Senegalese interpretations of Afro-Cuban and Afro-Borinqueño music have increased. Curiosity about the history of this cultural exchange has been noticeably on the upswing among intellectuals and musicians.

In 2006 I was present at the Skylight Studio in New Jersey when Ibrahima Sylla was recording the latest installment in the Africando series, *Ketukuba*.[55] The atmosphere in the recording studio was much more open to cultural interaction than during the 1997 recording session for *Baloba!*, which I also witnessed. The African and Caribbean musicians this time around joked with each other about food, language differences, and sex. During a short break in the recording, the Venezuelan arranger of the session, Nelson Hernandez, came over to me and asked me for a reading list on African music and also requested some leads on where he could purchase CDs of African percussion. "I *need* to know these things," he told me, illustrating that at long last the seemingly one-way transatlantic musical dialogue on Latin music is beginning to go both ways.

MONTUNO: THE TRANSATLANTIC ECHOES OF "YAYE BOY"

In 1996 in Latin dance clubs in New York, Bogota, Medellin, and Cali, one of the most popular musical pieces was a Colombian remix of a number sung in the Senegalese language Wolof to a rhythm derived from an Afro-Borinqueño song form. Before long, it had become a best seller in Colombian music stores despite its lyrics being in an African language from a country little known in Latin America. Undoubtedly the Colombian public was unaware that the song, "Yaye Boy" (or "Yay Boy"), had a long career and that Colombia was only the latest stop on a journey that crisscrossed the Atlantic basin. Indeed, the song continued to resonate around the Atlantic world, recorded in a significantly different version in Cuba several years later.

"Yaye Boy" has its origins in the song "Bomba de Corazón," originally recorded by the Nuyorican pianist, bandleader, and composer Eddie Palmieri in New York in 1964. Palmieri, an innovative figure in Latin music for half a century, has been a pioneer in adapting Cuban musical traditions to the social and cultural realities faced by post–World War II Puerto Rican migrants to the US mainland. He was one of the first Latin musicians of his era to experiment with avant-garde jazz and African American rhythm and blues and was famous in the early 1960s for being one of the first Latin band leaders to replace the blaring trumpets of the Cuban conjuntos of the 1950s with a chorus of trombones.

"Bomba del Corazón" represented another stylistic departure for Palmieri.[56] Recorded Puerto Rican music before the 1960s primarily drew its inspiration either from Afro-Cuban song forms like son or danzón or from musical forms like the *seis* and *aguinaldo* from the peasantry of the island's mountainous interior. Both the seis and aguinaldo genres display a marked Spanish influence and came to play an important role in the conceptualizing of a Puerto Rican nation by Borinqueño intellectuals in the twentieth century. Their vision of Puerto Rico was one of hardy European small-scale farmers thriving in a challenging tropical environment. What was missing from this vision was Puerto Rico's plantation heritage, with its enslaved African laborers. Equally absent was the proletarianization of Puerto Rico during the decades of US rule and the subsequent mass migration to the factories and workshops of the colonial power.

Given this prevailing foundational myth, it is not surprising that few, if any, Puerto Rican musicians recorded Afro-Borinqueño musical forms like the *bomba* before the 1950s. It thus was a daring gesture by Palmieri, who wasn't Afro-

Boriqueño, to record a bomba for a mass audience. In so doing, he was part of a broad-based movement in the 1960s to fashion a more inclusive Borinqueño identity in tune with the diverse strands of Puerto Rican history. Interestingly, Palmieri meshed his bomba with an Afro-Cuban arrangement with piano and a brass section predominating (bombas are traditionally a percussive tradition like the Cuban rumba). The result is a musical mix that thrilled listeners beyond the Puerto Rican public.

In 1978 the Senegalese band No. 1 traveled to Paris and recorded the Pape Seck composition "Yaye Boy," a praise song for Senegalese mothers.[57] Seck constructed his song around Palmieri's opening piano vamp for "Bomba del Corazón." While preserving the rhythmic structure of Palmieri's composition, the band's arrangement dispensed with piano and trombones and in their place substituted a saxophone solo by Tierno Koité, sounding more Moroccan than Caribbean, and a brief trumpet flourish by Ali Penda. More radically, No. 1 inserted some indigenous touches like tama drums and Seck's Wolof lyrics. The result is a song that stays within the parameters of Latin music but reconfigures previously existing elements into new patterns.

"Yaye Boy" assumed the status of a classic in the Senegalese popular music canon and became a staple of the band's repertoire. In 1991, when Ibrahima Sylla produced the first two Africando CDs, "Yaye Boy" was one of the songs the group recorded. In 1994 Sylla and Sterns released the album *Tierra Tradicional*, which contained the new recording of "Yaye Boy."[58] Under Sylla and his arranger Boncana Maïga's guidance, the Africando version turns the No. 1 original inside out. The aesthetic framework remains intact, but there is a reshuffling of musical elements. They recast Pape Seck's classic as a straight-ahead salsa piece. Where before Seck and Yahya Fall had included iconic signs of *Senegalismo* like tama drums, Sylla "re-Latinizes" the song with bongos and New York salsa horn lines to better accentuate its cosmopolitan underpinnings.

The song enjoyed a long life as an underground hit in New York dance clubs and began to circulate around the Caribbean basin, especially in Colombia. By the mid-1990s it attracted the attention of the Asefra brothers, Colombian music producers who closely followed the New York Latin music scene. In 1995, much to the bemusement of Sterns's management, the Asefras showed up at Sterns's New York offices and asked for permission to do a remix of "Yaye Boy." Gratified that the Colombians hadn't simply pirated the music, Sterns agreed and even offered them the rights without a fee.[59] The Asefra Brothers then hired a New York DJ, Baron Lopez, to do the remix in the then prevailing "Latin House" style. The

Asefras knew how to work the system in New York Latin music radio, and the song received extensive airplay. Before long it reached the Latin charts, where it remained for six weeks. In Colombia the remix was even more popular.[60] The Asefras obviously were fascinated by the song, because around the same time they recorded a second version of the piece, sung by the Peruvian salsero and comedian Melcochita, who had long been active in Ivorian Latin music circles.[61] He was backed on the recording by some of the same New York Latin session musicians who had played on the Africando project.

The Asefras probably intended the session with Melcochita for the West African and Peruvian markets. Trumpets dominate the opening, followed by a trombone chorus, and the song's melody is set to Spanish lyrics. The arrangement adheres closely to the New York "Fania" salsa style, with an emphasis on a strong dance beat. The music only deals peripherally with such matters as cultural self-definition. The remix for Colombian listeners, however, is different. Perhaps to evoke Palmieri's "Bomba del corazón," the piano returns to prominence. Colombia's music public is extremely knowledgeable about Latin recordings from the 1950s through the 1980s, and it is not inconceivable that many would recognize Palmieri's piano vamp.[62] The extensive use of reverb is reminiscent of many Colombian *champeta* recordings and perhaps is intended to attract the local champeta audience.[63] The presence of Pape Seck's vocals in Wolof reinforces this hypothesis. At the very least, combining salsa piano riffs and Senegalese vocals is part of a reimagining of Colombia, similar to Palmieri's project in the 1960s. The remix, like much of Colombian's extensive salsa recordings, shifts Colombia's narrative on its national identity from an Andean axis to a tropical one, in which previously excluded Afro-Colombians play a significant role. This redefinition of *Colombianismo* exclusively deploys cultural materials from outside of Colombia—from Cuba, Puerto Rico, and Senegal—bypassing the world's dominant cultural paradigms.

The next chapter in "Yaye Boy"'s migration is rife with irony. Orquesta Aragón, the venerable Cuban charanga group, recorded a version of "Yaye Boy" in 1998 for its album *Quien Sabe Sabe*.[64] Although a charanga's arrangements can be creative and innovative, Cubans prefer to regard charanga ensembles as the guardians of some of their more historic musical forms, such as the danzón. The popularity of charanga ensembles peaked in Cuba and the United States in the 1950s and 1960s. However, as their popularity declined in the United States and Cuba, it soared in Francophone West Africa.

Since the 1980s Orquesta Aragón has oriented its recordings toward the African market, working from time to time with African producers. The group's interpretation of "Yaye Boy" was released on Lusafrica, a Portuguese label that targets Francophone and Lusophone African listeners. It is one of the few Cuban recordings of African material. The ensemble's members claim they first heard the song over the radio in Colombia while they were on tour there.[65] It is highly likely that they heard the Asefra brothers' remix rather than the original Africando version or the Melcochita translation. The Orquesta Aragón's vocalists sing it persuasively in a Wolof learned phonetically, in the same way that African Latin musicians once learned Spanish. Interestingly, their recording emphasizes percussion more than any performance since the initial version by No. 1. Their recording brings the song full circle. What started out with Eddie Palmieri in New York as a nod toward Puerto Rican rural folklore passes through Senegal to end up with Aragón in Cuba as the epitome of musical urbanity.

In looking at the circulation history of "Yaye Boy," it is important to take note of the fact that none of the musicians playing the song regard their versions as musical hybrids or examples of méttisage. The Senegalese regarded their forays into Afro-Cuban music as a tool for cultural emancipation, a way of entering modernity on their own terms. The Colombians embraced "Yaye Boy" as a means of resituating their national identity in the wider context of a tropical south. The Cubans played "Yaye Boy" in a style that acknowledged the role that Africa has played in the last forty years in keeping the charanga tradition vital, even as that type of music has become archaic in its own homeland. In each case musicians knew that they were creating music in "the second degree," adding new layers of meaning to a cultural text that predated them and would outlast them.

CONCLUSION

Making Waves

In April 1966 the Senegalese government staged its first FESMAN, Festival Mondial des Arts Nègres (Global Festival of Black Arts). The program reflected the aesthetic sensibility of then president Léopold Senghor. Musically, it showcased culturally prestigious performers like the US jazzman Duke Ellington and essentially ignored Hispanic music of the Caribbean. In December 2010 a second FESMAN was held under the auspices of the incumbent Senegalese president, Abdoulaye Wade, highlighting what he saw as an African renaissance. Artists, writers, academics, dancers, and musicians from around the world converged in Dakar for weeks of performances, exhibitions, and seminars, underscoring the contributions of individuals from Africa or of African descent to world civilization. This time the festival emphasized Brazilian culture with a concert by the musician (and former Brazilian minister of culture) Gilberto Gil. Just like forty-four years before, the organizers of the official program largely excluded musicians from the Hispanic Caribbean.

However, in 2010 the generation of the 1950s and 1960s that saw in Cuban music a pathway to modernity and full inclusion in a black Atlantic was in a position to rectify government neglect. A number of Senegalese promoters put on what was in effect an alternative festival of Afro-Cuban music. They marshaled their resources to bring over some of the most beloved Latin ensembles. such as Orquesta Broadway. While Senegalese youth jammed shows by Akon and other hip-hop artists, and Senegalese politicians and foreign dignitaries made their presence felt at concerts by Angélique Kidjo and Youssou N'Dour, a counter public of intellectuals, fonctionnaires, and other middle-class Senegalese attended concerts of Afro-Cuban music.

As in 1966, two "black Atlantics" vied with one another for influence: an "official" version linking Senegal with economic and political powers like the United States (and now Brazil) and a contrasting vision stressing Senegal's historic connections with the Hispanic Caribbean, especially Cuba. Ironically, in 2010 a global hip-hop movement, emphasizing the spoken word over musical virtuosity, overshadowed both these conceptions of the black Atlantic. Streetwise posturing displaced tropical decorum. Beneath the stridency, however, lay the same commitment by hip-hop performers to cosmopolitanism and an inclusive national culture that characterized the Afro-Cuban generations. The Senegalese debates over which modernity best suits their nation continues, with no end in sight.

The history of Afro-Cuban music in Senegal, encapsulated by the two FESMANS, questions the uniformity of the black Atlantic. As an analytical concept, the black Atlantic is elusive, given that it is an ideological construct, not a geographic space. Different groups and places overlay their own versions of local racial politics, class tensions, and regional histories on a common foundation of the transatlantic slave economy. As a result, how groups have *used* the model of a black Atlantic varies significantly. There are various black Atlantics, depending on whether one's vantage point is Cambridge (Massachusetts), New York, Miami, London, Kingston, Havana, Cartagena, Salvador de Bahia, Lagos, or Dakar. Some emphasize the continuing impact of plantation economies; others focus on a virulent mix of racism and class oppression in Europe and the United States. Still others chart the contours of a diasporic imaginary, essentialist in orientation. The Senegalese Afro-Cuban black Atlantic conforms to none of these models. For many Senegalese, the black Atlantic was a mirror in which they saw their culture reflected back to them in a modern form. These roots in reverse allowed them to conserve values that they cherished, such as *teggin* and *kersa*, and alter social patterns that they found constraining, such as prohibitions on gender interaction. Anchoring themselves in the black Atlantic enabled them to claim full cultural and political citizenship in a cosmopolitan world wherein how one carried oneself, what one knew, and what one consumed determined a person's worth.

The strong presence of Latin music alongside FESMAN in 2010 shows that despite the efforts of colonial regimes and postcolonial African states to engineer and dominate the creation of cultural identities, groups like the Senegalese Afro-Cubanistas have persisted outside of government channels. In the 1950s and early 1960s young men in Dakar and other Senegalese cities forged a modern habitus through private realms of consumption (individual recorded music collections).

They displayed these "power goods" in sites of semipublic sociality (record club parties). Later, state-sponsored radio stations expanded this habitus through the increased broadcasting of Afro-Cuban and Puerto Rican music.

The increasing popularity and creativity of local Afro-Cuban-style bands also contributed to this process. A growing circuit of elegant Latin music nightclubs created new performing opportunities for local performers. Musicians also exploited new technologies like transistor radios and recording studios, which produced LP discs to enlarge the public for Afro-Cuban music. They helped bring this music to urban streets and rural areas through touring and a wide circulation of their recorded music. This history demonstrates how a cohort of youthful enthusiasts and professional musicians can fashion their own subjectivities and structures of feeling and have them reproduced on a wide scale in spite of culture dictated from above.

The growing public for Afro-Cuban music was more than just an audience. It involved the circulation of cultural materials (Latin music records), practices like male elegance, new behaviors like moral refinement, and new models of sociality—all of which brought relative strangers into relationships of affinity. Unlike Benedict Anderson's print-based "imagined communities," this public recognized itself through a shared love of Afro-Cuban music.[1] This awareness in Senegal was expressed through an articulation of generational solidarity and mission. As a public coalesced, its members became conscious that they were mastering a way of being in the world that allowed them to be African and modern without relying on French models. Later this public overlapped and fused with other emerging publics (fans of sports like wrestling and soccer, participants in Dakar's café and salon culture, followers of "cassette" Islam, practitioners of high fashion, radio listeners, and newspaper readers) to help create a postcolonial Senegalese public sphere that remains vibrant. Together these publics forged a national modern imaginary that draws on a stockpile of aural materials from the Hispanic Caribbean (and elsewhere) that eluded state control. Today, this imaginary still defines and shapes Senegalese society.

The public for Afro-Cuban music, however, differed from its North American and European counterparts at the time. African show business, of course, has been commercially oriented, but in Senegal, as in most other parts of Africa, it has never developed into a full-fledged entertainment industry.[2] Elsewhere in Africa, such as Mali and Guinea, state patronage in the 1960s and 1970s filled the gap left by the lack of a significant entertainment sector in the national economy. However, in Senegal, Afro-Cuban musicians have had to fend for themselves.

Record companies have largely been lone initiatives. Bands have lacked agents and capable managers. There have been no mediating institutions like artist and repertoire (A&R) men or media moguls shaping repertoires, "messages," or "images." To a certain extent local aficionados of Afro-Cuban music have played that role, but they have served more as tastemakers and occasional artistic advisers than as Svengali-like figures. Because an entertainment infrastructure has been lacking in Senegal, the relationship between major Afro-Cuban bands and their public has been more direct and interactive than in industrialized countries. As a result, Afro-Cuban music in Senegal has been more than a consumer object; it has become an integral part of Senegal's social memory. Through its continued existence, Senegal's centuries-long ties to the Caribbean "are not only recollected but also recalled and re-imagined through public rituals of remembrance."[3] Every performance implicitly has a transatlantic dimension, something of which the musicians and their audiences are keenly aware. To dance salsa in Senegal is to dance history and embody the black Atlantic.

Starting in the 1980s Senegalese Afro-Cuban music acquired another dimension as it started to reverberate across the Atlantic. Performers such as Joe Arroyo from Colombia and Orquesta Aragón from Cuba began recording Senegalese material. Senegalese Afro-Cuban musicians Laba Sosseh, Orchestre Baobab, and the Africando ensemble began recording and performing in the United States and Europe, and their music could be heard on radio stations throughout the Caribbean basin as well as in New York. Orchestre Baobab even appeared in a music documentary with the US jam band Phish on MTV. This global dissemination of Senegalese Cuban music coincided with the rise of world music in Europe and the United States and the implanting of hip-hop in Africa. Ironically, as Senegalese Latin musicians gained listeners abroad and acquired the prestige that only international popularity can bring, they lost most of their audience at home to m'balax and hip-hop. After helping revitalize the dialogue between Africans at home and in diaspora, they largely failed to reap the benefits of their efforts.

As the relationship between Afro-Cuban music and hip-hop demonstrates, modernity in Senegal has not been a monolithic project. Generational conflict, government cultural policy, Cold War politics, and an evolving Islam have splintered the modernity project into competing shards. However, nearly all of these vernacular modernities share two characteristics: they are concerned with cultural identity, and they define themselves as being either in opposition to or in concert with Afro-Cuban music and the sociality associated with it. For many Senegalese, Afro-Cuban music has been a bedrock of a tropical cosmopolitanism. In a culture in which the sonic environment is of primary importance and literacy rates remain low, sound acquires greater significance than in societies where visuality reigns supreme and print is a major mode of communication. In the former environment, the history of Afro-Cuban music is not just a curiosity. "El manisero" is more than a piece about selling peanuts on the street. It becomes a tool for resistance, a blueprint for a new conception of leisure and pleasure, and a means of embracing modernity. Songs like "El manisero" made waves of sound that resonated in Senegal's social, cultural, and political spheres for more than seventy years.

Today the music's volume may be turned down, but it still resounds. Senegalese Afro-Cuban musicians continue to record new music, although at a reduced rate.[4] Cuban rhythms and references to Senegalese Afro-Cuban culture even occasionally surface in Senegalese hip-hop. In 2003 the popular hip-hop group Daara J recorded the song "Esperanza," partially sung in Spanish with an unmistakable Cuban feel.[5] One year later the Senegalese French rapper Serigne Mbaye aka Disiz la peste recorded "N'Dioukel," an unabashed tribute to his father's generation and its passion for Afro-Cuban music.[6] Praising their style and elegance, Mbaye celebrates their music—"la musique nostalgique et presque magique" (their nostalgic music which was almost magical). As with Senghor's "Comme Je Passais," hearing the music as an adolescent in France stirred Mbaye's senses ("la musique remplit mes sens / Je lui suis reconnaissant / mets mes sens à l'unisson") and emotionally reconnected him with Senegal. Moreover, the music helped him set his life on a positive path, underlining that for the Senegalese, Afro-Cuban music always was more than entertainment. It was a compendium of cultural practices and a "structure of feeling" that enabled them to enter modernity and continue through postmodernity on their own terms, and with élan.

NOTES

Introduction

1. Nicholas Cook, cited in Denis-Constant Martin, *Sounding the Cape: Music, Identity and Politics in South Africa*, (Somerset, South Africa: African Minds, 2014), 10.

2. Ibid.

3. See Richard M. Shain, "Roots in Reverse: Cubanismo in Twentieth Century Senegalese Music," *International Journal of African Historical Studies* 35, no. 1 (2002): 83–101.

4. Néstor García Canclini, *Customers and Citizens: Globalization and Multicultural Conflicts*, trans. George Yúdice. (Minneapolis: University of Minnesota Press, 2001), 21.

5. Stern's Music (a British label) and Popular African Music (a German label) were especially scrupulous in paying the original musicians for their work. Often, however, this task proved difficult. A number of the original musicians had passed away, opening up the question of whom in the family to compensate. Sometimes the record labels would depend on one member of the group to distribute the royalty "checks." In some cases (No. 1 in Dakar) this method worked well. However, in others it led to acrimonious disputes. Another problem is that sometimes the revivalist record owners had to pay the original "owners" of the music and hope that these individuals would pass on some of the proceeds to the musicians. These individuals rarely did because they had no legal obligation to do so.

6. During my research, RTS radio aired an interview with me about my work. I also was twice a featured guest on the weekly RTS television show on salsa. I will deposit these visual documents at the African Music Archive in Mainz.

ONE Kora(son): *Africa and Afro-Cuban Music*

1. Pape Fall, interview by author, Dakar, January 23, 2003.

2. This section does not consider Puerto Rican music, which has had much less impact on Africa. Those Puerto Rican musicians who have enjoyed some popularity in Africa, such as Eddie Palmieri and the Fania Stars, for the most part played in the Cuban style. For more on the Puerto Rican contribution to Senegalese salsa, see the conclusion.

3. For a powerful theoretical statement on this model of culture formation, see Sally Price and Richard Price, *Maroon Arts: Cultural Vitality in the African Diaspora* (Boston: Beacon Press, 1999).

4. Interestingly, this layering was also characteristic of the Cuban baroque style in literature and architecture. See José Lezama Lima, *La expresión americana* (Mexico City: Fondo de Cultura Económica, 2010).

5. It is impossible to overemphasize the contributions of Arsenio Rodríguez to the development of Afro-Cuban music. For a comprehensive survey of his career, listen to *Arsenio Rodríguez: El alma de Cuba* (Tumbao TCD 315, 2007, CD). For an academic study of his work, see David García, *Arsenio Rodríguez and the Transnational Flows of Latin American Popular Music* (Philadelphia: Temple University Press, 2006).

6. Ned Sublette, *Cuba and Its Music: From the First Drums to the Mambo* (Chicago: Chicago Review Press, 2004), 77.

7. Listen to *Sexteto y Septeto Habanero: Grabaciones completas, 1925–1931* (recorded 1998; Tumbao TCD 300, CD).

8. The López family of Havana, a dynasty of bassists, played a crucial role in the establishment of the bass as a virtuoso instrument in Cuba. The most influential member of the family was Israel "Cachao" López, who helped revolutionize the danzón genre. To hear Cachao at his best, listen to *Cachao Master Sessions, Volume II* (recorded 1995; CineSon EK67319, CD). The actor Andy Garcia also made a superb documentary on López in 1993: *Cachao: Como su ritmo no hay dos* (dir. Andy Garcia, USA, CineSon Productions, 1993, VHS).

9. See Simon Broughton, Mark Ellingham, David Muddyman, and Richard Trillo, eds., *World Music: The Rough Guide* (London: The Rough Guides, 1994), 250.

10. The kora (sometimes spelled cora) is a twenty-one-string African lute. It became popular as an instrument for "traditional" music in the twentieth century and has spread from the Gambia and Guinea-Bissau to Mali, Senegal, and beyond. Until recently it was only appropriate for griots, a hereditary caste of musicians, poets, and oral historians found in a number of West African societies, to play the kora.

11. The Carabalí encompassed a number of different language groups, including, among others, the Efik, the Ibibio, the Anaang, the Oron, the Ejagham, and the Ekit.

12. For more on the history of Cross River peoples in Cuba, see Ivor Miller, *The Voice of the Leopard: African Secret Societies and Cuba* (Jackson: University Press of Mississippi, 2008). To my knowledge, no one has yet intensively studied the history of the Fon/Ewe peoples in Cuba. The most celebrated efflorescence of Fon culture in the New World has been in Haiti, but the Fon/Ewe speakers' contributions to Cuban cultural history have been cruciaol and need to be further researched.

13. Extensive work has been done on the Yoruba in Cuba. Most of this research focuses

on the impact of Yoruba religious practices on Cuban culture. For an example of this scholarship, see Katherine J. Hagedorn, *Divine Utterances: The Performance of Afro-Cuban Santeria* (Washington, DC: Smithsonian Institution Press, 2001). There also is a vast literature on the impact of the Yoruba on New World African-based cultures generally. For a particularly rich treatment of this subject, see Sandra T. Barnes, *Africa's Ogun: Old World and New* (Bloomington: Indiana University Press, 1989).

14. Philip A. Howard, *Changing History: Afro-Caribbean Cabildos and Societies of Color in the Nineteenth Century* (Baton Rouge: Louisiana University Press, 1998), 17.

15. For more on cabildos, see ibid.

16. Cuba didn't abolish slavery until 1886. Brazil only abolished slavery two years later, in 1888. The Anti-Slavery Squadron attempted to limit the transport of captives to both countries, but smugglers used specially designed ships to elude European interdiction.

17. These rhythms still play a vital role in Cuban music through the genre *tumba francesa.*

18. To hear a recording of one of these bands in which a number of black Cuban musicians have played, listen to *Fanfare cubaine: La banda municipale de Santiago de Cuba* (Buda 92724, 1998, CD).

19. For more on rumba, see Yvonne Daniel, *Rumba: Dance and Social Change in Contemporary Cuba* (Bloomington: Indiana University Press, 1995). To hear a classic rumba recording, listen to *Guaguancó Matancero* (Tumbao 707, 2001, CD).

20. With the exception of one or two aficionados of Cuban music, I found few Senegalese who had any knowledge of or interest in classic Cuban rumba. When I played recordings of this genre for them, few found it compelling.

21. For an important discussion of the cultural and sexual contexts of boleros in Latin America, see Frances R. Aparicio, *Listening to Salsa: Gender, Latin Popular Music and Puerto Rican Cultures* (Middletown, CT: Wesleyan University Press, 1998), 123–42.

22. I am grateful to the late El Hadj Amadou Ndoye for his clarifications about the place of boleros in Senegalese musical culture. The Senegalese include French ballads in their definition of what constitutes this musical genre. The French tradition lacks the intensity and tone of suffering that characterize the classic Cuban bolero.

23. Ariana Hernandez-Reguant has pointed out, however, that in Spain and Mexico, audiences associated Cuban boleros with blackness (personal communication, June 18, 2010).

24. Reissued recordings of Rossi abound. For a good sampling of his style, listen to *Tino Rossi: Les plus grandes chansons* (recorded 2004; Coppelia B00001VQeaI, CD).

25. Fernando Alvarez's *Se feliz: Fernando Alvarez y Descemer Bueno* (Egrem 964, 2008, CD) is a superb recent example of the Cuban bolero tradition.

26. Ochoa was one of the mainstays of the Buena Vista Social Club (see chapter 6). He

recorded an album, *CubAfrica*, with the noted Cameroonian saxophonist Manu Dibango (Mélodie 79593.2, 1998, CD).

27. For an excellent example of Portabales's artistry, listen to *Lo mejor de Guillermo Portabales* (Disco Hit Productions DHCD 1520, 1999, CD).

28. "Guantanamera" ("The Country Girl from Guantánamo") vies with "El manisero" as the most famous Cuban song of all time. Its author, Joseíto Fernández, who was a Havana shoemaker and performer, not a farmer or rancher, originally wrote the song in 1928. Fernández would improvise fresh lyrics each time he sang it. In the 1950s the Cuban composer Julián Orbón incorporated part of a famous poem by José Martí into the song, giving it a nationalist political dimension. Orbón's additional lyrics gave the piece new life, and it became a staple in many groups' repertoires in the years immediately before the Castro takeover. The song became famous in the United States in the early 1960s in an ebullient if musically and linguistically compromised version by the folksinger Pete Seeger. Seeger's interpretation recast the song as a defense of the Cuban Revolution. In Africa, the popularity of "Guantanamera" has been based on its haunting melody and poetic language. Few musicians dwell on its political subtext. For more on "Guantanamera," see Peter L. Manuel, "The Saga of a Song: Authorship and Ownership in the case of Guantanamera," *Latin American Music Review* 27, no. 2 (Fall 2006): 121–47.

29. For an informative primer on Cuban rhythms by the Puerto Rican pianist and band leader Eddie Palmieri, see *The Note, Episode 2—Eddie Palmieri: A Revolution on Harlem River Drive*, at www.redbull.tv/search/thenote.

30. Fernando Ortiz, *Cuban Counterpoint: Tobacco and Sugar* (Durham, NC: Duke University Press, 1995).

31. Robin D. Moore, *Nationalizing Blackness: Afro-Cubanismo and Artistic Revolution in Havana, 1920–1940* (Pittsburgh: University of Pittsburgh Press, 1997), 93–94.

32. To hear a fine example of early bongo playing, listen to *Sexteto y Septeto Habanero: Grabaciones completas, 1925–1931*. The high pitch of the bongos seems well suited for the primitive recording equipment of the 1920s. Their sound comes through explosively on the old records.

33. Moore, *Nationalizing Blackness*, 90.

34. Isabelle Leymarie, *Cuban Fire: The Story of Salsa and Latin Jazz* (London: Continuum, 2002), 33–34.

35. Boncana Maïga, interview by author, New York, July 18, 1997. Maestro Maïga has worked with many Senegalese musicians and record producers and is a noted arranger of both Afro-Cuban and African music (see chapter 6).

36. For a major study of the danzón in Cuba (and Mexico), see Alejandro L. Madrid and Robin D. Moore, *Danzón: Circum-Caribbean Dialogues in Music and Dance* (Oxford: Oxford University Press, 2013).

37. Sublette, *Cuba and Its Music*, 134. This same tango rhythmic cell later in the century was the foundation of the Cuban dance music form the habanera. By the end of the nineteenth century the habanera had "traveled" to Buenos Aires, where it became known as the tango. The tango has had minimal popularity in Africa.

38. To hear danzón played in the classic Cuban manner, listen to the two excellent anthologies *The Cuban Danzón: Before There was Jazz: 1906–1929* (Arhoolie 7032, 1999, CD) and *Early Cuban Danzón Orchestras, 1916–1920* (recorded 1999; Harlequin HQ CD 131, CD). An excellent film, *Danza Charanguero: Popular Dances of Cuba* (*Danza Charanguero: Popular Dances of Cuba*) (USA/Cuba, Boogalu Productions, 2006, DVD), documents the various dances associated with danzón and its variants and shows the performance style of a typical charanga francesa (the renowned Orquesta Estrellas Cubanas). It also contains three informative interviews providing useful context and detail.

39. For an excellent analysis of the rise of charanga orchestras, see Madrid and Moore, *Danzón: Circum-Caribbean Dialogues*, 50.

40. For a review of this debate, see Sublette, *Cuba and Its Music*, 307. The French historically have been famous in musical circles for the excellence of their flutists, a fact that would have been well known to early twentieth-century Cubans.

41. In Francophone West Africa, it has been common for listeners to label danzón music as charanga. Senegal is no exception. Following Senegalese practice, I use the two terms interchangeably.

42. Garang Coulibaly, interview by author, Dakar, May 13, 2003.

43. Pozo met the trumpeter Dizzy Gillespie in Harlem in 1947. The two played together for a year before Pozo died in 1948.

44. The mambo actually originated with Arcaño's ensemble in a song composed by the López brothers in the 1930s. However, it first rose to global popularity in the 1940s with the Pérez Prado Orchestra, which relieved heavily on its brass sections in its arrangements. In the 1950s the black Cuban singer Beny Moré assembled a virtuoso group, the Banda Gigante, which excelled at playing mambos. It, too, gained much of its power and drive from its explosive brass section. For a retrospective on Beny Moré, see *Benny Moré y su Banda Gigante: Grabaciones completas 1953–1960* (Tumbao 309, 2003, CD). For a collection of Pérez Prado's most popular work, see Pérez Prado, *Mondo Mambo*! (RCA R2 71889/DRCI-1242, 1995, CD).

45. Helio Orovio, *Cuban Music from A to Z* (Durham, NC: Duke University Press, 2004), 50. It is doubtful that Jorrín "invented" the cha-cha-chá. Like most Cuban rhythms, it probably had been circulating for a number of years before Jorrín wrote "La engañadora." However, through his prowess as an arranger and composer, he brought it to the forefront of Cuban music.

46. Madrid and Moore, *Danzón: Circum-Caribbean Dialogues*, 57.

47. For a documentary on the cha-cha-chá epoch and the genre's subsequent history

in Cuban music that includes some informative interviews with Jorrín, see *Por siempre cha cha chá* (dir. Jesús Dámaso González, Cuba, EGREM, 2007.)

48. Aziz Dieng, interview by author, Dakar, June 13, 2006.

49. The Senegalese's embrace of charanga ensembles gradually eroded their interest in other types of Latin music. Early recordings of Senegalese Latin music reveal that Senegalese musicians initially had catholic tastes in Caribbean Hispanic music and were willing to experiment with a variety of genres. Probably driven by their public's passion for pachanga, they began to search for a Senegalese equivalent of the charanga sound.

TWO *Havana/Paris/Dakar: Itineraries of Afro-Cuban Music*

1. Zarzuela is an operetta-like Spanish theatrical genre. It took root in Cuba and developed its own distinct traditions, reflecting the racial complexity of the Caribbean.

2. The legendary Cuban troubadour Sindo Garay also was part of her troupe. See Moore, *Nationalizing Blackness*, 160, for a photograph of Ortiz and Richards in their stage garb. Their outlandish costumes clearly indicate that Montaner was situating her presentation of Cuban music more in a tradition of tropical exoticism and *teatro bufo* than in "authentic" Afro-Cuban culture. However, at that point in time few other traditions existed for performing Afro-Cuban music in public. The costumes were typical for the time and place. Neither dancer was of African ancestry. According to Ariana Hernandez-Reguant, that was also the norm on stage during this period (personal communication, June 18, 2012).

3. The population of expatriate Cubans in Paris in the 1920s was so large that it alarmed French authorities. Among this group were a number of prominent artists and intellectuals. The writers Alejo Carpentier and Lydia Cabrera, both of whom pioneered the literary representation of Afro-Cuban culture, were in Paris during this period. The composers Alejandro García Caturla and Amadeo Roldán, famous for incorporating Afro-Cuban music into their symphonic works, had lived and worked in Paris a decade earlier. The great Cuban painter Wifredo Lam fled to Paris in 1938 to escape the Spanish Civil War (1936–1939). Interestingly, Moisés Simons, the composer of "El manisero," lived in Paris in the 1930s.

4. To hear Rita Montaner's version of "El manisero" (there are multiple spellings of the song's title), listen to her recording with La Orquesta de J. M. La Calle on *25 versiones clásicas de "El manisero"* (Tumbao Cuban Classics TCD-801, 1997, CD).

5. The all-woman Anacaona orchestra and The Lecuona Cuban Boys were two famous Cuban ensembles that played in Paris in the 1930s, among many others.

6. Later on that year, Azpiazú and Phil Fabiello, the leader of the orchestra at the RKO Coliseum, another leading vaudeville venue, added to the visual spectacle by having Machin make his entrance dressed as a street vendor, pushing a cart filled with peanuts, some of which he threw to the audience.

7. For more on Don Azpiazú and "El manisero," see John Storm Roberts, *The Latin Tinge: The Impact of Latin American Music on the United States* (Tivoli, NY: Original Music, 1985), 76–79.

8. In 1931 Azpiazú and his orchestra traveled to Paris, where they caused as great a sensation as they had in New York. See Sublette, *Cuba and Its Music*, 402.

9. To hear a reissue of Azpiazú's historic recordings, listen to *Don Azpiazu* (Harlequin HQCD 10, 1991, CD).

10. According to the music historian John Collins, the major record companies sold eight million records in West Africa alone between 1930 and 1933. It is safe to assume that "El manisero" accounted for a significant proportion of these sales. See John Collins, *Highlife Time* (Accra, Ghana: Anansesem Publications, 1994), 245.

11. Léopold Sédar Senghor, "Éléments constitutifs d'une civilization d'inspiration négro-africaine," in *L'unité des cultures négro-africaines.* Proceedings of Deuxième Congrès des Écrivains et Artistes Noirs, nos. 24–25 (Paris: Présence Africaine, 1959), 1:251–81.

12. For a comprehensive narrative on the impact of the Depression on Cuban musical expression, see Sublette, *Cuba and Its Music*, 403–15. For another account of the Depression in Cuba with a wider focus, see Louis A. Pérez, *Cuba: Between Reform and Revolution* (New York: Oxford University Press, 1995), 252–56.

13. For more on these clubs, see Moore, *Nationalizing Blackness*, 176. Moore mentions Melody's Bar and the Cabaña Bambú as two of the more popular nightspots.

14. Interestingly, one of these migrants was Moisés Simons, the composer of "El manisero."

15. For an incisive analysis of the contradictions and complexities of French colonial policy, see Gary Wilder, *The French Imperial Nation-State: Negritude and Colonial Humanism between the Two World Wars* (Chicago: University of Chicago Press, 2005).

16. To hear what a typical evening at La Cabane Cubaine might have sounded like, listen to *Cuba en Paris: Oscar Calle—Señor Tentación* (Iris Musique HMCD 79, 1998, CD). Calle's band had an extended engagement at La Cabane Cubaine as the house band. Listen also to *Cuba 1926–1937 Bal à La Havane* (Frémeaux & Associés FA 5134, 2006, CD), on which one of the cuts features another house band at La Cabane Cubaine, led by Castellanos and his brothers.

17. Ousmane Socé Diop, *Mirages de Paris: Roman* (Paris: Nouvelles Éditions, 1965), 55–56.

18. For a superb study of how Latin American writers have textualized Paris as a city of desire, see Marcy E. Schwartz, *Writing Paris: Urban Topographies of Desire in Contemporary Latin American Fiction* (Albany: State University of New York Press, 1999).

19. Janet G. Vaillant, *Black, French and African: A Life of Léopold Sédar Senghor* (Cambridge, MA: Harvard University Press, 1990), 88.

20. Ibid., 102.

21. For a critical assessment of Senghor's ability as a dancer, see Tyler Edward Stovall,

Paris Noir: African Americans in the City of Light (Boston: Houghton Mifflin, 1996), 107. For Senghor's subsidiary career as a dance instructor, see Wilder, *French Imperial Nation-State*, 215.

22. Wilder, *French Imperial Nation-State*, 264.

23. In a recent study of Senghor's thought, the Senegalese scholar Cheikh Thiam argues that Senghor was more oriented toward cultural authenticity than cosmopolitanism. Here I argue the opposite. See Cheikh Thiam, *Return to the Kingdom of Childhood: Re-envisioning the Legacy and Philosophical Relevance of Negritude* (Columbus: Ohio University Press, 2014).

24. Wilder, *French Imperial Nation-State*, 211.

25. For an analysis of Paris's role as a world capital of literary prestige, see Pascale Casanova, *The World Republic of Letters* (Cambridge, MA: Harvard University Press, 2004). For a more wide-ranging assessment, see David Harvey, *Paris, Capital of Modernity* (New York: Routledge, 2003).

26. For an influential analysis of how Senghor's cultural and political philosophies overlapped, see Wilder, *French Imperial Nation-State*.

27. This phrase is taken from the title of Pascale Casanova's book, *The World Republic of Letters*.

28. Christopher L. Miller, *Nationalists and Nomads: Essays on Francophone African Literature and Culture* (Chicago: University of Chicago Press, 1998), 60.

29. Léopold Sédar Senghor, *Léopold Sédar Senghor: The Collected Poetry*, trans. and ed. Melvin Dixon (Charlottesville: University Press of Virginia, 1991), 589.

30. Ibid., 248. The English translation by Dixon overlooks some of the poem's nuances.

31. Senghor received a "*supérieure*" for his thesis "Exoticism in Baudelaire." Wilder, *French Imperial Nation-State*, 153.

32. Charles Baudelaire, *Les fleurs du mal* (Paris: Gallimard, 1972).

33. The two leading popular music ensembles of the Congo around the time of independence were called OK Jazz and Grand Kallé & L'African Jazz. However, neither played jazz. Their repertoire initially leaned heavily toward Afro-Cuban music.

34. Elizabeth Harney, *In Senghor's Shadow: Art, Politics, and the Avante-garde in Senegal, 1960–1995* (Durham, NC: Duke University Press, 2004), 12.

35. Senghor was fascinated by latinité, a word and concept he used instead of Hispanic.

36. According to the late novelist and librarian Cheikh "Charles" Sow: "People have told me that Senghor really liked Latin music. His son, in fact, told me, Francis Senghor who was a jazz musician. He lives in France and he said his father had Cuban records and he listened to them." Interview by author, Dakar, June 20, 2003.

37. In the 1950s and 1960s Senghor experimented with having his poems read with jazz accompaniment. Mercer Cook, "Afro-Americans in Senghor's Poetry" in *Hommage á Léopold Sédar Senghor: Homme de culture* (Paris: Présence Africaine, 1976), 156–58.

38. See, for example, the multivolume autobiography of Birago Diop, *A rebrousse-gens: Épissures entrelacs et reliefs, Mémoires IV* (Paris: L'Harmattan, 1987); and *Et les yeux pour me dire*, Mémoires V (Paris: L'Harmattan, 1989).

39. My thanks to the late Cheikh "Charles" Sow for bringing this novel to my attention as a rich source for reconstructing the early Senegalese response to Afro-Cuban music. Some of the notable scholarly analyses of this novel, such as Christopher L. Miller's, fail to mention the significance of Afro-Cuban music in the book. See, for example, Miller, *Nationalists and Nomads*, 59–65. Gary Wilder misidentifies La Cabane Cubaine as a jazz club in *French Imperial Nation-State*, 199. Senghor would have been pleased by these omissions and confusions.

40. Cheikh Hamidou Kane, *L'aventure ambiguë* (Paris: René Julliard, 1962).

41. Diop, *Mirages de Paris*, 62.

42. For a recent ethnography of an African jazz "scene," see Steven Feld, *Jazz Cosmopolitanism in Accra: Five Musical Years in Accra* (Durham, NC: Duke University Press, 2012).

43. Diop in his *Mirages de Paris*, for example, writes about the impact that Afro-Cuban music had on Fara at La Cabane Cubaine:

> Les tam-tams se ressouvinrent de leurs cadences ancestrales. Ils martelèrent les cerveaux, en chassant toute autre idée, jusqu'à l'hypnose.
>
> The tam-tams remembered their ancestral cadences. They hammered the brain, chasing out all other ideas, until hypnosis set in.

44. Camou Yandè, interview by author, Dakar, February 20, 2003.

45. During my research I had numerous informal conversations with Senegalese from a wide variety of backgrounds about why they loved Cuban music. What I heard during these spontaneous encounters confirmed what I had learned during formal interviews with Afro-Cuban music "professionals."

46. Balla Sidibè, interview by author, Dakar, February 18, 2003. Sidibè has been one of the leaders of Orchestre Baobab since the 1970s (see chapters 4 and 6). For many years he also sang with Pape Fall's African Salsa.

47. Djibril Gaby Gaye, interview by author, Dakar, June 12, 2003.

48. Mbaye Seck, interview by author, Dakar, July 29, 2003.

49. Antoine Dos Reis, interview by author, Dakar, June 6, 2003.

50. Pierre Gomis, interview by author, Dakar, June 6, 2006.

51. Ibid.

52. Aleysia Whitmore, "Cuban Music Is African Music: Productive Frictions in the World Music Industry," *MUSICultures* 40, no. 1 (2013): 122–44.

53. Pascal Dieng, interview by author, Dakar, February 25, 2003.

54. El Hadj Amadou Ndoye, interview by author, Dakar, June 19, 2003. For more on these student dance contests, see chapter 3.

55. Aminata Laye, interview by author, Dakar, June 9, 2003.

56. Mas Diallo, interview by author, Dakar, June 6, 2006.

57. Mbaye Seck, interview by author, Dakar, July 29, 2003.

58. Arjun Appadurai, *Modernity at Large: Cultural Dimensions of Globalization* (Minneapolis: University of Minnesota Press, 1996), 8. Appadurai's work in this area draws heavily on Benedict R. O'G. Anderson, *Imagined Communities: Reflections on the Origin and Spread of Nationalism* (London: Verso, 1991).

59. Pape Fall, interview by author, Dakar, January 23, 2003.

60. Baye Sy, interview by author, Dakar, June 9, 2003.

61. Nicolas Menheim, interview by author, Dakar, February 25, 2003.

62. Cheikh "Charles" Sow, interview by author, Dakar, June 20, 2003.

63. Appadurai, *Modernity at Large*, 8.

THREE *Son and Sociality: Afro-Cuban Music, Gender, and Cultural Citizenship, 1950s–1960s*

1. Ibid., 7.

2. For more on Mbelekete, see Graeme Ewens, *Congo Colossus: The Life and Legacy of Franco & OK Jazz* (North Walsham, Norfolk, UK: Buku Press, 1994), 51–52.

3. Marissa Jean Moorman, *Intonations: A Social History of Music and Nation in Luanda Angola, from 1945 to Recent Times* (Athens: Ohio University Press, 2008), 91. For the Nigerian "cowboys," see Carolyn Brown, "Creating the Western, Seizing the Streets: Nigerian 'Cowboys' and Urban Masculinity Identity During World War II" (paper presented at the Annual Meeting of the African Studies Association, New Orleans, LA, November 11–14, 2004). For Tanzania, see Andrew Ivaska, *Cultured States: Youth, Gender, and Modern Style in 1960s Dar es Salaam* (Durham, NC: Duke University Press, 2011). For more on African masculinities, see Lisa A. Lindsay and Stephan Miescher, eds., *Men and Masculinities in Modern Africa* (Portsmouth, NH: Heinemann, 2003); and Lahoucine Ouzgane and Robert Morrell, eds., *African Masculinities: Men in Africa from the Late 19th Century to the Present* (Houndmills, UK: Palgrave Macmillan, 2005). For a detailed study of the role of colonial policy in creating new masculinities, see Lisa A. Lindsay, *Working with Gender: Wage Labor and Social Change in Southwestern Nigeria* (Portsmouth, NH: Heinemann, 2003). To date, the research on masculinities in Africa has had a distinct emphasis on Anglophone Africa and has for the most part shied away from looking at popular culture, with Moorman's *Intonations* being the exception.

4. Salons have been a conspicuous feature of Senegalese cultural life since at least the twentieth century. Some still exist in Dakar, though they are less active than in the past.

5. The Argentinean sociologist Néstor García Canclini, who first used this phrase, was revising Claude Levi-Strauss's famous axiom that "kinship is good for thinking." See Néstor García Canclini, *Consumers and Citizens: Globalization and Multicultural Conflicts*, trans. George Yúdice (Minneapolis: University of Minnesota Press, 2001), 20.

6. For an especially influential statement of this argument, see Fredric Jameson, *Postmodernism; or, The Cultural Logic of Late Capitalism* (Durham, NC: Duke University Press, 1991).

7. Timothy Burke, *Lifebuoy Men, Lux Women: Commodification, Consumption, and Cleanliness in Modern Zimbabwe* (Durham, NC: Duke University Press, 1996), 12.

8. García Canclini, *Consumers and Citizens*, 21.

9. For another perspective on cultural citizenship, see Nadine Dolby, "Popular Culture and Public Space in Africa: The Possibilities of Cultural Citizenship," *African Studies Review* 49, no. 3 (2006): 31–49. Dolby deemphasizes consumption as a central component of cultural citizenship. Her article's ahistorical approach also implies that cultural citizenship has only come to the forefront in Africa as a result of the economic and political crises of the 1980s.

10. Richard Fardon, *Raiders & Refugees: Trends in Chamba Political Development, 1750–1950* (Washington, DC: Smithsonian Institution Press, 1988), 24.

11. Ibid.

12. Wilder, *French Imperial Nation-state*, 159.

13. Ibid.

14. Raymond F. Betts, "Dakar: Ville Impériale (1857–1960)," in *Colonial Cities: Essays on Urbanism in a Colonial Context*, ed. Robert Ross and Gerard J. Telkamp (Dordrecht: Springer, 1985), 204.

15. Ibid., 203.

16. John D. Hargreaves, *Decolonization in Africa* (London: Longman, 1988), 78.

17. Betts, "Dakar: Ville Impériale (1857–1960)," 200.

18. Patrick Manning has pointed out that a significant amount of FIDE's budget came from African taxation. See Patrick Manning, *Francophone Sub-Saharan Africa, 1880–1995* (Cambridge, UK: Cambridge University Press, 1998), 124.

19. Hargreaves, *Decolonization in Africa*, 96.

20. Cité ouvrières are barrack-like housing for laborers. Betts, "Dakar: Ville Impériale (1857–1960)," 204.

21. Many of these factories already existed in the 1930s, but they increased in size during the postwar period. For a detailed and fascinating look at the economy of Dakar in the 1930s, see Ousseynou Faye, "L'urbanisation et les processus sociaux au Sénégal: Typologie descriptive et analytique des deviances à Dakar, d'après les sources d'archives, de 1885 à 1940" (PhD diss., Départèment D'Histoire, Université Cheikh Anta Diop De Dakar, 1988).

22. In Nafissatou Diallo's memoir of growing up in Dakar in the 1940s and 1950s, *A*

Dakar Childhood, she mentions that in the family compound her father "sheltered countless country folk who came to the capital to look for work." Nafissatou Diallo, *A Dakar Childhood*, trans. Dorothy S. Blair (Harlow, Essex, UK: Longman, 1982), 2.

23. Gail P. Kelly, "Colonialism, Indigenous Society and School Practices: French West Africa and Indochina 1918–1939," in *Education and the Colonial Experience*, ed. Philip G. Altbach and Gail P. Kelly (New Brunswick, NJ: Transaction, 1984), 9.

24. Lauren K. Locraft, "Senegalese Novel, African Voice: Examining the French Educational System through Aminata Sow Fall's *L'appel des arènes* and Cheikh Hamidou Kane's *L'aventure ambiguë*" (master's thesis, Department of History, Virginia Polytechnic University, 2005), 20.

25. Manning, *Francophone Sub-Saharan Africa*, 165.

26. Ironically, this was when sales of phonographs plummeted in the United States and Western Europe because of competition from radio.

27. Mark Katz incisively discusses these characteristics of the record in *Capturing Sound: How Technology Has Changed Music* (Berkeley: University of California Press, 2004), 8–47.

28. For an extensive discussion of the impact that phonographs had on world music, see Michael Denning, *Noise Uprising: The Audiopolitics of a World Musical Revolution* (London: Verso, 2015).

29. Ibid., 71.

30. Much of this music came from the EMI's HMV GV series, which started in 1933. For more on this series, see Janet Topp Fargion's liner notes for *Out of Cuba: Latin American Music Takes Africa by Storm* (Topic Records, 2004).

31. Collins, *Highlife Time*, 245.

32. Michael Chanan, *Repeated Takes: A Short History of Recording and Its Effects on Music* (London: Verso, 1995), 87.

33. This increasing availability of phonographs to all social classes was a global phenomenon. See Denning, *Noise Uprising*, 110–15.

34. Betts, "Dakar: Ville Impériale (1857–1960)," 203.

35. For an account of what these parties might have been like, see Youssouf Doumbia, "Total Atmosphere with Garrincha!," in André Magnin, *Malick Sidibé* (Zurich: Scalo, 1998), 163–67. Doumbia's account describes the record clubs in Bamako, Mali, not Dakar or St.-Louis. However, it is highly likely that the record clubs in both countries (in the 1950s they were part of the same section of the French colonial empire) organized themselves in similar ways and staged parties in the same manner. These parties bear a striking resemblance to the parties the Congolese sapeurs, young men who organized associations centered around European fashion and Congolese music, staged more than a generation later in Brazzaville and Kinshasa; see Justin-Daniel Gandoulou, *Dandies á Bacongo: Le culte de L'élegance dans la société congolaise contemporaire* (Paris: L'Harmattan,

1989), 105–17. While many individuals in Dakar with whom I spoke were nostalgic about the record clubs, few wanted to talk in detail about their activities. Their reticence may have arisen from their now prominent positions in Senegalese society. Reminiscing about their youthful hijinks to a foreigner like myself might have struck them as undignified.

36. Boris B. Diop, *Les Petits de Guenon* (Paris: Philippe Rey, 2009), 14.

37. Ça Twiste à Poponguine (Moussa Sene Absa, Senegal, Library of African Cinema, 1993, DVD).

38. Record clubs tended to have names. For an invaluable list of some of these names in Bamako taken from the file of the famous Malian photographer Malick Sidibé, see Magnin, *Malick Sidibé*, 4–5. To my knowledge, no such resource exists for Senegal.

39. Serigne Mbacké Fall, interview by author, Dakar, June 10, 2003. Fall later went on to become an authority on the history of the Cuban ensemble Orquesta Aragón.

40. Sylla's collection ultimately grew to thousands of records. See Ibrahima Sylla, interview by author, Belleville, New Jersey, August 16, 2006. Latin music on 45 rpm recordings does not seem to have circulated to any great extent in Senegal.

41. Garang Coulibaly, interview by author, Dakar, May 13, 2003; and El Hadj Amadou Ndoye, interview by author, Dakar, June 19, 2003. Professor Ndoye went on to become one of the leading African scholars of Hispanic literature and head of the Department of Spanish and Portuguese at Université Cheikh Anta Diop in Dakar.

42. The more intensely Islamicized cultures in Senegal discouraged dancing in any form.

43. Hélène Neveu Kringelbach has unearthed some eighteenth-century sources that suggest that such rigid segregation of the sexes during dance events is a relatively recent phenomenon in Senegal. If so, I argue that the more complete Islamization of Senegal during the nineteenth century and the colonial period would have curtailed these interactions between male and female dances, a process reversed by the rise of Cuban dancing. See Hélène Neveu Kringelbach, *Dance Circles: Movement, Morality and Self-Fashioning in Urban Senegal* (Oxford: Berghahn Books, 2013), 29.

44. Catherine M. Cole, *Ghana's Concert Party Theatre* (Bloomington: Indiana University Press, 2010), 74 and 111. El Hadj Amadou Ndoye recalled that dance academies existed in 1950s Dakar on the rue Escoffier (personal communication, August 2010). For a fascinating description of what dance academies were like in Southeastern Nigeria, see Christopher Abani, *GraceLand* (New York: Farrar, Straus, and Giroux, 2004), 84–87.

45. Diallo, *Dakar Childhood*, 68.

46. It is not clear what Diallo meant by gumbe music. Today, gumbe music is an important popular music form in Guinea-Bissau, a country bordering on Senegal, but it is possible that in the 1950s the term described a broader range of music, including rhythms from Casamance (Southern Senegal). See Diallo, *Dakar Childhood*, 85.

47. For the kalela dancers, see J. Clyde Mitchell, *The Kalela Dance: Aspects of Social

Relationships among Urban Africans in Northern Rhodesia (Manchester: Published on Behalf of the Rhodes-Livingstone Institute by the Manchester University Press, 1956).

48. For the sapeurs, see Ch. Didier Gondola, "Dream and Drama: The Search for Elegance among Congolese Youth," *African Studies Review* 42, no. 1 (April 1999): 23–48; and Gandoulou, *Dandies á Bacongo*. Gandoulou's book is a detailed ethnography, while Gondola's account combines local knowledge with a semiotic approach. For another perspective on sapeurs, see Jonathan Friedman, *Cultural Identity and Global Process* (London: Sage Publications, 1994), 155–63. Friedman's analysis sees the *sapes* as the children of globalization.

49. Gondola, "Dream and Drama," 37.

50. The anthropologist Hudita Nura Mustafa coined this phrase to describe the Senegalese fascination with contemporary fashion.

51. The advertisements in *Bing* magazine comprise an invaluable visual archive of evolving male taste in fashion in Dakar during this period.

52. "Mod" fashion enjoyed great popularity throughout Africa in the early 1960s. For a visual record of this fashion trend during this period, see the iconic photographs of Malian youths by Malick Sidibé in Magnin, *Malick Sidibé*.

53. Ibrahima Sylla, liner notes to *Cuba: Una noche en La Habana* (Syllart Productions 6132952, 2007, CD). For more on record collecting during this period, see Serigne Mbacké Fall, interview by author, Dakar, June 10, 2003. See also Ibrahima Sylla, interview by author, Belleville, New Jersey, August 16, 2006.

54. According to Lise A. Waxer in *The City of Musical Memory: Salsa, Record Grooves, and Popular Culture in Cali, Colombia* (Middletown, CT: Wesleyan University Press, 2002), 72, sailors working on ships that docked in Colombia in the 1950s set themselves up as peddlers of Cuban records during this period. This same phenomenon seems to have occurred with ships docking in Dakar.

55. Jacques Attali, *Noise: The Political Economy of Music*, trans. Brian Massumi (Minneapolis: University of Minnesota Press, 1985), 100.

56. Jean Baudrillard, "The System of Collecting," in *The Cultures of Collecting*, ed. John Elsner and Roger Cardinel (London: Reaktion Books, 1994), 7.

57. García Canclini, *Consumers and Citizens*, 20.

58. Martin Stokes, Introduction to *Ethnicity, Identity and Music: The Musical Construction of Place*, ed. Martin Stokes. (Oxford: Berg 1994), 4.

59. Ibid.

60. Ibid., 4–5.

61. Néstor García Canclini, *Hybrid Cultures: Strategies for Entering and Leaving Modernity* (Minneapolis: University of Minnesota Press, 20001), 21.

62. As mentioned previously, El Hadj Amadou Ndoye was a professor of Hispanic literature at Université Cheikh Anta Diop; Djibril Gaby Gaye has achieved national fame

as a broadcaster with RTS (RadioTelevisionSenegal); and Garang Coulibaly was a retired civil servant who specialized in sports and culture. He is widely recognized as among the most knowledgeable figures in Senegal on the history of Afro-Cuban music.

63. This same type of encyclopedic knowledge of Cuban music has also been characteristic of Latin music enthusiasts in Colombia, a "scene" that bears an uncanny resemblance to Senegal's. See Waxer, *City of Musical Memory*, 111–52. Several New York salsa musicians have told me that Colombian Latin music fans are among the most well informed that they have ever encountered. It is commonplace for audiences there to know the words of every song the musicians play, even the most obscure numbers. Senegalese audiences are the same.

64. These debates remain a feature of Senegalese cultural life today. At cafés, receptions, baptisms, and music clubs and in private homes, Latin music aficionados test one another's expertise and evaluate each other's taste. As a newcomer to these long-standing discussions, I was expected to plunge in without warning and make a convincing case, for example, about why Miguelito Cuní was a better sonero for the Arsenio Rodríguez conjunto style than René Scull. If my response had been inadequate, many in the Latin music community in Senegal would have restricted their interactions with me to polite, aloof, and brief encounters.

65. Wilder, *French Imperial Nation-state*, 157–61.

66. For the British colonial regime's policy toward music, see John Collins and Paul Richards, "Popular Music in West Africa," in *World Music, Politics and Social Change*, ed. Simon Firth (Manchester, UK: Manchester University Press, 1989), 12–47. For Portuguese policies, see Moorman, *Intonations*.

67. For at least two individuals I interviewed, memories of these generational clashes over what was correct moral behavior were almost too painful to recall, much less discuss. One interview ended abruptly when I brought up the issue.

68. Mame Cheikh Kounta, interview by author, Thiés, March 25, 2003.

69. A legend has arisen that cruise ships in the twentieth century frequently docked in Dakar or Conakry and that some Afro-Cuban musicians who played in the ships' orchestras would go on shore and have a descarga with their Senegalese and Guinean counterparts. It is unlikely that this myth has any validity. No one in the Dakar Latin musical community has any recollection of jamming in the 1950s or 1960s with visiting Cuban musicians. Moreover, in the interviews that exist with Cuban musicians of this generation, no one mentions playing in Africa in this fashion. Few cruise ships traditionally have gone to West Africa. In 2006, for example, less than 1 percent of the ships that docked at Dakar were cruise ships (www.worldportsource.com/ports/SEN_Port_of_Dakar). For two versions of this myth, see Matt Rogers, "Viva Cuba Y Senegal," *Village Voice*, November 12, 2002; and Eric S. Charry, *Mande Music: Traditional and Modern Music of the Maninka and Mandinka of Western Africa* (Chicago: University of Chicago Press,

2000), 263. Neither Rogers nor Charry identifies his source for the assertion that cruise ships carrying Cuban Orquestas regularly visited West Africa. However, on Colombia's Pacific coast, cruise ship orchestras were important transmitters of Cuban music; see Waxer, *City of Musical Memory*.

70. Septeto Habanero was one of the earliest and greatest son groups to record in the 1920s. Though not as famous in Africa as Trio Matamoros, African Latin music aficionados hold its music in high regard. Remarkably, the group still exists.

71. There were a number of nightclubs in Dakar during this period, but all were too small to profitably accommodate an overseas star like Pacheco. They featured instead local talent.

72. For more on the entertainment business in Nigeria, see Christopher Alan Waterman, *Jùjú: A Social History Ethnography of an African Popular Music* (Chicago: University of Chicago Press, 1990). For Ghana, see Catherine M. Cole, *Ghana's Concert Party Theatre* (Bloomington: Indiana University Press, 2001). For Africa as a whole, two useful sources are Gary Stewart, *Rumba on the River: A History of the Popular Music of the Two Congos* (London: Verso, 2000); and Louise Meintjes, *Sound of Africa! Making Music Zulu in a South African Studio* (Durham, NC: Duke University Press, 2003).

73. This absence of trained personnel continues to be a problem for concert promoters in Senegal. The famous Senegalese singer and band leader Youssou N'Dour was able to get a grant from the European Economic Community in the 1990s to train a cadre of show business support staff, but the results to date have been disappointing.

74. Daniel Cuxac, interview by author, Yoff, July 20, 2004.

75. Stokes, Introduction to *Ethnicity, Identity and Music*, 4.

76. Eddy Zervigón, interview by author, Maspeth, NY, July 17, 2003. For an illuminating interview with Zervigón, see Mary Kent, *Salsa Talks: A Musical Heritage Uncovered* (Altamonte Springs, FL: Digital Domain, 2005), 212–18.

77. Pacheco was also a record producer of note. He was cofounder of Fania Records, the most famous salsa label. For a documentary film of his performance style in Africa, see *Soul Power* (Jeffrey Levy-Hinke, Sony Pictures Classics, 2008). Shot by Leon Gast, the film is a visual record of Pacheco's set with the Cuban singer Celia Cruz in 1974 in Kinshasa, which was attended by eighty thousand Congolese.

78. My thanks to Serigne Mbacké Fall for the gift of a carefully preserved ticket from this 1964 concert by Pacheco.

79. The musical director for this project was the Cuban flutist Gonzalo Fernández, who earlier in his career had collaborated with the Congolese musician Joseph "Grand Kallé" Kabasele on African Team, one of the first African Cuban bands.

80. Penny M. Von Eschen, *Satchmo Blows up the World: Jazz Ambassadors Play the Cold War* (Cambridge, MA: Harvard University Press, 2006).

81. This mindset still dominates US State Department thinking in the twenty-first

century. While the US government has sent Hispanic jazz musicians like Miguel Zenon to West Africa, it largely overlooks salsa orquestas, charanga ensembles, and Latin jazz groups.

82. Eric Charry claims Orquesta Aragón toured Guinea in 1968, citing as his source the notes to the government-issued recording *Neuvième Festival National des Arts de la Culture* (SLP 42); see Charry, *Mande Music*, 263. While this source should be reliable, it conflicts with all other scholarship on Aragón, including Héctor Ulloque Germán's authoritative *Orquesta Aragón* (Bogota: Editorial Nomos S.A., 2004). However, even Ulloque Germán's documentation of Aragón's African tours is incomplete. He fails to mention, for example, the ensemble's 1984 concert in Dakar.

83. This timing may have been connected with the Senghor regime's improving its relations with neighboring Guinea in 1978.

84. I am indebted to Raquel Romberg for clarifying this part of my analysis.

FOUR *From Sabor to Sabar: The Rise of Senegalese Afro-Cuban Orchestras, 1960s–1970s*

1. Denning, *Noise Uprising*, 137.

2. "Foundational" in this case doesn't mean "original." There were other ensembles in Senegal playing Afro-Cuban music before the Star Band, such as Lyre Africaine, a group sponsored by the Dakar municipal government, in the 1940s, and Les Déménageurs in the 1950s. See Tim Mangin, "Mbalax: Cosmopolitanisms in Senegalese Popular Music" (PhD diss., Department of Music, Columbia University, 2012), 79.

3. For more on the history of the Star Band, see Cornelia Panzacchi, *Mbalax mi: Musikszene Senegal* (Wuppertal, Germany: Peter Hammer, 1996), 46–51.

4. Amara Touré stayed in Senegal until 1970, when he left for Cameroon. The Senegalese revered him for what they regarded as his deep Cuban style. He migrated to Cameroon in 1970 and was still active in musical circles until at least the early 1980s. To hear his vocals, listen to *Amara Touré* (Analog Africa No. 18, 2015).

5. Garang Coulibaly, interview by author, Dakar, May 13, 2003.

6. Such official orchestras were common in West African Francophone nations like Guinea and Mali. Senegal, however, has only had its Orchestre National, which traditionally has received a low level of state support.

7. This Caribbean mélange was typical of Francophone Africa as a whole. The early Congolese bands largely played this same repertoire. What Africans called rhumba was not the same as the Cuban genre, which usually only involves singing and drumming, often with African religious overtones. The rhumba in a 1960s variété repertoire was a ballroom dance then popular in North America and Western Europe.

8. Tino Rossi (Constantino Rossi), born in Corsica, was one of the most famous French

singers of popular music from the 1930s through the 1960s. Though his stylistic range was vast, he specialized in romantic ballads. He was enormously popular in Francophone Africa during the 1950s.

9. Cuní sang with the Conjunto Chappotin and also with Beny Moré in the 1950s. He is a favorite of Senegalese Cuban music aficionados.

10. Franco was respected for his scrupulousness in paying salaries. He also meted out fines for any infractions of OK Jazz's rules. In the chaotic whirl of the Congolese entertainment world, OK Jazz stood for stability and reliability. For more on Franco and OK Jazz, see Stewart, *Rumba on the River*, esp. 204–5.

11. This equating of the capacity of some musicians to successfully run large, popular musical outfits with the ability of an entire people to function efficiently and confidently in a modern economy has been a common cultural analogy in the black Atlantic. This perspective emerged in such disparate environments as 1920s Harlem with the Fletcher Henderson and Duke Ellington Orchestras, 1960s Guinea with Bembeya Jazz and other "national" orchestras, and 1960s and 1970s Kinshasa with OK Jazz and Africa International.

12. When the US singer James Brown toured Africa in the 1960s, African musicians were entranced by his music (especially his horn arrangements) but found his hyperactive stage manner disturbing.

13. This constraint is still true today for Afro-Cuban bands. Dance displays, however, are an integral part of many m'balax ensembles' performances. M'balax groups like Fallou Dieng's and Thione Seck's usually appear at much larger clubs with more expansive stages than Afro-Cuban orchestras. Dancers always have been part of Youssou N'Dour's stage show as well. Both Senegalese audiences and musicians perceive m'balax dancing as having a folkloric dimension, underscoring m'balax's claim to be a culturally "authentic" Senegalese cultural form.

14. This assumption is totally without basis and reflects Cuban racist ideologies. For more on the complicated and constantly shifting Cuban attitudes toward Afro-Cuban percussion, see Moore, *Nationalizing Blackness*, esp. 169–70. See also the illuminating notes by Jordi Pujol for the boxed set *El tambor de Cuba*, devoted to the percussionist Chano Pozo (Tumbao 305, 2001).

15. Chano Pozo pioneered Latin jazz with the trumpeter Dizzy Gillespie in the 1940s. He was also a recognized composer.

16. Despite these expectations, the griot percussionists frequently circulate among the audience before and after performances, soliciting *cadeaux* (gifts), a typical griot gesture but one embarrassing to other Senegalese Afro-Cuban musicians.

17. Before embarking on a solo career, Patato was the conguero with the Orquesta Casino de la Playa in the 1930s. Changuito was the conguero with the *songo* group Los Van Van for nearly two decades.

18. Unfortunately the exact date of this recording and the personnel are unknown.

Thanks to Saliou Lamine Diop for making this rare recording from his collection available to me.

19. To hear a recording of Johnson in his prime, listen to *Dexter Johnson & Le Super Star de Dakar Live à L'Étoile* (Teranga Beat TBLP 019, 2014).

20. Mbaye Seck, interview by author, Dakar, July 29, 2003.

21. Youssou N'Dour's Étoile de Dakar was the exception to this pattern. Very quickly after its organization in 1977, it began championing m'balax music. Afro-Cuban music figured less in its repertoire.

22. For more on Fela's high school and university student following, see Nkiru Nzegwu, "School Days in Lagos—Fela, Lady and 'Arcada,'" in *Fela: From West Africa to West Broadway*, ed. Trevor Schoonmaker (New York: St. Martin's Press, 2003), 135–49.

23. In Raoul Peck's film *Lumumba* (2000), Lumumba and his close advisers celebrate Independence in Kinshasa by dancing in a nightclub to Kasabele's band playing its famous "Independence Chachacha." According to Congolese music chronicler Gary Stewart, Kasabele campaigned with Lumumba in 1959–1960, using his luxurious US-manufactured car. See Stewart, *Rumba on the River*, 90. For a retrospective of Kabasele's career, see *Le Grand Kallé: His Life, His Music* (Sterns Music STCD3058–59, 2013).

24. For more on E. T. Mensah and other Ghanaian highlife bands, see Collins, *Highlife Time*. Collins has little information on highlife music's audience. However, the book is more informative on the complicated relationship between Ghanaian musical ensembles and the Ghanaian state.

25. The present generation of Senegalese Afro-Cuban musicians insisted that I intensively research Xalam "un," making it clear that they regarded the group as an essential precursor.

26. Charles Dieng, interview by author, Dakar, June 27, 2003.

27. Thiam describes the experience of singing Cuban music in public as "sublime." Tidiane Thiam, interview by author, Dakar, May 5, 2003.

28. Magay Niang, interview by author, Dakar, May 7, 2003. Pape Seck of No. 1 (discussed later in this chapter) and Africando (discussed in chapter 6) also came out of an art school background.

29. This remarkable film deals with the struggles of a young Senegalese couple to amass the necessary funds to migrate to Paris, for them the capital of modernity. Once they finally succeed in buying their boat tickets to France, the character played by Magay cannot bring himself to leave Dakar. Though Djibril Diop Mambéty was a connoisseur of Latin music, there is none in the film. Instead, the sound track features Josephine Baker singing a song about Paris.

30. The guitarist Cheikh Tidiane Tall, who played with both Xalam ensembles, confirmed that the audience for Xalam "un" included many artists, writers, actors, and university students and staff. Cheikh Tidiane Tall, interview by author, Dakar, June 11, 2006.

31. There is a song by Xalam "un," "A Comer Lechón," in the anthology *AfroLatin Via Dakar* (Syllart 3237562, 2011).

32. For more on Congolese musical debates within modernity, see Stewart, *Rumba on the River*, 88–90; and Bob W. White, *Rumba Rules: The Politics of Dance Music in Mobutu's Zaire* (Durham, NC: Duke University Press, 2008), 42–45. The stylistic battle lines in this Congolese debate were not hard and fast. Franco frequently evoked Afro-Cuban music, and Kabasele excelled at playing African material. In the Congo, at least, the debate had just as much to do with politics as music. Kabasele was a Lumumba supporter, and Franco was more or less in the Mobutu camp, albeit often uncomfortably so.

33. UCAS Jazz, formed in 1959, might be the oldest continuous popular music ensemble of any type in Senegal. Though it was eclipsed during the 1990s as a result of political problems in Casamance, it reemerged after the turn of the century, its creative prowess undiminished. In 2006 the group released a CD, *Casa di mansa*, on the Parisian Africa Productions label. UCAS Jazz claims to be the first "modern" Senegalese band to incorporate traditional instruments like the kora and the *balafon* into its music. Casamance also spawned the Touré Kunda ensemble in the 1970s, one of the first African popular music orchestras to have a significant global musical impact. It was especially popular in France where, at its peak, the group filled stadiums for live performances.

34. Bala Sidibé was born in 1942 in Casamance. His father was a small merchant who had migrated from Mali. As a teenager, Sidibé sang with UCAS Jazz and joined the Senegalese army. After his discharge he settled in Dakar and sang with such bands as Harlem Jazz and the University Sextet. Bala Sidibé, interview by author, Yoff, February 18, 2003.

35. Gomis was born in 1947, the son of a prosperous shellfish wholesaler in Ziguinchor. After finishing lycée, he attended the University of Dakar as a literature student. However, Gomis was more attracted to the entertainment world than academia. He found steady work as a singer with many of the leading Afro-Cuban bands in Dakar and eventually started a second career as a language instructor at the Centre Baobab in Dakar for foreign students, researchers, businesspeople, and diplomats. Radolphe Gomis, personal communication, November 2006. (Gomis is unusually reticent about revealing personal information and tends to give varying accounts of his life. Therefore this biography is provisional.)

36. Attisso varies the spelling of his name, sometimes eliminating the second "s."

37. In the 1980s, when the group's prospects diminished, Attisso returned home to Togo to work as a lawyer.

38. In June 2005 I encountered Geloune at one of the leading salons in Dakar, where he is a regular and highly valued participant.

39. Diallo also was an alumnus of the Star Band. He later went on to be part of the Africando project. Medioune Diallo, interview by author, New York, July 27, 1997.

40. In Mali, for example, the *jalo* Kanté Manfila (a Guinean) played a crucial role in

the creation of a "modern" Malian popular music. In Guinea many Latin-influenced orchestras, such as Bembeya Jazz, were filled with musicians, like the guitarist Sekouba "Bembeya" Diabaté, from a jeli background.

41. The singer N'Diouga Dieng also joined the band during this period, giving Baobab three frontline Wolof singers.

42. Attisso, like many Senegalese guitarists of this period, was influenced by Carlos Santana and, to a lesser extent, by Jimi Hendrix. Like both of those musicians, Attisso used wah-wah pedals and feedback. To West African ears, Hendrix and Santana sounded modern, not psychedelic. For the most part, African musicians were unaware of the drug use and alternative lifestyles associated with this guitar style in North America. From an African perspective, these new guitar technologies allowed a more percussive guitar style, evocative of traditional African music.

43. The image is the cover photo from the album *Orchestre du Baobab* (Vol. 1, Bao 001, 1972). The photographer is unidentified. For more on this recording, see below.

44. The photograph is from the band's archives. The photographer is unknown. The image was reproduced for the 1989 World Circuit Record release of *Pirate's Choice* and the 2002 World Circuit CD re-release of the same material. In the 1989 release, the photo is incorrectly dated as 1982. Seck was no longer with the band at that point, so it is highly likely that the photo is from a previous point in the ensemble's history. The music on these releases was originally recorded on cassette form in 1982. For more on this music, see below.

45. See, for example, the insightful analyses in Kelly Michelle Askew, *Performing the Nation: Swahili Music and Cultural Politics in Tanzania* (Chicago: University of Chicago Press, 2002); and Stewart, *Rumba on the River*.

46. See the CD *Baobab—N'Wolof* (Dakar Sound DKS 014, 1998).

47. Many of Franco and OK Jazz's early recordings can be heard on the RetroAfric CD *Originalité* (Retro 2XCD).

48. *Franco et le tout puissant OK Jazz* (Sonodisc SD40, [1989] 1994).

49. Descargas (jam sessions), of course, are an exception to this pattern. However, Senegalese audiences were not drawn to this variety of Cuban music.

50. These songs originally appeared in cassette form in Senegal in 1982. Later, during the mid-1980s, the songs appeared on a long-playing record in France. In 1989 the British label World Circuit released the material as a CD entitled *Pirate's Choice* and promoted it in English-speaking markets. The CD acquired cult-like status and was re-released in 2001 to critical and popular acclaim in Europe and North America.

51. Jules Sagna, interview by author, Yoff, July 20, 2004. These recordings were sold on the band's Bao label. Later, they were released abroad on the Buur label.

52. Sylla and his partner Richard Diek reputedly never paid the band for the recordings, nor have the musicians ever received any royalty payments for their Parisian work aside

from some copyright fees. The members of Baobab returned to Dakar after five months in France with no financial gain to show from their trip abroad.

53. Ledoux Records asl7001, 1978. The LP has been re-released on CD several times; first as Mélodie 79559-2 and later as World Circuit wcd 027.

54. In 2002 the band produced another version of the song "Hommage à Tonton Ferrer" for the CD *Specialists in All Styles* (Nonesuch 79685). The recording features solo vocals by Ibrahim Ferrer, the Cuban star of *Buena Vista Social Club*, and Youssou N'Dour in addition to the band's singers. The notes accompanying the song in the album spell the title "Utrus Oras."

55. Radolphe Gomis, personal communication, November 2002.

56. Mário Chamie "The Entropic Tropic of Tropicália," in *Tropicália: A Revolution in Brazilian Culture [1967–1972]*, ed. Carlos Basualdo (São Paulo: Cosac & Naify Edicoes Ltda., 2005), 261. This essay has great relevance for African cultural history.

57. Pape Seigne Seck was born in Dakar on July 20, 1946. He attended the Lycées Faidherbe and De Gaulle in St.-Louis and afterward spent some time at art school. In 1961 he began performing with a local St.-Louis ensemble, St.-Louis Jazz. He played with a number of other bands in the 1960s, including Star Jazz de St.-Louis, before joining the Star Band of Dakar in 1969. Originally a saxophonist, Seck gradually became a lead singer.

58. Yahya Fall was born in Thiès in 1950. His musical career began while he was still a student. After teaching himself guitar, he became part of a local yéyé group and found that music could be a profitable activity. Before long his taste shifted toward Afro-Cuban music, and he joined a Latin band. When his father died Fall, an excellent student, had to withdraw from secondary school. He became a full-time professional guitarist. In 1970 he joined the Star Band.

59. The Sahel band during this period was creatively exploring this same artistic terrain with the guitarist Cheikh Tidiane Tall, formerly of "un," and the singer Idrissa Diop. To hear the band, listen to *Diamonoye Tiopité: L'époque de l'évolution* (Teranga Beat TBCD 013). The Sahel band was one of the first Senegalese ensembles to incorporate US funk music into its sound.

60. Christina Roden, "Pape Seck: A Remembrance," www.rootsworld.com.

61. To hear an early version of "Yaye Boy," listen to Volume 6, *No. 1 de No. 1* (Dakar Sound 2002969, 1998). The writer and musical historian Mark Hudson anthologized "Nongui, Nongui" in *The Music in My Head*, an album of Senegalese music that accompanies his book (Sterns Music STCD 1081, 1998).

62. See *No. 1 de No. 1* (2002969, 1998).

63. Ibid.

64. In recent years Fall has been filling in for Attisso on Orchestre Baobab's international tours as well as in its local gigs.

65. Yahya Fall, interview by author, Dakar, April 2, 2003.

66. For a retrospective of Mar Seck's career, listen to *Mar Seck: Vagabonde: From Super Cap-Vert to Number One* (Teranga Beat TBCD 018, 2013).

67. Many of the same conditions resulted in the dominance of *soukous* music in Zaire in the 1980s, in which the driving *sebene* segment of a piece, previously in the middle of a song, expanded at the expense of the extended opening melodic rumba section.

68. Several Senegalese friends told me about the Mercedes Benzes during a number of informal conversations. I have not been able to verify the truth of their claims.

69. Yahya Fall, interview by author, Dakar, April 2, 2003; Mar Seck, interview by author, Dakar, January 17, 2003; and Doudou Sow, interview by author, Dakar, February 18, 2003.

70. Griots (jeli in the Mande languages) are the hereditary poets, historians, praise singers, and musicians of the Mande cultures in West Africa. Most jeli of Sosseh's generation retained some adherence to their "traditional" functions and status. Sosseh is unusual in how little his jeli background figured in his artistic development and presentation of self. However, his bohemian lifestyle and lifelong excessive alcohol consumption were much more characteristic of Senegambian griots than of the region's Latin musicians, who have tended to be steady, sober individuals. For more on griots, see Charry, *Mande Music*; and Thomas A. Hale, *Griots and Griottes: Masters of Words and Music* (Bloomington: Indiana University Press, 1998).

71. Laba Sosseh, interview by author, Dakar, July 31, 2003.

72. Some reports indicate that Sosseh's father was already employed in Dakar and that Sosseh had established himself as a performer in both cities. See John Child, "Laba Sosseh Obituary," *Descarga*, March 9, 2007, www.descarga.com. Child doesn't indicate the source of this information.

73. Laba Sosseh, interview by author, Dakar, July 31, 2003.

74. See Philip Hayward, *Widening the Horizon: Exoticism in Post-war Popular Music* (Sydney: John Libbey, 1999). This style of hotel music still exists in Senegal.

75. Senegalese music usually calls for more full-voiced singing than does Afro-Cuban music. Dakar Latin musicians claim that during the first phase of his career in the 1970s Youssou N'Dour gravitated toward m'balax music because his voice wasn't well suited for the Afro-Cuban sound.

76. During this period there were lively Afro-Cuban music scenes in the administrative town Ziguinchor in southern Senegal, the railway center Thiès, and the market town Kaolack.

77. For an ethnography of a South African recording studio, see Meintjes, *Sound of Africa!*

78. Daniel Cuxac, interview by author, Yoff, July 20, 2004.

79. Sosseh and Cuxac both had roots in Southern Senegal (Casamance), where Cuxac was born and which was the home of Sosseh's father. In addition Cuxac, a purist when it came to Afro-Cuban music, is a great admirer of Sosseh's artistry and fidelity to the Afro-

Cuban style. Lassissi started in the music business as an assistant to Cuxac. According to Cuxac, Lassissi signed Sosseh to his label behind Cuxac's back (personal communication, July 2, 2012). Sosseh's defection created bad feelings between the two men that lasted until Lassissi's death.

80. Eddy Zervigón, interview by author, Maspeth, NY, July 17, 2003. Zervigón was the head of Orquesta Broadway, a charanga ensemble immensely popular in New York and Francophone Africa.

81. John Child, "Sergio George—'We Will Never Return to the Horse and Buggy,'" *Descarga*, September 18, 2007, www.descarga.com. Africando was an African salsa group put together by the Senegalese impresario Ibrahima Sylla in the 1990s (see chapter 6). Laba Sosseh recorded two songs—"Ayo Nene" and "Aminata"—for Africando's album *Baloba!* (Sterns Africa STCD 1082, 1998, CD).

82. See Randy Weston and Willard Jenkins, *African Rhythms: The Autobiography of Randy Weston* (Durham, NC: Duke University Press, 2010).

83. For more on the issue of race and racial self-definition in Afro-Cuban music, see Moore, *Nationalizing Blackness*; Robin Moore, *Music and Revolution: Cultural Change in Socialist Cuba* (Berkeley: University of California Press, 2006), 170–96; García, *Arsenio Rodríguez and the Transnational Flows*, 32–63; and Ariana Hernandez-Reguant, "Havana's Timba: A Macho Sound for Black Sex," in *Globalization and Race: Transformation in the Cultural Production of Blackness*, ed. Kamari M. Clarke and Deborah Thomas (Durham, NC: Duke University Press, 2006), 249–78.

84. Reggae was beginning to attract Ivorian youth. In 1982 the Ivorian reggae artist Alpha Blondy released his first album, *Jah Glory*, which made reggae the sound of modernity in Abidjan, eclipsing Afro-Cuban music. For more on reggae in the Ivory Coast, see Simon Akindes, "Playing It 'Loud and Straight': Reggae, Zouglou, Mapouka and Youth Insubordination in Côte D'Ivoire," in *Playing with Identities in Contemporary Music in Africa*, ed. Mai Palmberg and Annmette Kirkegaard (Uppsala: Nordic Africa Institute, 2002), 86–104; and Yacouba Konaté, *Alpha Blondy: Reggae et société en Afrique noire* (Abidjan: CEDA, 1987).

85. Laba Sosseh, interview by author, Dakar, July 31, 2003.

86. Sosseh insisted to me that his stay in New York was uninterrupted. However, Daniel Cuxac says that Sosseh was shuttling back and forth between New York and West Africa (personal communication, July 2, 2012).

87. Sacodisc International LS 26-80, vinyl recording.

88. Attali, *Noise*. Attali was making a theoretical point. He was unaware of the Sosseh-Monguito collaboration.

89. Paul Gilroy, *The Black Atlantic: Modernity and Double Consciousness* (Cambridge, MA: Harvard University Press, 1993). Afro-Cuban music is strangely absent from Gilroy's book.

90. Laba Sosseh, interview by author, Dakar, July 31, 2003.

91. Thanks to the Senegalese guitarist and bandleader Yahya Fall, I was able to watch Sosseh teach the younger generation of Senegalese Latin musicians several times between 2003 and 2006.

92. Senegalese in the music business told me repeatedly that this record "went gold." However, I have not been able to verify this information or learn what constituted "gold status" in West Africa in the 1980s. Reportedly, in 1980 the Ivorian minister of agriculture presented Monguito with a gold-plated disc in recognition of his having a "gold record." Monguito, however, made a number of records for Lassissi around that time, and it's not clear which one of his albums was being recognized at this ceremony. According to Ariana Hernandez-Reguant, Daniel Cuxac traveled to Cuba in 1990 and 1991 to give golden record plaques to the Cuban performers Barbarito Diez and Pio Leyva (personal communication, May 26, 2008). As with Monguito, the criteria for golden disc status remain unspecified.

93. *Roberto Torres Presenta Laba Sosseh* (recorded 1981; SAR 1020, vinyl recording); and *Laba Sosseh* (recorded 1982; SAR 1029, vinyl recording).

94. The musicians on the album included the tresero Charlie Rodríguez, the pianist Alfredo Valdés Jr., and the renowned trumpeter Alfredo "Chocolate" Armenteros.

95. Joe Arroyo, *Echao Pa'lante* (Disco Fuentes 11242, 1987, vinyl recording).

96. Daniel Cuxac produced this session, which according to him was never officially released, though pirated cassette versions have had a limited circulation (personal communication, July 2, 2012). The cassette was titled *Maestro Laba Sosseh con Orquesta Aragón.*

97. Celso Velez and Rafael Lay Jr. (of Orquesta Aragón), interview by author, New Brunswick, NJ, November 14, 2003; and Laba Sosseh, interview by author, Dakar, July31, 2003.

98. Celso Velez and Rafael Lay Jr., interview by author, New Brunswick, NJ, November 14, 2003. Reliable information on the history of the Orquesta Aragón's touring of Africa is unavailable. Velez and Lay were vague about it, and there is no consensus in Senegal about when the group first played there and how many times it has since returned.

99. For a trenchant analysis of salsa romántica, see Christopher Washburne, "Salsa Romántica," in *Situating Salsa: Global Markets and Local Meaning in Latin Popular Music*, ed. Lise A. Waxer (New York: Routledge, 2002), 101–35. This type of Latin music has proven unpopular in Africa. For a comprehensive view of merengue, see Paul Austerlitz, *Merengue: Dominican Music and Dominican Identity* (Philadelphia: Temple University Press, 1997).

100. Sosseh and Fall had played together in the Vedette band in the 1960s in Dakar. In 1995 Fall launched his own ensemble, African Salsa. He is regarded in Dakar as the inheritor of Sosseh's mantle and closely models his style on that of his mentor.

101. Laba Sosseh, *El Maestro: 40 Años de Salsa* (Mélodic 00022, 2002, CD).

102. This section's subheading is a wordplay on the title of Gustavo Pérez Firmat's *Life on the Hyphen: The Cuban-American Way* (Austin: University of Texas Press, 1994).

FIVE *ReSONances Senegalaises: Authenticity, Cosmopolitanism, and the Rise of Salsa M'balax, 1980s–1990s*

1. Other nations faced similar anxieties during this period. For a cultural analysis of Turkey in this era, see Martin Stokes, *The Republic of Love: Cultural Intimacy in Turkish Popular Music* (Chicago: University of Chicago Press, 2010).

2. This phrase comes from ibid., 20.

3. Salons have long been important cultural institutions in Dakar, although they are gradually dying out. They are organized gatherings at someone's house, usually with food and drink, at which people discuss literature, music, philosophy, politics, and painting. Often each "session" of a salon will have one common topic around which all conversation revolves. The guests at a salon tend to be intellectuals and cultural producers, with some business leaders, civil servants, and politicians attending as well. I attended several salons in Dakar between 2003 and 2005.

4. This phrase comes from Stokes, *Republic of Love*, 2.

5. See Timothy Dean Taylor, *Global Pop: World Music, World Markets* (New York: Routledge, 1997), 21–28.

6. There have been many important statements on authenticity in the last hundred years. In literary studies, Lionel Trilling's *Sincerity and Authenticity* (Cambridge, MA: Harvard University Press, 1972) remains influential. In philosophy, Charles Taylor's "The Politics of Recognition," in *Multiculturalism: Examining the Politics of Recognition*, ed. Charles Taylor (Princeton, NJ: Princeton University Press, 1994), has provoked a great deal of comment. In anthropology, see Raquel Romberg's *Witchcraft and Welfare: Spiritual Capital and the Business of Magic in Modern Puerto Rico* (Austin: University of Texas Press, 2003), 257–69.

7. This phrase comes from George Yúdice's "Postmodernity and Transnational Capitalism in Latin America," in *On Edge: The Crisis of Contemporary Latin American Culture*, ed. George Yúdice, Jean Franco, and Juan Flores (Minneapolis: University of Minnesota Press, 2002), 18.

8. RetroAfric has released an anthology of Pino's work. See Geraldo Pino, *Heavy Heavy Heavy* (Retro-Afric20CD, 2005, CD). Fela's music is widely available, and the musician has been the subject of a successful Broadway musical.

9. See "Cosmopolitanism," special issue, *Public Culture* 12, no. 3 (Fall 2000). For some recent discussions of these issues in African musical studies, see Thomas Turino, *Nationalists, Cosmopolitans and Popular Music in Zimbabwe* (Chicago: University of Chicago Press, 2000); Ivaska, *Cultured States: Youth, Gender, and Modern Style*; and Alex Perullo, *Live from Dar es Salaam: Popular Music and Tanzania's Music Economy* (Bloomington: Indiana University Press, 2011)

10. For an overview of the social and cultural impacts of globalization during this

decade, see Saskia Sassen, "Organized Religions in Our Global Modernity," *PMLA* 126, no. 2 (March 2011): 455–60.

11. Achille Mbembe, "The New Africans: Between Nativism and Cosmopolitanism," in *Readings in Modernity in Africa*, ed. Peter Geschiere, Birgit Meyer, and Peter Pels (Bloomington: Indiana University Press, 2008), 107–11. Mbembe refers to Africa in general, but his remarks pertain to Senegal as well, a country he knows well.

12. For a major statement of Deleuze and Guattari's theoretical position, see Gilles Deleuze and Félix Guattari, *Kafka: Toward a Minor Literature*, trans. Dana B. Polan (Minneapolis: University of Minnesota, 1986). Explications of Deleuze and Guattari's dense philosophical arguments abound. For a particularly enlightening exegesis, see François Cusset, *French Theory: How Foucault, Derrida, Deleuze, & Co. Transformed the Intellectual Life of the United States* (Minneapolis: University of Minnesota, 2008).

13. The struggle to contain in one's self the compound and sometimes contradictory truths of Islam and European "rationality" is the subject of Cheikh Hamidou Kane's masterwork, *L'aventure Ambigüe* (Paris: René Julliard, 1962). Mamadou Diouf has written on the challenge of synchronizing these clashing temporalities in "The Senegalese Murid Trade Diaspora and the Making of a Vernacular Cosmopolitanism," *Public Cultures* 12, no. 3 (Fall 2000): 679–702.

14. The phrase "vernacular cosmopolitanism" comes from the work of Stuart Hall. See "A Conversation with Stuart Hall," *Journal of the International Institute* 7, no. 1 (Fall 1999).

15. The Murids have fascinated African and non-African scholars alike. The amount of research on their history, political ideology, and economic organization is staggering, and much of it is excellent. For the role of the Murids in twentieth-century Senegalese history, see Cheikh A. Babou, *Fighting the Greater Jihad: Amadu Bamba and the Founding of the Muridiya of Senegal, 1883–1913* (Athens: Ohio University Press, 2007); and David Robinson, *Paths of Accommodation: Muslim Societies and French Colonial Authorities in Senegal and Mauritania, 1880–1920* (Athens: Ohio University Press, 2000). For an analysis of the Murid impact on Senegalese visual culture, see Allen F. Roberts, Mary Nooter Roberts, Gassia Armenian, and Ousmane Guèye, *A Saint in the City: Sufi Arts of Urban Senegal* (Los Angeles: UCLA Fowler Museum of Cultural History, 2003). For Murid economic organization, see Momar C. Diop, "La confrérie Mouride: Organisation économique et mode d'implanation urbaine" (PhD diss., Université De Lyon, 1980); and Diouf, "Senegalese Murid Trade Diaspora," 679–702. For a study of the urban design of Touba, the Murid "capital," see Eric Ross, *Sufi City: Urban Design and Archetypes in Touba* (Rochester, NY: University of Rochester Press, 2006).

16. Pap Khouma, *I Was an Elephant Salesman: Adventures between Dakar, Paris, and Milan*, trans. Oreste Pivetta and Rebecca Crockett Hopkins (Bloomington: Indiana University Press, 2010).

17. Kwame Anthony Appiah, *Cosmopolitanism: Ethics in a World of Strangers* (New York: W. W. Norton, 2006), xv.

18. A full-scale scholarly monograph on m'balax has yet to be published. However, there are two informative texts that open up avenues for future work. In 1996 Panzacchi published *Mbalax Mi: Musikszene Senegal*, and in 2010 the Austrian ethnomusicologist Anja Brunner published her initial research on the topic: *Die Anfänge des Mbalax: Zur Entstehung einer senegalesischen Popularmusik* (Wien: Institut Fur Musikwissenschaft, 2010). Oumar Sankhare, a classicist at Université Cheikh Anta Diop, has written two interpretations of Youssou N'Dour's oeuvre: *Youssou Ndour: Artiste et artisan du développement* (Dakar, Senegal: Éditions du Livre Universel, 2002); and *Youssou Ndour: Le poète* (Dakar: Nouvelles Éditions Africaines du Sénégal, 1998). Patricia Tang has a chapter on m'balax in *Masters of the Sabar: Wolof Griot Percussionists of Senegal* (Philadelphia: Temple University Press, 2007). Mark Hudson has written what might be called an m'balax novel, *The Music in My Head* (London: Jonathan Cape, 1998), a roman à clef about Youssou N'Dour. For an early analysis of N'Dour's work, see Lucy Duran, "Key to N'Dour: Roots of the Senegalese Star." *Popular Music* 8, no. 3 (1989): 275–84.

19. Listen to Orchestre Baobab on *Baobab—N'Wolof*, with the remarkable griot singer Laye M'Boup (Dakar Sound DKS 014, 1998, CD). To hear the historically important music of Super Eagles, listen to *Super Eagles: Senegambian Sensation* (Retro Afric 17CD, 2001, CD).

20. My thanks to one of my anonymous external readers, who pointed out to me that m'balax was already a phenomenon in the 1970s with the influential band Super Diamono.

21. Habib Faye, personal communication, June 2006. Faye was the bass player for Youssou N'Dour's band for many years.

22. For a summary of the Diouf era, see Momar C. Diop and Mamadou Diouf, eds., *Le Sénégal sous Abdou Diouf* (Paris: Karthala, 1990).

23. See Harney, *In Senghor's Shadow*.

24. This complaint arose repeatedly in my conversations with Senegalese Latin musicians, who told me that their colleagues who played traditional music faced similar harsh working conditions.

25. There was a similar debate in the Congo in the 1960s and 1970s between the music of Tabu Ley "Rochereau" and that of François Luambo Makiadi "Franco." The Congolese associated Tabu Ley with cosmopolitanism and Franco with authenticity. The Congolese debate, however, differed greatly from the one in Senegal. Under President Mobutu, the Congolese state entered the fray, throwing its support behind Franco. In Senegal the government has had minimal interest in intervening in the music world, apart from its desultory support for a national orchestra, created in the 1980s. For more on the Congolese debate, see Ewens, *Congo Colossus*; Stewart, *Rumba on the River*; and White, *Rumba Rules*.

26. For an overview of this period, see Ibrahima Thioub, Momar C. Diop, and Catherine

Boone, "Economic Liberalization in Senegal: Shifting Politics of Indigenous Business Interests," *African Studies Review* 41, no. 2 (September 1998): 63–85.

27. For a retrospective of Étoile de Dakar, listen to *Once Upon a Time in Senegal—The Birth of Mbalax 1979–1981* (Sterns Music STCD 3054–55, 2010, CD).

28. See Juan Flores, *From Bomba to Hip-hop: Puerto Rican Culture and Latino Identity* (New York: Columbia University Press, 2000).

29. Although this song was recorded in 1994, N'Dour has done material like this throughout his career.

30. For more on m'balax lyrics, see Fiona McGaughlin, "Islam and Popular Music in Senegal: The Emergence of a New Tradition," *Africa* 67, no. 4 (1997): 560–81.

31. For more on the cassette revolution, see Panzacchi, *Mbalax mi: Musikszene Senegal*.

32. Interestingly, this type of percussion initially was not featured in the "new wave" bands like Étoile de Dakar. An audience in the late 1970s or early 1980s would have been far more likely to encounter sabar drumming in an Afro-Cuban ensemble like No. 1.

33. Mar Seck, interview by author, Dakar, January 17, 2003.

34. Patrick Nancy, interview by author, Dakar, June 28, 2003. Nancy, from Guadeloupe, is one of the leading Latin dance teachers in Dakar. My wife and I studied with him in 2003.

35. El Hadj Amadou Ndoye, interview by author, Dakar, June 19, 2003.

36. Garang Coulibaly, interview by author, Dakar, May 13, 2003.

37. I am only one of many researchers who has benefited from the late Mr. Coulibaly's generosity in sharing his work with fellow scholars.

38. For a description of a performance by the World Melody Makers, see Richard M. Shain, "The Re(Public) of Salsa: Afro-Cuban Music in Fin-de-Siècle Dakar," *Africa* 79, no. 2 (2009): 186–205. The group is now disbanded.

39. Djibril Gaby Gaye, interview by author, Dakar, May 13, 2003; and Djibril Gaby Gaye, interview by author, Dakar, June 19, 2003.

40. *Senegal Salsa* (dir. Moustapha Ndoye, Senegal RTS, 2000, VHS). Le Centre Cultural Français (CCF), one of the French government's cultural institutions in Dakar, helped finance this documentary. It contains a rare filmed interview with Laba Sosseh and has some footage of a descarga in Dakar showing Orquesta Aragón and many of the leading musicians in the 1990s salsa revival, such as Nicolas Menheim, Pape Fall, and Yahya Fall.

41. Mas Diallo and Pierre Gomis, interview by author, Dakar, June 6, 2006.

42. See Amadou Ndoye, *En torno a la literatura hispanoamericana*, trans. Yolanda González Pacciotti (Bogotá: Universidad Autónoma de Colombia, Departamento de Humanidades, 2008), 11–17.

43. El Hadj Amadou Ndoye, interview by author, Dakar, June 19, 2003.

44. I have talked extensively with all three individuals. However, they preferred to keep their conversations with me private and informal. None of the three would consent

to an interview. Their reticence probably stems from their reluctance to talk about the financial dimensions of their activities.

45. Ibrahima Sylla, interview by author, Belleville, NJ, August 16, 2006.

46. Isseu Niang in *Senegal Salsa*.

47. The pachanga had its origins in the late 1950s and early 1960s. Max Salazar is an excellent source of information on its history; see Primero Max Salazar, *Mambo Kingdom: Latin Music in New York* (New York: Schirmer Trade Books, 2002).

48. Djibril Gaby Gaye in *Senegal Salsa*. It would have been impossible for the Senegalese to see authentic merengue dancing in the 1950s and 1960s. The Dominican *caudillo* Rafael Leonidas Trujillo Molina's bizarre obsession with merengue inhibited its international circulation before his death in 1961. Trujillo believed that all music should be performed live and banned the recording of merengue during his regime. After he died Latin bandleaders in New York, such as Johnny Pacheco (a Dominican musician popular in Senegal for his renditions of Afro-Cuban music), incorporated merengue into their repertoire. However, the Senegalese have never shown interest in New York styles of Latin dancing. It is unlikely that developments there would have shaped their evolving Latin dance style. For more on Trujillo and merengue, see Austerlitz, *Merengue: Dominican Music*.

49. Patrick Nancy, interview by author, Dakar, June 28, 2003.

50. Lamine Faye, one of the earliest masters of m'balax guitar, emphasized to me in a conversation in 2005 in Dakar that this 12/8 time signature is one of the foundations of the m'balax style. M'balax bands play in 4/4 time as well.

51. These terms are Wolof. They are widespread in Senegalese society and have their equivalents in other Senegalese languages.

52. For an illuminating comparison of danzón dancing styles in Cuba and Mexico, see Madrid and Moore, *Danzón: Circum-Caribbean Dialogues*, 205–6.

53. This point came up often in off-the-record conversations but never in a formal interview situation.

54. This backlash against perceived Wolof cultural and political dominance was rarely spoken about publicly. However, it is a matter of great concern among some of the Afro-Cuban generation and their allies.

55. Ironically, Youssou N'Dour, the leading m'balax musician, is not Wolof, a well-known fact inside of Senegal, if not internationally. One of his parents was a Tukulor speaker, and the other spoke Serer.

56. When a Casamance secessionist movement during the 1990s brought Senegal to the brink of civil war, the model of peaceful national integration symbolized by Afro-Cuban music played a role in reducing political tensions. Pape Fall, a Wolof speaker from Rufisque, for example, recorded a cassette in 2002 entitled *Que vive la paix!*

57. Senegal is one of the few Islamic countries in the world without a state religion. Senegal is even more unique in having elected Léopold Senghor, a Christian, head of state.

58. Svetlana Boym, *The Future of Nostalgia* (New York: Basic Books, 2001), 251.

59. Ironically, Afro-Cuban groups like Orchestre Baobab and No. 1 also had many praise songs of Senegalese historical figures in their repertoires, such as Baobab's "Lat Dior" and No. 1's "Nongui Nongui," later covered by Youssou N'Dour.

60. Boym, *Future of Nostalgia*, 342.

61. Stokes, *Republic of Love*, 3.

62. Birame Cissé, rhythm guitarist for the salsa m'balax group Super Cayor, as interviewed in the *New York Times*. See David Hecht, "Senegal Takes Salsa, Adds Mbalax and Gets Magic," *New York Times*, December 8, 1999.

63. Menheim, in fact, had been a member of Youssou N'Dour's band early in his career.

64. Hecht, "Senegal Takes Salsa".

65. For more on Mapathé "James" Gadiaga, see chapter 6 and Mapathé "James" Gadiaga, interview by author, Dakar, February 21, 2003. Though it is a universal belief outside of Africa that Senegalese salsa is meant solely for the rich and well connected, the truth is more complicated. While walking around some of the grittier neighborhoods in Dakar with a number of Dakar's salsa musicians, I was surprised by how often they were stopped by fans who didn't fit the profile of a member of the elite. Similarly, after I appeared as a guest on an RTS program on salsa, many Dakarois from the "popular" classes would come up to me to say how much they enjoyed my show.

66. Le Super Cayor, *Sopenté* (Popular African Music Pam Oa 206, 1997, CD); and Pape Fall in *African Salsa* (Sterns/Earthworks STEW41CD, 1998, CD).

67. Gawlo, who is a griotte and a self-proclaimed emancipated woman, is also notorious for her racy videos, which have frequently been aired on RTS.

68. Once while at a Dakar salsa club, I ran into a woman I knew who was a cashier at the upscale Score supermarket chain. Accompanied by a group of women like herself, she was not in the least embarrassed to encounter me in such a venue. The women, however, left well before closing time to ensure that they wouldn't be confused with sex workers, who generally hovered into the late hours.

69. For an anthology that covers the full artistic range of Senegal's salsa bands of the 1990s, see *African Salsa* (Sterns/Earthworks STEW41CD, 1998, CD).

70. Only one international CD of Super Sabador exists. See Nicolas Menheim & Le Super Sabador, *Commandante Ché Guevara* (Popular African Music Pam Oa 209, 2002, CD).

71. Menheim has vocal polyps, a common problem among Senegalese singers, almost all of whom have little or no vocal training. The Cuban government arranged for him to have an operation in Havana. Unfortunately, the operation failed to cure his condition.

72. Fall's one international release is *Artisanat* (Sterns/Earthworks STEW47CD, 2002, CD).

73. For a description of a Pape Fall performance, see Shain, "The Re(Public) of Salsa."

74. See Le Super Cayor, *Sopenté* (Popular African Music Pam Oa 206, 1997, CD); and Super Cayor, *Embouteillage* (Popular African Music Pam Oa 210, 2002, CD).

75. Former president of Senegal Abdoulaye Wade, for example, was a well-known habitué of Dakar's Afro-Cuban nightclubs in the 1960s during the early phases of his career.

76. This famous phrase comes from Raymond Williams, *Marxism and Literature* (London: Oxford University Press, 1997), 132.

SIX *"Music Has No Borders": The Global Marketing of a Local Musical Tradition, 1990s–2006*

1. Ian Anderson, "World Music History," *fRoots*, March 2000, 201, www.frootsmag.com/content/features/world_music_history. This use of the term refers to the marketing of music. Its academic use goes back further in ethnomusicological circles.

2. José Quiroga, *Cuban Palimpsests* (Minneapolis: University of Minnesota Press, 2005), 157.

3. Dave Matthews and guitarist Trey Anatasio from Phish traveled to Dakar in 2004 to appear in a music documentary with members of Orchestre Baobab. The film *(Inside) Out: Trey and Dave Go to Africa*, directed by Jenna Rosher, was broadcast on VH1, the music video network. Orchestre Baobab also appeared with some of the musicians on a late-night talk show in the United States. The carefully rehearsed Orchestre Baobab, with its tight arrangements, bears little similarity to a "jam band."

4. Gomis is from the Mandiack language community, who live on both sides of the Senegalese–Guinea-Bissau border.

5. Attisso, who is a practicing lawyer, has no known history of drug use.

6. Orchestre Baobab's official Web site states that Attisso came to Dakar in 1968. The 1966 date is from an interview he did with the independent music Web site Pitchfork. Joe Tangari, "Orchestre Baobab," *Pitchfork*, August 5, 2008, www.pitchfork.com. Attisso came to Dakar in part because he had an uncle living there. The influence of the guitarist Carlos Santana may have spread to Senegal earlier than elsewhere in Africa as a result of documented interactions between music-loving US Peace Corp volunteers and Senegalese musicians. Ken Braun dates Santana's impact on Ghana to 1971 and the "Soul to Soul" festival in Accra (personal communication, June 3, 2012).

7. Gomis was briefly my language tutor in Dakar. He was a rigorous teacher. The resurgence of Orchestre Baobab cut short my time as his student.

8. Saudade seems largely absent in music from Mozambique, although the noted *fado* singer Maritza is half Mozambican.

9. Orchestre Baobab, *Pirates Choice: The Legendary 1982 Session* (recorded 1982; World Circuit WCD014, 1989, CD).

10. This section's subheading is a translation of the title of a short story, "Un arte de

hacer ruinas," by the exiled Cuban author Antonio José Ponte, in *Tales from the Cuban Empire* (San Francisco: City Lights Press, 2002), 21–45. Ponte's story deals with the same images of tropical decay that Nick Gold and the German film director Wim Wenders traffic in, but he subtly situates these images within their political, historical, and cultural contexts in a way that is totally absent from Gold's and Wender's narratives.

11. Lucy Durán, "Orchestre Baobab," www.worldmusiccentral.org. Durán has worked with Nick Gold as both a producer and an author of album notes.

12. Gold bought out his former employers in the early 1990s. Farquharson went on to help found the Mexican label Corason, which mostly recorded Mexican regional music. Some of Corason's most successful CDs, however, were releases featuring the Cuban son group Cuarteto Patria, led by the guitarist Eliades Ochoa. Ochoa went on to become one of the mainstays of Nick Gold's Buena Vista Social Club project in 1997 and Afrocubism in 2010.

13. Ali Farka Toure and Ry Cooder, *Talking Timbuktu* (World Circuit HNCD 1381, 1994, CD). The World Circuit Web site claims sales of 500,00 units for the album.

14. The US government fined Cooder $25,000 for his participation in the project. His traveling to Cuba violated the US trade and travel embargo of the island nation. See www.afrocubaweb.com.

15. Some say the Malians couldn't get the necessary travel papers. Others say they missed the plane. Still others claim that the untimely arrival of a rich and generous patron of the Malian musicians led them to stay in Bamako rather than go to Havana. From their point of view, keeping a patron happy was more important than recording a world music CD that might only bring them limited financial gain. The third hypothesis is the most convincing, though conclusive evidence is lacking to confirm any of the three theories. See Banning Eyre, *In Griot Time: An American Guitarist in Mali* (Philadelphia: Temple University Press, 2000), 181.

16. Buena Vista Social Club, *The Buena Vista Social Club* (World Circuit/Nonesuch 79478-2, 1997, CD). In Eugene Robinson's *Last Dance in Havana. The Final Days of Fidel and the Start of the New Cuban Revolution* (New York: Free Press, 2004), Marcos states that he had already recruited the BVSC musicians to make an album that he alone was going to direct (28–29). This album, *A toda Cuba le gusta* (recorded 1997; World Circuit/Nonesuch 79476-2, 1997), featured a 1940s–1950s jazzy big band sound. It was recorded at the same time as *Buena Vista Social Club*.

17. Quiroga, in *Cuban Palimpsests*, 159–65, has written an assessment of the Buena Vista Social Club phenomenon obviously influenced by Ariana Hernandez-Reguant's analysis in her *Cuba in the Special Period: Culture and Ideology in the 1990s* (New York: Palgrave Macmillan, 2009).

18. *Buena Vista Social Club* (dir. Wim Wenders, USA, Artisan Entertainment, 1999, DVD).

19. A number of Cuban commentators have rightfully pointed out that the CD and the film exaggerate the neglect and obscurity experienced by many of the musicians. See, for example, Pedro De la Hoz's perceptive article "Buenavavista Social Club," *Granma*, August 14, 2000.

20. Linda Hutcheon, "Irony, Nostalgia and the Postmodern," in *University of Toronto English Library*, last modified January 1998, www.library.utoronto.ca/utel/criticism/hutchinp.

21. Appadurai, *Modernity at Large*, 77–78.

22. Hutcheon, "Irony, Nostalgia and the Postmodern."

23. For more on the poetics and cultural politics of ruins in Latin America, see Michael J. Lazzara and Vicky Unruh, *Telling Ruins in Latin America* (New York: Palgrave Macmillan, 2009).

24. Robinson, *Last Dance in Havana*, 27.

25. "Mystic chords of memory" is a phrase from Abraham Lincoln's first inaugural address, on March 4, 1861. The quote from Juan de Marcos González is from Robinson, *Last Dance in Havana*, 27.

26. See *Baobab Guy-Gui* and *Toon Baaxul*. There are no dates for these cassettes. However, they were recorded at Dakar's Studio 2000, which was only established in the 1990s. Neither of these cassettes made a dent in Senegal's music market.

27. Orchestra Baobab, *Pirate's* Choice (recorded 2001 [1982]; World Circuit 79643-2, CD).

28. Orchestra Baobab, *Specialist in All Styles* (recorded 2002; World Circuit 79685-2, CD).

29. This reworking of the song, with the exception of the two additional singers and a new title, "Hommage á Tonton Ferrer," varied only slightly from the 1982 version. Gold's decision to include an m'balax singer and an Afro-Cuban sonero on the most Lusophone song in Baobab's playlist was an odd one. The singers requited themselves well enough but brought little new to the song.

30. This conforming to the sound of old records carried over to its live performances as well. I have seen the ensemble live on three occasions in the United States. Its work closely adhered to the recorded version on each song played. Guitarist Barthélémy Attisso's solos were almost the same note for note as on his recordings. According to an interview Attisso gave to the Pitchfork website, his solos are not improvised, but composed. See Tangari, "Orchestre Baobab."

31. Many musicians in the Senegalese Afro-Cuban music world resent the insertion of N'Dour into Gold's narrative. They consider N'Dour hostile to Afro-Cuban music, in part because they claim his voice was never right for singing Afro-Cuban music. They believe that he envies the artistry of the Dakar salseros. N'Dour, according to Gold, always was a big fan of Orchestre Baobab. However, in Dakar it is well known that he was much

more influenced by the singing of Mar Seck of No. 1 and the proto-funk style of Idrissa Diop's and Cheikh Tidiane Tall's 1970s Sahel Band. Another version of this narratives emphasizes Gold's role in "rediscovering" Orchestre Baobab. Aleysia Whitmore quotes Ben Mandelson: "They disappeared and [Gold] went to find them. We put the band back together again. It's like '*The Blues Brothers.*'" Aleysia Whitmore, "The Art of Representing the Other: Personnel in the World Music Industry," *Ethnomusicology* 60, no. 2 (Spring/Summer 2016): 329–55.

32. Car rapides provide the bulk of transportation for Dakar's workers and small traders. This photograph of Orchestre Baobab was originally taken by the well-known portrait photographer Jonas Karlsson for the magazine *Vanity Fair*.

33. For a different perspective on Orchestre Baobab and World Circuit, see Whitmore, "Art of Representing the Other," 329–55. She situates her discussion of Baobab's transformation into a world music icon within the debates about musical authenticity and purity.

34. Lassissi also was a former employee of Cuxac.

35. *Las Maravillas de Mali* (recorded 2001; re-release, Maestro Sound 004 08968-2, CD). For more on Las Maravillas, see Andy Morgan, "Afrocubism: An Old Transatlantic Love Story," www.andymorganwrites.com.

36. Boncana Maïga, interview by author, New York. July 27, 1997.

37. The smooth Africando percussion, for example, would have sounded perfect on a 1980s salsa romántica recording.

38. Sylla was criticized for this omission in Senegal. In a later Africando CD, he did have Sosseh sing on one track, but by and large Sylla steered clear of the most famous African sonero of all, probably because Sosseh in his later years had become difficult to work with as a result of his excessive alcohol consumption.

39. Ken Braun, interview by author, New York, July 26, 2006.

40. Salif Keïta, *Soro* (Celluloid CD 66883–2, 1987, CD).

41. The source of this information prefers to remain anonymous. Individuals involved in the project, including Sylla, had no idea that conditions at the hotel housing the musicians were less than ideal.

42. Ibrahima Sylla, interview by author, Belleville, NJ, August 16, 2006.

43. Africando, *Trovador* (Sterns Music STCD 1045, 1993).

44. Ibrahima Sylla, interview by author, Belleville, NJ, August 16, 2006.

45. To date Africando has recorded seven albums: Vol. 1, *Trovador* (Sterns Music STCD 1045, 1993, CD); Vol. 2, *Tierra tradicional* (Sterns Music STCDS 1054, 1994, CD); *Gombe Salsa* (Sterns Music STCD 1071, 1996, CD); *Baloba!* (Sterns Music STCD 1082, 1998, CD); Africando All Stars, *Mandali* (Sterns Music STCD 1092, 2000, CD); *Martina* (Sterns Music STCD 1096, 2003, CD); and *Ketukuba* (Sterns Music STCD 1103, 2006, CD).

46. Sylla died in 2013. A month before his death, Sterns released the latest Africando recording, *Viva Africando*. Sylla's daughter, Binetou, who has been a PhD candidate in

African history at the Sorbonne, has taken over his label. Under her leadership, the Africando project may continue. See Africando, *Viva Africando* (Sterns STCD 1120, 2013).

47. Robinson, *Last Dance in Havana*, 31.

48. Moore, *Music and Revolution.*

49. For more on the Castroite state and its complicated response to the prevalence of racism in Cuba, see Robinson, *Last Dance in Havana*; Hagedorn, *Divine Utterances*; and Daniel, *Rumba: Dance and Social Change*. For cultural policy in Cuba in the post-Soviet era, see Hernandez-Reguant, *Cuba in the Special Period.*

50. Moore, *Music and Revolution*, 107–35.

51. This account of the tour is taken from Gunter Gretz's liner notes to *los afro-salseros de senegal en la Habana* (Popular African Music 407, Frankfurt, 2001, CD). Gretz accompanied the Senegalese musicians to Cuba.

52. Yahya Fall, personal communication, June 2003.

53. *Los afro-salseros de senegal en la Habana* (Popular African Music 407, Frankfurt, 2001, CD).

54. www.afrocubaweb.com.

55. Skylight Studio was renowned for its recordings of Latin music. Many prominent salsa musicians, including Eddie Palmieri, chose to record there. It closed sometime after the Africando recording.

56. "Bomba del Corazón," on Eddie Palmieri, *Lo que trago es sabroso* (Alegre LPA 8320, 1964, CD).

57. *Orchestre Number One de Dakar 78, Volume 1* (Barclay No-001, 1978, CD).

58. Africando, *Tierra Tradicional* (Sterns Music STCD 1054, 1994, CD).

59. Ken Braun, interview by author, New York, July 26, 2006.

60. The version of the song that I have heard is on *African Salsa* (Sterns Music/Earthworks STEW1CD, 1998, CD).

61. "Yaye Boy," on *Máscara Salera: Gozando!* (Asefra Productions CD1012, 1995, CD).

62. Cuban and Puerto Rican musicians who have toured Colombia have been astonished by the discographic expertise of Colombian audiences. See Waxer, *City of Musical Memory.*

63. Champeta is an Afro-Colombian music that blends Afro-Colombian musical genres with rhythms from contemporary African popular music, especially from the Congo and Nigeria. It has been popular on Colombia's Caribbean coast.

64. Orquesta Aragón, *Quien sabe sabe* (Candela/LusAfrica 42855492, 1998, CD).

65. Album notes to *Quien sabe sabe.*

Conclusion

1. Anderson, *Imagined Communities.*

2. South Africa is an exception to this generalization. See Meintjes, *Sound of Africa.* To a certain extent, Nigeria in the 1960s and 1970s was also.

3. Richard Elliott and Nanette De Jong, "Ritual, Remembrance and Recorded Sound" (course syllabus, Newcastle University, Newcastle upon Tyne, UK, 2010–2011).

4. Listen to, for example, Alsassane Ngom's "La Ravin." Alassane Ngom et la Salsa Stars, *Le Ravin* (private label, 2016, CD).

5. Daara J., "Esperanza," on *Boomrang* (BMG France 74321 983932, 2003, CD).

6. Serigne Mbaye (Disiz la peste), "N'Dioukel," on *Itineraire d'un enfant bronze* (Def Jam France B00063920A, 2004, CD). My thanks to Eric Charry for bringing "N'Dioukel" to my attention.

GLOSSARY OF SPANISH AND LATIN MUSIC TERMS

bugaloo A mélange of Cuban and African American music (rhythm and blues and soul), developed in New York by Puerto Rican youth in the 1960s. It became popular in Africa but had little sustained influence on the development of Senegalese Afro-Cuban music.

bongos Twin connected small wooden drums (now made with modern materials). Bongos are played between the legs and have a higher pitched sound than other drums. Bongos are rarely played in Senegal.

cha-cha-chá A variation of danzón that swept the world in the 1950s and has been hugely popular in Senegal. Its simplified rhythms made it easier to dance to than other forms of Cuban music. Usually, a charanga ensemble plays cha-cha-chás.

charanga A type of ensemble associated with danzón, cha-cha-chá, and pachanga. In its classic form, it consists of a wooden flute, piano, three violins, bass, conga, and three singers. In more recent years, timbales also have been included.

conga drum A large, single-head wooden drum (now made with modern materials). The Conga drum produces a deeper sound than bongos. Senegalese Afro-Cuban musicians frequently use conga or its local equivalent.

conjunto A type of ensemble that emerged in the late 1920s and early 1930s. Originally it featured a piano, bass, trumpets, conga and bongo drums, a tres, and singers. Conjuntos have a heavier sound than charangas; augmented with more brass and a drum kit, they have become the basis of salsa orchestras.

danzón A dance widely considered to be the national dance of Cuba. It emerged in the last part of the nineteenth century. It is danced at a leisurely pace to an orchestra that usually consists of brass, violins, and percussion.

Fania A record company founded in the 1960s, was famous for recording salsa ensembles. The Dominican musician Johnny Pacheco, greatly beloved in Senegal, was one of its founders. The Fania sound is brassy and tough.

pachanga A dance craze of the late 1950s and 1960s. It is usually played at a fast pace by ensembles that are combinations of charangas and conjuntos. The Senegalese have a special affinity for it.

rumba/rhumba A term with three different meanings depending on the context. In Cuba, rumba is a folkloric music form with percussion ensembles, dancers, and singers, often performed in the streets. Outside Cuba the term has referred to a ballroom dance linked to Latin music. In Africa, as a result of early recordings of Cuban music being labeled as rumbas (they were not), rumba became a generic term describing a number of different Cuban musical forms.

salsa A term much in dispute, but most commentators agree that salsa emerged in the United States and Puerto Rica after the Cuban Revolution. It is a combination of Cuban music (son and guaracha) and Puerto Rican music (bomba and plena) with rock, jazz, Colombian, and Dominican elements. In contemporary Senegal, it is common to conflate Afro-Cuban music and salsa.

salsa romántica A form of salsa that became dominant in the 1980s; it emphasized romantic ballads. It has had little impact on Senegal.

salsero A lead singer in a salsa ensemble.

sonero A lead singer in a son (see chapter 1) ensemble.

songo A type of music associated with the postrevolutionary Cuban group Los Van Van. It incorporated rumba, danzón, and funk elements with complex jazzy horn arrangements. Senegalese have paid little attention to it.

timbales Twin shallow, tin-encased drums mounted on a metal stand. They are played with wooden sticks. Senegalese Afro-Cuban musicians frequently play timbales.

típica Folksy, rootsy, and "authentic." It also refers to ensembles in the nineteenth century that played danzóns.

tumbao A Cuban riff or groove.

INTERVIEWS

Braun, Ken. Interview by author. New York, July 26, 2006.
Coulibaly, Garang. Interview by author. Dakar, May 13, 2003.
Cuxac, Daniel. Interview by author. Yoff, July 20, 2004.
Diallo, Alias. Interview by author. Dakar, February 20, 2003.
Diallo, Mas, and Pierre Gomis. Interview by author. Dakar, June 6, 2006.
Diallo, Medoune. Interview by author. New York, November 1, 1997.
Diallo, Ousmane "Ouza." Interview by author. Dakar, May 22, 2003.
Dieng, Aziz. Interview by author. Dakar, June 13, 2006.
Dieng, Charles. Interview by author. Dakar, June 27, 2003.
Dieng, Pascal. Interview by author. Dakar, February 25, 2003.
Dione, Maguette. Interview by author. Dakar, February 25, 2003.
Diop, Fatou, and Alioune Kassé. Interview by author. Dakar, June 1, 2006.
Dos Reis, Antoine. Interview by author. Dakar, June 6, 2003.
Fall, Pape. Interview by author. Dakar, January 23, 2003.
Fall, Serigne Mbacké "Aragón." Interview by author. Dakar, June 10, 2003.
Fall, Yahya. Interview by author. Dakar, April 2, 2003.
Gadiaga, Mapathé "James." Interview by author. Dakar, February 21, 2003.
Gaye, Djibril Gaby. Interviews by author. Dakar, June 12, 2003 and June 19, 2003.
Konaté, Ibou. Interview by author. Dakar, June 5, 2006.
Kounta, Mame Cheikh. Interview by author. Thiés, March 25, 2003.
Lô, Cheikh. Interview by author. Lac Rose, June 7, 2003.
Maïga, Boncana. Interview by author. New York, July 29, 1997.
Menheim, Nicolas. Interview by author. Dakar, February 25, 2003.
Nancy, Patrick. Interview by author. Dakar, June 28, 2003.
Ndiaye, Khady. Interview by author. Dakar, May 31, 2006.
Ndoye, El-Hadj Amadou. Interview by author. Dakar, June 19, 2003.
Ndoye, Mamadou "Dr. Baccouche." Interview by author. Dakar, June 10, 2006.

Niang, Magaye. Interview by author. Dakar, May 7, 2003.
Nuñez, Marcel. Interview by author. Dakar, May 16, 2003.
Sagna, Jules. Interview by author. Dakar, July 20, 2004.
Seck, Adama "Secka." Interview by author. Dakar, April 29, 2003.
Seck, Mar. Interview by author. Dakar, January 17, 2003.
Seck, Mbaye. Interview by author. Dakar, July 29, 2003.
Sidibè, Balla. Interview by author. Dakar, February 18, 2003.
Sosseh, Laba. Interview by author. Dakar, July 31, 2003.
Sow, Cheikh "Charles." Interview by author. Dakar, June 20, 2003.
Sow, Doudou. Interview by author. Dakar, February 18, 2003.
Sy, Baye, and Aminata Gaye. Interview by author. Dakar, June 9, 2003
Sylla, Ibrahima. Interviews by author. New York, August 1, 1997; and Belleville, NJ, August 16, 2006.
Tall, Cheikh Tidiane. Interview by author. Dakar, June 11, 2006.
Thiam, Tidiane. Interview by author. Dakar, May 5, 2003.
Velez, Celso, and Rafael Lay Jr. Interview by author. New Brunswick, NJ, November 14, 2003.
Yandé, Camou. Interview by author. Dakar, February 20, 2003.
Zervigón, Eddy. Interview by author. Maspeth, NY, December 17, 2003.

BIBLIOGRAPHY

Abani, Christopher. *GraceLand*. New York: Farrar, Straus, and Giroux, 2004.

Akindes, Simon. "Playing It 'Loud and Straight': Reggae, Zouglou, Mapouka and Youth Insubordination in Côte d'Ivoire." In *Playing with Identities in Contemporary Music in Africa*, edited by Mai Palmberg and Annmette Kirkegaard, 86–104. Uppsala: Nordic Africa Institute, 2002.

Anderson, Benedict R. O'G. *Imagined Communities: Reflections on the Origin and Spread of Nationalism*. London: Verso, 1991.

Anderson, Ian. "World Music History." In *fRoots* 201, March 2000. www.frootsmag.com/content/features/world_music_history/.

Aparicio, Frances R. "Women as Absence: Hetero(homo) Sexual Desire in the Bolero." In *Listening to Salsa: Gender, Latin Popular Music and Puerto Rican Culture*, 125–42. Middletown, CT: Wesleyan University Press, 1988.

Appadurai, Arjun. *Modernity at Large: Cultural Dimensions of Globalization*. Minneapolis: University of Minnesota Press, 1996.

Appiah, Anthony. *Cosmopolitanism: Ethics in a World of Strangers*. New York: W. W. Norton, 2006.

Askew, Kelly Michelle. *Performing the Nation: Swahili Music and Cultural Politics in Tanzania*. Chicago: University of Chicago Press, 2002.

Attali, Jacques. *Noise: The Political Economy of Music: The Political Economy of Music*. Translated by Brian Massumi. Minneapolis: University of Minnesota Press, 1985.

Austerlitz, Paul. *Merengue: Dominican Music and Dominican Identity*. Philadelphia: Temple University Press, 1997.

Babou, Cheikh A. *Fighting the Greater Jihad: Amadu Bamba and the Founding of the Muridiya of Senegal, 1883–1913*. Athens: Ohio University Press, 2007.

Barnes, Sandra T. *Africa's Ogun: Old World and New*. Bloomington: Indiana University Press, 1989.

Baudelaire, Charles. *Les fleurs du mal*. Paris: Gallimard, 2004.

Baudrillard, Jean. "The System of Collecting." In *The Cultures of Collecting*, edited by John Elsner and Roger Cardinel, 7–25. London: Reaktion Books, 1994.

———. *The System of Objects*. Translated by James Benedict. London: Verso, 1996.

Betts, Raymond F. "Dakar: Ville impériale (1857–1960)." In *Colonial Cities: Essays on Urbanism in a Colonial Context*, edited by Robert Ross and Gerard J. Telkamp, 193–206. Dordrecht: Springer, 1985.

Bolster, W. Jeffrey. *Black Jacks: African American Seamen in the Age of Sail*. Cambridge, MA: Harvard University Press, 1997.

Boym, Svetlana. *The Future of Nostalgia*. New York: Basic Books, 2001.

Breckenridge, Carol A., Dipesh Chakrabarty, Homi Bhabha, and Sheldon Pollock, eds. *Cosmopolitanism*. Durham, NC: Duke University Press, 2002.

Broughton, Simon, and Kim Burton, eds. *World Music: The Rough Guide*. London: The Rough Guides, 1994.

Brown, Carolyn. "Creating the Western, Seizing the Streets: Nigerian 'Cowboys' and Urban Masculinity Identity During World War II." Paper presented at the Annual Meeting of the African Studies Association, New Orleans, LA, November 11–14, 2004.

Buena Vista Social Club. Directed by Wim Wenders. Santa Monica, CA: Artisan Entertainment, 1999. DVD.

Brunner, Anja. *Die Anfänge des Mbalax: Zur Entstehung einer senegalesischen Popularmusik*. Vienna: Institut für Musikwissenschaft, 2010.

Burke, Timothy. *Lifebuoy Men, Lux Women: Commodification, Consumption, and Cleanliness in Modern Zimbabwe*. Durham, NC: Duke University Press, 1996.

Ça twiste à Poponguine. Directed by Moussa Sene Absa. San Francisco: California Newsreel, 1993. DVD.

Cachao: Como su ritmo no hay dos. Directed by Andy Garcia. New York: Epic Music Video, 1993. VHS.

Casanova, Pascale. *The World Republic of Letters*. Cambridge, MA: Harvard University Press, 2004.

Chamie, Mário. "The Entropic Tropic of Tropicália." In *Tropicália: A Revolution in Brazilian Culture [1967–1972]*, edited by Carlos Basualdo, 261–65. São Paulo: Cosac and Naify Edicções, 2005.

Chanan, Michael. *Repeated Takes: A Short History of Recording and Its Effects on Music*. London: Verso, 1995.

Charry, Eric S. *Mande Music: Traditional and Modern Music of the Maninka and Mandinka of Western Africa*. Chicago: University of Chicago Press, 2000.

Child, John. "Laba Sosseh Obituary." *Descarga*, March 9, 2007. www.descarga.com.

———. "Sergio George—'We Will Never Return to the Horse and Buggy.'" *Descarga*, September 18, 2007. www.descarga.com.

Christopher, Emma. *Slave Ship Sailors and Their Captive Cargoes, 1730–1807*. New York: Cambridge University Press, 2006.

Cobley, Alan. "Migration and Remigration between the Caribbean and Africa." In *The African-Caribbean Connection: Historical and Cultural Perspectives*, edited by Alan G. Cobley and Alvin Thompson, 49–68. Bridgetown, Barbados: University of the West Indies, 1990.

Cole, Catherine M. *Ghana's Concert Party Theatre*. Bloomington: Indiana University Press, 2001.

Collins, John, and Paul Richards. "Popular Music in West Africa." In *World Music, Politics and Social Change*, edited by Simon Firth, 12–47. Manchester, UK: Manchester University Press, 1989.

Collins, John. *Highlife Time*. Ghana: Anansesem Publications, 1994.

Cook, Mercer. "Afro-Americans in Senghor's Poetry." In *Hommage à Léopold Sédar Senghor: Homme de culture*. 151–61. Paris: Présence Africaine, 1976.

Cusset, François. *French Theory: How Foucault, Derrida, Deleuze, and Co. Transformed the Intellectual Life of the United States*. Minneapolis: University of Minnesota Press, 2008.

Daniel, Yvonne. *Rumba: Dance and Social Change in Contemporary Cuba*. Bloomington: Indiana University Press, 1995.

Danza Charanguero: Popular Dances of Cuba. Sebastopol, CA: Boogalu Productions, 2006. DVD.

Davies, Rick. *Trompeta: Chappottín, Chocolate, and the Afro-Cuban Trumpet Style*. Lanham, MD: Scarecrow Press, 2003.

Dávila, Jerry. *Hotel Trópico: Brazil and the Challenge of African Decolonization, 1950–1980*. Durham, NC: Duke University Press, 2010.

De Boeck, Filip. "Tales of the 'Invisible City' and the Second World." In *Readings in Modernity in Africa*, edited by Peter Geschiere, Birgit Meyer, and Peter Pels, 124–35. Bloomington: Indiana University Press, 2008.

De La Hoz, Pedro. "Buenavavista Social Club." *Granma*, August 14, 2000.

Deleuze, Gilles, and Félix Guattari. *Kafka: Toward a Minor Literature*. Translated by Dana B. Polan. Minneapolis: University of Minnesota, 1986.

Denning, Michael. *Noise Uprising: The Audiopolitics of a World Musical Revolution*. London: Verso, 2015.

Diallo, Nafissatou. *A Dakar Childhood*. Translated by Dorothy S. Blair. Harlow, Essex, UK: Longman, 1982.

Diop, Birago I. *Du temps de L'Harmattan*. Vol. 4 of *Mémoires*. Paris: L'Harmattan, 1987.

———. *Et les yeux pour me dire*. Vol. 5 of *Mémoires*. Paris: L'Harmattan, 1989.

———. *A rebrousse-gens: Épissures, entrelacs et reliefs*. Vol. 3 of *Mémoires*. Paris: Présence Africaine, 1985.

Diop, Boris B. *Les petits de la guenon*. Paris: Philippe Rey, 2009.

Diop, Momar C. "La confrérie Mouride: Organisation économique et mode d'implanation urbaine." PhD diss., Université de Lyon, 1980.

Diop, Momar C., and Mamadou Diouf, eds. *Le Sénégal sous Abdou Diouf.* Paris: Karthala, 1990.

Diouf, Mamadou. "The Senegalese Murid Trade Diaspora and the Making of a Vernacular Cosmopolitanism." *Public Cultures* 12, no. 3 (Fall 2000): 679–702.

Dolby, Nadine. "Popular Culture and Public Space in Africa: The Possibilities of Cultural Citizenship." *African Studies Review* 49, no. 3 (2006): 31–49.

Doumbia, Youssouf. "Total Atmosphere with Garrincha!" In *Malick Sidibé*, edited by André Magnin, 163–67. Zurich: Scalo, 1998.

Duran, Lucy. "Key to N'Dour: Roots of the Senegalese Star." *Popular Music* 8, no. 3 (1989): 275–84.

———. "Orchestra Baobab." In *World Music Central.* n.d. www.worldmusiccentral.org.

Elliott, Richard, and Nanette De Jong. "Ritual, Remembrance and Recorded Sound." Course syllabus at Newcastle University, Newcastle upon Tyne, UK, 2010–2011.

Ewens, Graeme. *Congo Colossus: The Life and Legacy of Franco & OK Jazz.* North Walsham, Norfolk, UK: Buku Press, 1994.

Eyre, Banning. *In Griot Time: An American Guitarist in Mali.* Philadelphia: Temple University Press, 2000.

Fardon, Richard. *Raiders & Refugees: Trends in Chamba Political Development, 1750–1950.* Washington, DC: Smithsonian Institution Press, 1988.

Faye, Ousseynou. "L'urbanisation et les processus sociaux au Sénégal: Typologie descriptive et analytique des déviances à Dakar, d'après les sources d'archives, de 1885 à 1940." PhD diss., Département d'Histoire, Université Cheikh Anta Diop De Dakar, 1988.

Feld, Steven. *Jazz Cosmopolitanism in Accra: Five Musical Years in Accra.* Durham, NC: Duke University Press, 2012.

Flores, Juan. *From Bomba to Hip-hop: Puerto Rican Culture and Latino Identity.* New York: Columbia University Press, 2000.

Friedman, Jonathan. *Cultural Identity and Global Process.* London: Sage Publications, 1994.

Gandoulou, Justin-Daniel. *Dandies à Bacongo: Le culte de l'élégance dans la société congolaise contemporaine.* Paris: L'Harmattan, 1989.

García, David F. *Arsenio Rodríguez and the Transnational Flows of Latin Popular Music.* Philadelphia: Temple University Press, 2006.

García Canclini, Néstor. *Consumers and Citizens: Globalization and Multicultural Conflicts.* Translated by George Yúdice. Minneapolis: University of Minnesota Press, 2001.

German, Héctor Ulloque. *Orquesta Aragón.* Havana: Pablo de la Torriente, 2004.

Gilroy, Paul. *The Black Atlantic: Modernity and Double Consciousness.* Cambridge, MA: Harvard University Press, 1993.

Gondola, Ch. Didier. "Dream and Drama: The Search for Elegance among Congolese Youth." *African Studies Review* 42, no. 1 (April 1999): 23–48.

———. "The Tropical West: The Young 'Bills' of Kinshasa and the Politics of Masculinity." Paper presented at the Annual Meeting of the African Studies Association, New Orleans, LA, November 11–14, 2004.

Hafkin, Nancy J., and Edna G. Bay, eds. *Women in Africa: Studies in Social and Economic Change*. Stanford, CA: Stanford University Press, 1976.

Hagedorn, Katherine J. *Divine Utterances: The Performance of Afro-Cuban Santería*. Washington, DC: Smithsonian Institution Press, 2001.

Hale, Thomas A. *Griots and Griottes: Masters of Words and Music*. Bloomington: Indiana University Press, 1998.

Hall, Stuart. "A Conversation with Stuart Hall." *Journal of the International Institute* 7, no. 1 (Fall 1999).

Hargreaves, John D. *Decolonization in Africa*. London: Longman, 1988.

Harney, Elizabeth. *In Senghor's Shadow: Art, Politics, and the Avant-garde in Senegal, 1960–1995*. Durham, NC: Duke University Press, 2004.

Harvey, David. *Paris, Capital of Modernity*. New York: Routledge, 2003.

Hayward, Philip. *Widening the Horizon: Exoticism in Post-war Popular Music*. Sydney: John Libbey, 1999.

Hecht, David. "Senegal Takes Salsa, Adds Mbalax and Gets Magic." *New York Times*, December 8, 1999.

Hernández-Reguant, Ariana. *Cuba in the Special Period: Culture and Ideology in the 1990s*. New York: Palgrave Macmillan, 2009.

———. "Havana's Timba: A Macho Sound for Black Sex." In *Globalization and Race: Transformation in the Cultural Production of Blackness*, edited by Kamari M. Clarke and Deborah Thomas, 249–78. Durham, NC: Duke University Press, 2006.

———. "World Music Producers and the Cuban Frontier." In *Music and Globalization: Critical Encounters*, edited by Bob W. White, 111–35. Bloomington: Indiana University Press, 2012.

Howard, Philip A. *Changing History: Afro-Cuban Cabildos and Societies of Color in the Nineteenth Century*. Baton Rouge: Louisiana State University Press, 1998.

Hudson, Mark. *The Music in My Head*. London: Jonathan Cape, 1998.

Hutcheon, Linda. "Irony, Nostalgia and the Postmodern." In *University of Toronto English Library*. Last modified January 19, 1998. www.library.utoronto.ca/utel/criticism/hutchinp.

Ivaska, Andrew. *Cultured States: Youth, Gender, and Modern Style in 1960s Dar es Salaam*. Durham, NC: Duke University Press, 2011.

Jameson, Fredric. *Postmodernism; or, The Cultural Logic of Late Capitalism*. Durham, NC: Duke University Press, 1991.

Kane, Cheikh Hamidou. *L'aventure ambiguë*. Paris: René Julliard, 1962.

Katz, Mark. *Capturing Sound: How Technology Has Changed Music*. Berkeley: University of California Press, 2004.

Kelly, Gail P. "Colonialism, Indigenous Society and School Practices: French West Africa and Indochina 1918–1939." In *Education and the Colonial Experience*, edited by Philip G. Altbach and Gail P. Kelly. 9–32. New Brunswick, NJ: Transaction, 1984.

Kent, Mary. *Salsa Talks: A Musical Heritage Uncovered*. Altamonte Springs, FL: Digital Domain, 2005.

Khouma, Pap. *I Was an Elephant Salesman: Adventures between Dakar, Paris, and Milan*. Translated by Oreste Pivetta and Rebecca Crockett-Hopkins. Bloomington: Indiana University Press, 2010.

Konaté, Yacouba. *Alpha Blondy: Reggae et société en Afrique noire*. Abidjan: CEDA, 1987.

Kringelbach, Hélène Neveu. *Dance Circles: Movement, Morality and Self-Fashioning in Urban Senegal*. Oxford: Berghahn, 2013.

Larkin, Brian. *Signal and Noise: Media, Infrastructure, and Urban Culture in Nigeria*. Durham, NC: Duke University Press, 2008.

Lazzara, Michael J., and Vicky Unruh. *Telling Ruins in Latin America*. New York: Palgrave Macmillan, 2009.

Leymarie, Isabelle. *Cuban Fire: The Story of Salsa and Latin Jazz*. London: Continuum, 2002.

Lezama Lima, José. *La expresión americana*. Mexico City: Fondo de Cultura Económica, 2010.

Lindsay, Lisa A. *Working with Gender: Wage Labor and Social Change in Southwestern Nigeria*. Portsmouth, NH: Heinemann, 2003.

Lindsay, Lisa A., and Stephan Miescher, eds. *Men and Masculinities in Modern Africa*. Portsmouth, NH: Heinemann, 2003.

Locraft, Lauren K. "Senegalese Novel, African Voice: Examining the French Educational System through Aminata Sow Fall's *L'appel des arènes* and Cheikh Hamidou Kane's *L'aventure ambigüe*." Master's thesis, Department of History, Virginia Polytechnic University, 2005.

Lumumba. Directed by Raoul Peck. New York: Zeitgeist Films, 2002. DVD.

Madrid, Alejandro L., and Robin D. Moore. *Danzón: Circum-Caribbean Dialogues in Music and Dance*. Oxford: Oxford University Press, 2013.

Magnin, André. *Malick Sidibé*. Zurich: Scalo, 1998.

Makeba, Miriam, and James Hall. *Makeba: My Story*. New York: New American Library, 1989.

Mangin, Tim. "Mbalax: Cosmopolitanisms in Senegalese Popular Music." PhD diss., Department of Music, Columbia University, 2012.

Manning, Patrick. *Francophone Sub-Saharan Africa, 1880–1995*. Cambridge, UK: Cambridge University Press, 1998.

Manuel, Peter L. "The Saga of a Song: Authorship and Ownership in the Case of Guantamera." *Latin American Music Review* 27, no. 2 (Fall 2006): 121–47.

Martin, Denis-Constant. *Sounding the Cape: Music, Identity and Politics in South Africa*. Somerset West, South Africa: Africa Mind, 2013.

Mbembe, Achille. "The New Africans: Between Nativism and Cosmopolitanism." In *Readings in Modernity in Africa*, edited by Peter Geschiere, Birgit Meyer, and Peter Pels, 107–11. Bloomington: Indiana University Press, 2008.

———. "The Senegalese Murid Trade Diaspora and the Making of a Vernacular Cosmopolitanism." *Public Culture* 12, no. 3 (Fall 2000): 679–702.

McLaughlin, Fiona. "Islam and Popular Music in Senegal: The Emergence of a New Tradition." *Africa* 67, no. 4 (1997): 560–581.

Meintjes, Louise. *Sound of Africa! Making Music Zulu in a South African Studio*. Durham, NC: Duke University Press, 2003.

Miller, Christopher L. *Nationalists and Nomads: Essays on Francophone African Literature and Culture*. Chicago: University of Chicago Press, 1998.

Miller, Ivor. *The Voice of the Leopard: African Secret Societies and Cuba*. Jackson: University Press of Mississippi, 2008.

Mitchell, J. Clyde. *The Kalela Dance: Aspects of Social Relationships among Urban Africans in Northern Rhodesia*. [Manchester, UK]: Published on Behalf of the Rhodes-Livingstone Institute by the Manchester University Press, 1956.

Moore, Robin. *Music and Revolution: Cultural Change in Socialist Cuba*. Berkeley: University of California Press, 2006.

———. *Nationalizing Blackness: Afrocubanismo and Artistic Revolution in Havana, 1920–1940*. Pittsburgh, PA: University of Pittsburgh Press, 1997.

Moorman, Marissa Jean. *Intonations: A Social History of Music and Nation in Luanda, Angola, from 1945 to Recent Times*. Athens: Ohio University Press, 2008.

Morgan, Andy. "Afrocubism: An Old Transatlantic Love Story." *Andy Morgan Writes*, March 31, 2011. http://www.andymorganwrites.com/afrocubism-a-transatlantic-love-affair/.

Ndoye, Amadou. *En torno a la literatura hispanoamericana*. Translated by Yolanda González Pacciotti. Bogotá: Universidad Autónoma de Colombia, Departamento de Humanidades, 2008.

Nzegwu, Nkiru. "School Days in Lagos—Fela, Lady and 'Arcada.'" In *Fela: From West Africa to West Broadway*, edited by Trevor Schoonmaker, 135–49. New York: St. Martin's Press, 2003.

Orovio, Helio. *Cuban Music from A to Z*. Durham, NC: Duke University Press, 2004.

Ortiz, Fernando. *Cuban Counterpoint, Tobacco and Sugar.* Durham, NC: Duke University Press, 1995.

Ouzgane, Lahoucine, and Robert Morrell, eds. *African Masculinities: Men in Africa from the Late 19th Century to the Present.* Houndmills, UK: Palgrave Macmillan, 2005.

Palmieri, Eddie. *The Note, Episode 2—Eddie Palmieri: A Revolution on Harlem River Drive.* Red Bull Music Academy, 2016. http://www.redbull.tv/thenote.

Panzacchi, Cornelia. *Mbalax Mi: Musikszene Senegal.* Wuppertal, Germany: Peter Hammer, 1996.

Pérez, Louis A. *Cuba: Between Reform and Revolution.* New York: Oxford University Press, 1988.

Pérez Firmat, Gustavo. *Life on the Hyphen: The Cuban-American Way.* Austin: University of Texas Press, 1994.

Perullo, Alex. *Live from Dar es Salaam: Popular Music and Tanzania's Music Economy.* Bloomington: Indiana University Press, 2011.

Ponte, Antonio José. *Tales from the Cuban Empire.* San Francisco: City Lights Press, 2002.

Por siempre Cha cha chá. Directed by Jesús Dámaso González. Havana: Mundo Latino/EGREM, 2007. DVD.

Price, Sally, and Richard Price. *Maroon Arts: Cultural Vitality in the African Diaspora.* Boston: Beacon Press, 1999.

Quiroga, José. *Cuban Palimpsests.* Minneapolis: University of Minnesota Press, 2005.

Rediker, Marcus. *Between the Devil and the Deep Blue Sea: Merchant Seamen, Pirates, and the Anglo-American Maritime World, 1700–1750.* Cambridge, UK: Cambridge University Press, 1987.

Roberts, Allen F., Mary Nooter Roberts, Gassia Armenian, and Ousmane Guèye. *A Saint in the City: Sufi Arts of Urban Senegal.* Los Angeles: UCLA Fowler Museum of Cultural History, 2003.

Roberts, John Storm. *The Latin Tinge: The Impact of Latin American Music on the United States.* Tivoli, NY: Original Music, 1985.

Robinson, David. *Paths of Accommodation: Muslim Societies and French Colonial Authorities in Senegal and Mauritania, 1880–1920.* Athens: Ohio University Press, 2000.

Robinson, Eugene. *Last Dance in Havana: The Final Days of Fidel and the Start of the New Cuban Revolution.* New York: Free Press, 2004.

Rogers, Matt. "Viva Cuba y Senegal." *Village Voice,* November 12, 2002.

Romberg, Raquel. *Witchcraft and Welfare: Spiritual Capital and the Business of Magic in Modern Puerto Rico.* Austin: University of Texas Press, 2003.

Ross, Eric. *Sufi City: Urban Design and Archetypes in Touba.* Rochester, NY: University of Rochester Press, 2006.

Salazar, Primero Max. *Mambo Kingdom: Latin Music in New York.* New York: Schirmer Trade Books, 2002.

Sankharé, Oumar. *Youssou Ndour: Artiste et artisan du développement.* Dakar, Senegal: Éditions du Livre Universel, 2002.

———. *Youssou Ndour: Le poète.* Dakar: Nouvelles Éditions Africaines du Sénégal, 1998.

Sassen, Saskia. "Organized Religions in Our Global Modernity." *PMLA* 126, no. 2 (March 2011): 455–60.

Schwartz, Marcy E. *Writing Paris: Urban Topographies of Desire in Contemporary Latin American Fiction.* Albany: State University of New York Press, 1999.

Scott, Julius S., III. "The Common Wind: Currents of Afro-American Communication in the Era of the Haitian Revolution." PhD diss., Department of History, Duke University, 1986.

Senegal Salsa. Directed by Moustapha Ndoye. Dakar: Radio Diffusion Télévision Sénégalaise (RTS), 2000. VHS.

Senghor, Léopold Sédar. "Éléments constitutifs d'une civilization d'inspiration négro-africaine." In *L'unité des cultures négro-africaines.* Proceedings of Deuxième Congrès des Écrivains et Artistes Noirs, nos. 24–25. Vol. 1. Paris: Présence Africaine, 1959.

———. *Léopold Sédar Senghor: The Collected Poetry.* Edited and translated by Melvin Dixon. Charlottesville: University of Virginia Press, 1998.

———. *Œuvre poétique.* Paris: Editions du Seuil, 1990.

Shain, Richard. "The Re(Public) of Salsa: Afro-Cuban Music in Fin-de-Siècle Dakar." *Africa* 79, no. 2 (2009): 186–205.

———. "Roots in Reverse: *Cubanismo* in Twentieth Century Senegalese Music." *International Journal of African Historical Studies* 35, no. 1 (2002): 83–101.

Socé Diop, Ousmane. *Mirages de Paris: Roman.* Paris: Nouvelles Éditions Latines, 1965.

Sommer, Doris. *Foundational Fictions: The National Romances of Latin America.* Berkeley: University of California Press, 1993.

Soul Power. Directed by Jeffrey Levy-Hinte. Amsterdam: Homescreen, 2009. DVD.

Stewart, Gary. *Rumba on the River: A History of the Popular Music of the Two Congos.* London: Verso, 2000.

Stokes, Martin. Introduction to *Ethnicity, Identity and Music: The Musical Construction of Place*, edited by Martin Stokes. Oxford: Berg, 1994.

———. *The Republic of Love: Cultural Intimacy in Turkish Popular Music.* Chicago: University of Chicago Press, 2010.

Stovall, Tyler Edward. *Paris Noir: African Americans in the City of Light.* Boston: Houghton Mifflin, 1996.

Sublette, Ned. *Cuba and Its Music: From the First Drums to the Mambo.* Chicago: Chicago Press Review, 2004.

Tang, Patricia. *Masters of the Sabar: Wolof Griot Percussionists of Senegal.* Philadelphia: Temple University Press, 2007.

Tangari, Joe. "Orchestre Baobab." *Pitchfork*, August 5, 2008. http://pitchfork.com/features/interview/7144-orchestra-baobab/.

Taylor, Charles. "The Politics of Recognition." In *Multiculturalism: Examining the Politics of Recognition*, edited by Charles Taylor and Amy Gutmann, 25–75. Princeton, NJ: Princeton University Press, 1994.

Taylor, Timothy Dean. *Global Pop: World Music, World Markets*. New York: Routledge, 1997.

Thiam, Cheikh. *Return to the Kingdom of Childhood: Re-envisioning the Legacy and Philosophical Relevance of Negritude*. Columbus: Ohio University Press, 2014.

Thioub, Ibrahima, Momar C. Diop, and Catherine Boone. "Economic Liberalization in Senegal: Shifting Politics of Indigenous Business Interests." *African Studies Review* 41, no. 2 (September 1998): 63–85.

Touki Bouki. Directed by Djibril Diop Mambéty. New York: Kino on Video, (1973) 2005. DVD.

Trilling, Lionel. *Sincerity and Authenticity*. Cambridge, MA: Harvard University Press, 1972.

Turino, Thomas. *Nationalists, Cosmopolitans and Popular Music in Zimbabwe*. Chicago: University of Chicago Press, 2000.

Vaillant, Janet G. *Black, French, and African: A Life of Léopold Sédar Senghor*. Cambridge, MA: Harvard University Press, 1990.

Von, Eschen Penny M. *Satchmo Blows Up the World: Jazz Ambassadors Play the Cold War*. Cambridge, MA: Harvard University Press, 2006.

Warner, Michael. *Publics and Counterpublics*. New York: Zone Books, 2005.

Washburne, Christopher. "Salsa romántica." In *Situating Salsa: Global Markets and Local Meaning in Latin Popular Music*, edited by Lise A. Waxer, 101–35. New York: Routledge, 2002.

Waterman, Christopher Alan. *Jùjú: A Social History Ethnography of an African Popular Music*. Chicago: University Chicago Press, 1990.

Waxer, Lise. *The City of Musical Memory: Salsa, Record Grooves, and Popular Culture in Cali, Colombia*. Middletown, CT: Wesleyan University Press, 2002.

Weston, Randy, and Willard Jenkins. *African Rhythms: The Autobiography of Randy Weston*. Durham, NC: Duke University Press, 2010.

White, Bob W. *Rumba Rules: The Politics of Dance Music in Mobutu's Zaire*. Durham, NC: Duke University Press, 2008.

Whitmore, Aleysia. "The Art of Representing the Other: Personnel in the World Music Industry." *Ethnomusicology* 60 no. 2 (Spring/Summer 2016): 329–55.

———. "'Cuban Music Is African Music': Productive Frictions in the World Music Industry." *MUSICultures* 40 no. 1 (2013): 122–44.

Wilder, Gary. *The French Imperial Nation-state: Negritude and Colonial Humanism between the Two World Wars*. Chicago: University of Chicago Press, 2005.
Williams, Raymond. *Marxism and Literature*. London: Oxford University Press, 1997.
Xala. Directed by Ousmane Sembène. New York: New Yorker Films, (1975) 2005. DVD.
Yohannès, D. "Addis by Night." *Menen* 10, no. 8 (May 1966): 18–21.
Yúdice, George. "Postmodernity and Transnational Capitalism in Latin America." In *On Edge: The Crisis of Contemporary Latin American Culture*, edited by George Yúdice, Jean Franco, and Juan Flores. 1–28. Minneapolis: University of Minnesota Press, 2002.

DISCOGRAPHY

African Salsa. Sterns/Earthworks, STEW41CD, 1998. CD.

Africando. *Baloba!* Sterns Africa STCD 1082, 1998. CD.

Africando. *Gombe Salsa*. Sterns Africa STCD 1071, 1996. CD.

Africando. *Ketukuba*. Sterns Africa STCD 1103, 2006. CD.

Africando. *Martina*. Sterns Africa STCD 1096. 2003. CD.

Africando. *Tierra tradicional*. Sterns Africa STCDS 1054, 1994. CD.

Africando. *Trovador*. Sterns Africa STCD 1045, 1993. CD.

Africando *Viva africando*. Sterns Africa STCD 1120, 2013.

Africando All Stars. *Mandali*. Sterns Africa STCD 1092, 2000. CD.

AfroLatin Via Dakar. Syllart 3237562, 2011.

Afro-Salseros de Senegal, Los. *Los Afro-salseros de Senegal en La Habana*. Popular African Music 407, 2001. CD.

Álvarez, Fernando. *Se feliz*. Fernando Álvarez y Descemer Bueno. Egrem 964, 2008. CD.

Arroyo, Joe. *Echao Pa'lante*. Disco Fuentes 11242, 1987. Vinyl recording.

Azpiazu, Don. *Don Azpiazu*. Harlequin HQCD 10, 1991. CD.

Banda Municipale de Santiago de Cuba, La. *Fanfare cubaine*. Buda 92724, 1998. CD.

Buena Vista Social Club, The. *The Buena Vista Social Club*. World Circuit/Nonesuch 79478-2, 1997. CD.

Buena Vista Social Club. *A toda Cuba le gusta*. Recorded 1997. World Circuit/Nonesuch 79476-2. CD.

Cachao. *Master Sessions, Volume II*. Recorded 1995. CineSon EK67319. CD.

Calle, Oscar. *Cuba en Paris: Oscar Calle—Señor Tentació*. Iris Musique HMCD 79, 1998. CD.

Cuba: Una Noche en La Habana. Syllart Productions 6132952, 2007. CD.

Cuba 1926–1937 Bal à La Havane. Frémeaux & Associés FA 5134, 2006. CD.

The Cuban Danzón: Before There Was Jazz: 1906–1929. Arhoolie 7032, 1999. CD.

Early Cuban Danzón Orchestras, 1916–1920. Recorded 1999. Harlequin HQ CD 131. CD.

Daara J. *Boomrang*. BMG France 74321 983932, 2003. CD.

Diop, Idrissa, and Cheikh Tidiane Tall. *Diamonoye Tiopité: L'époque de l'évolution*. Teranga Beat TBCD 013, 2010. CD.

El Manisero. *25 versiones clásicas de El Manisero*. Tumbao Cuban Classics TCD-801, 1997. CD.

Étoile de Dakar. *Étoile de Dakar, Volume 1 "absa Gueye."* Recorded 1979. Sterns Music STCD 3004, 2002. CD.

Étoile de Dakar. *Once Upon a Time in Senegal—The Birth of Mbalax 1979–1981*. Sterns Music STCD 3054–55, 2010. CD.

Fall, Pape. *Artisanat*. Sterns/Earthworks, STEW 47CD, 2002. CD.

Fall, Pape. *Que vive la paix!* Recorded 2002. Cassette.

Farka Touré, Ali, and Ry Cooder. *Talking Timbuktu*. World Circuit HNCD 1381, 1994. CD.

Franco and OK Jazz. *Franco et le tout-puissant OK Jazz*. Sonodisc SD40, 1994. CD.

Franco and OK Jazz. *Originalité*. RetroAfric Retro 2XCD, 2006. CD.

Gomis, Rudy. *Toon Baaxul*. N.d. Cassette.

Johnson & le Super Star de Dakar. *Live à l'Étoile*. Terenga Beat TBLP 019, 2014.

Kabasele, Joseph. *le Grand Kalle: His Life, His Music; Joseph Kabasele and the Creation of Modern Congolese Music*. Sterns Music STCD 3058–59, 2013.

Keita, Salif. *Soro*. Celluloid CD 66883-2, 1987. CD.

Lloyd, A. L., and Ewan MacColl. *Blow Boys Blow*. Recorded 1967. Tradition TCD 1024, 1996. CD.

Makeba, Miriam. *The Many Voices of Miriam Makeba*. Kapp KTL41040, 1960. Vinyl recording.

Maravillas de Mali, Las. *Las Maravillas de Mali*. Maestro Sound 004 08968-2, 2001. CD.

Mbaye, Serigne (Disiz la peste). "N'Dioukel," on *Itinéraire d'un enfant bronzé*. Def Jam France B00063920A, 2004. CD.

Melochita. *Máscara Salera: Gozando!* Asefra Productions CD 1012, 1995. CD.

Moré, Benny. *Grabaciones completas, 1953–1960*. Benny Moré y su Banda Gigante. Tumbao 309, 2003. CD.

Muñequitos de Matanzas, Los. *Guaguancó Matancero*. Tumbao 707, 2001. CD.

Music in My Head, The. Compiled by Mark Hudson. Sterns Music STCD 1081, 1998. CD.

Menheim, Nicolas, and Le Super Sabador. *Commandante Ché Guevara*. Popular African Music Pam Oa 209, 2002. CD.

Ngom, Alassane, et la Salsa Stars. *Le ravin*. Private label, 2016. CD.

No. 1. *No. 1 De No. 1*. Dakar Sound, Volume 6, 2002969, 1998. CD.

No. 1. *Orchestra Number One de Dakar 78, Volume 1*. Barclay No-001, 1978. Vinyl recording.

Ochoa, Eliades, and Manu Dibango. *CubAfrica*. Mélodie 79593.2, 1998. CD.

Orchestre Baobab. *Baobab—N'Wolof*. Dakar Sound DKS 014, 1998. CD.

Orchestre Baobab. *Baobab Guy-Gui*. N.d. Cassette.

Orchestre Baobab. *On verra ça*. Recorded 1978. Ledoux Records Asl7001. Vinyl recording.

Orchestre Baobab. *Orchestre du Baobab, Vol. 1*. Bao 001, 1972. Vinyl recording.

Orchestre Baobab. *Pirate's Choice*. Recorded 2001. World Circuit 79643-2. CD.

Orchestre Baobab. *Pirates Choice: The Legendary 1982 Session*. Recorded 1982. World Circuit WCD014, 1989. CD.

Orchestre Baobab. *Specialist in All Styles*. Recorded 2002. Nonesuch 79685. CD.

Orquesta Aragón. *Quien sabe sabe*. Candela/LusAfrica 42855492, 1998. CD.

Out of Cuba: Latin American Music Takes Africa by Storm. Topic Records TSCD927, 2004. CD.

Palmieri, Eddie. *Lo que traigo es sabroso*. Alegre LPA 8320, 1964. CD.

Pina, Geraldo. *Heavy Heavy Heavy*. Retro-Afric20CD, 2005. CD.

Portabales, Guillermo. *Lo mejor de Guillermo Portabales*. Disco Hit Productions DHCD 1520, 1999. CD.

Pozo, Chano. *El tambor de Cuba*. Recorded 2001. Tumbao 305. CD.

Prado, Pérez. *Mondo Mambo!* RCA R2 71889/DRCI-1242, 1995. CD.

Rodríguez, Arsenio. *El alma de Cuba*. Tumbao TCD 315, 2007. CD.

Rossi, Tino. *Les plus grandes chansons*. Recorded 2004. Coppelia B00001VQeaI. CD.

Seck, Mar. *Vagabonde: From Super Cap-Vert to Number One*. Teranga Beat TBCD 018, 2013.

Sexteto y Septeto Habanero. *Grabaciones completas, 1925–1931*. Recorded 1998. Tumbao TCD 300. CD.

Sosseh, Laba. *El Maestro: 40 años de salsa*. Mélodie 00022, 2002. CD.

Sosseh, Laba. *Laba Sosseh*. Recorded 1982. SAR 1029. Vinyl recording.

Sosseh, Laba. *Roberto Torres presenta Laba Sosseh*. Recorded 1981. SAR 1020. Vinyl recording.

Sosseh, Laba, and Monguito. *Salsa Africana, Vol. 1, Monguito el unico and Laba Sosseh in U.S.A.* Recorded 1980. Sacodisc International LS 26-80. Vinyl recording.

Super Cayor. *Embouteillage*. Popular African Music Pam Oa 210, 2002. CD.

Super Cayor. *Sopenté*. Popular African Music Pam Oa 206, 1997. CD.

Super Eagles. *Super Eagles: Senegambian Sensation*. RetroAfric 17CD, 2001. CD.

Touré, Amara. *Amara Touré*. Analog Africa No.18, 2015. CD.

Touré Kunda. *Live—Paris-Ziguinchor*. Recorded 1983. M.I.L. Multimedia ESP 8516, 1996. CD.

Touré Kunda. *Natalia*. Recorded 1985. Charley CPCD 8268. CD.

UCAS Jazz Band de Sedhiou. *Casa di Mansa*. 2006. Africa Productions 03076-2.

INDEX

MUSIC / CULTURE

A series from Wesleyan University Press
Edited by Deborah Wong, Sherrie Tucker, and Jeremy Wallach
Originating editors: George Lipsitz, Susan McClary, and Robert Walser

Marié Abe
Resonances of Chindon-ya: Sounding Space and Sociality in Contemporary Japan

Frances Aparicio
Listening to Salsa: Gender, Latin Popular Music, and Puerto Rican Cultures

Paul Austerlitz
Jazz Consciousness: Music, Race, and Humanity

Harris M. Berger
Metal, Rock, and Jazz: Perception and the Phenomenology of Musical Experience

Harris M. Berger
Stance: Ideas about Emotion, Style, and Meaning for the Study of Expressive Culture

Harris M. Berger and Giovanna P. Del Negro
Identity and Everyday Life: Essays in the Study of Folklore, Music, and Popular Culture

Franya J. Berkman
Monument Eternal: The Music of Alice Coltrane

Dick Blau, Angeliki Vellou Keil, and Charles Keil
Bright Balkan Morning: Romani Lives and the Power of Music in Greek Macedonia

Susan Boynton and Roe-Min Kok, editors
Musical Childhoods and the Cultures of Youth

James Buhler, Caryl Flinn, and David Neumeyer, editors
Music and Cinema

Thomas Burkhalter, Kay Dickinson, and Benjamin J. Harbert, editors
The Arab Avant-Garde: Music, Politics, Modernity

Patrick Burkart
Music and Cyberliberties

Julia Byl
Antiphonal Histories: Resonant Pasts in the Toba Batak Musical Present

Daniel Cavicchi
Listening and Longing: Music Lovers in the Age of Barnum

Susan D. Crafts, Daniel Cavicchi, Charles Keil, and the Music in Daily Life Project
My Music: Explorations of Music in Daily Life

Jim Cullen
Born in the USA: Bruce Springsteen and the American Tradition

Anne Danielsen
Presence and Pleasure: The Funk Grooves of James Brown and Parliament

Peter Doyle
Echo and Reverb: Fabricating Space in Popular Music Recording, 1900–1960

Ron Emoff
Recollecting from the Past: Musical Practice and Spirit Possession on the East Coast of Madagascar

Yayoi Uno Everett and Frederick Lau, editors
Locating East Asia in Western Art Music

Susan Fast and Kip Pegley, editors
Music, Politics, and Violence

Heidi Feldman
Black Rhythms of Peru: Reviving African Musical Heritage in the Black Pacific

Kai Fikentscher
"You Better Work!" Underground Dance Music in New York City

Ruth Finnegan
The Hidden Musicians: Music-Making in an English Town

Daniel Fischlin and Ajay Heble, editors
The Other Side of Nowhere: Jazz, Improvisation, and Communities in Dialogue

Wendy Fonarow
Empire of Dirt: The Aesthetics and Rituals of British "Indie" Music

Murray Forman
The 'Hood Comes First: Race, Space, and Place in Rap and Hip-Hop

Lisa Gilman
My Music, My War: The Listening Habits of U.S. Troops in Iraq and Afghanistan

Paul D. Greene and Thomas Porcello, editors
Wired for Sound: Engineering and Technologies in Sonic Cultures

Tomie Hahn
Sensational Knowledge: Embodying Culture through Japanese Dance

Edward Herbst
Voices in Bali: Energies and Perceptions in Vocal Music and Dance Theater

Deborah Kapchan
Traveling Spirit Masters: Moroccan Gnawa Trance and Music in the Global Marketplace

Deborah Kapchan, editor
Theorizing Sound Writing

Max Katz
Lineage of Loss: Counternarratives of North Indian Music

Raymond Knapp
Symphonic Metamorphoses: Subjectivity and Alienation in Mahler's Re-Cycled Songs

Laura Lohman
Umm Kulthūm: Artistic Agency and the Shaping of an Arab Legend, 1967–2007

Preston Love
A Thousand Honey Creeks Later: My Life in Music from Basie to Motown—and Beyond

René T. A. Lysloff and
Leslie C. Gay Jr., editors
Music and Technoculture

Allan Marett
Songs, Dreamings, and Ghosts: The Wangga of North Australia

Ian Maxwell
Phat Beats, Dope Rhymes: Hip Hop Down Under Comin' Upper

Kristin A. McGee
Some Liked It Hot: Jazz Women in Film and Television, 1928–1959

Rebecca S. Miller
Carriacou String Band Serenade: Performing Identity in the Eastern Caribbean

Tony Mitchell, editor
Global Noise: Rap and Hip-Hop Outside the USA

Christopher Moore and
Philip Purvis, editors
Music & Camp

Rachel Mundy
Animal Musicalities: Birds, Beasts, and Evolutionary Listening

Keith Negus
Popular Music in Theory: An Introduction

Johnny Otis
Upside Your Head!: Rhythm and Blues on Central Avenue

Kip Pegley
Coming to You Wherever You Are: MuchMusic, MTV, and Youth Identities

Jonathan Pieslak
Radicalism and Music: An Introduction to the Music Cultures of al-Qa'ida, Racist Skinheads, Christian-Affiliated Radicals, and Eco-Animal Rights Militants

Matthew Rahaim
Musicking Bodies: Gesture and Voice in Hindustani Music

John Richardson
Singing Archaeology: Philip Glass's Akhnaten

Tricia Rose
Black Noise: Rap Music and Black Culture in Contemporary America

David Rothenberg
and Marta Ulvaeus, editors
The Book of Music and Nature: An Anthology of Sounds, Words, Thoughts

Nichole Rustin-Paschal
The Kind of Man I Am: Jazzmasculinity and the World of Charles Mingus Jr.

Marta Elena Savigliano
Angora Matta: Fatal Acts of North-South Translation

Joseph G. Schloss
Making Beats: The Art of Sample-Based Hip-Hop

Richard M. Shain
Roots in Reverse: Senegalese Afro-Cuban Music and Tropical Cosmopolitanism

Barry Shank
Dissonant Identities: The Rock 'n' Roll Scene in Austin, Texas

Jonathan Holt Shannon
Among the Jasmine Trees: Music and Modernity in Contemporary Syria

Daniel B. Sharp
Between Nostalgia and Apocalypse: Popular Music and the Staging of Brazil

Helena Simonett
Banda: Mexican Musical Life across Borders

Mark Slobin
Subcultural Sounds: Micromusics of the West

Mark Slobin, editor
Global Soundtracks: Worlds of Film Music

Christopher Small
The Christopher Small Reader

Christopher Small
Music of the Common Tongue: Survival and Celebration in African American Music

Christopher Small
Music, Society, Education

Christopher Small
Musicking: The Meanings of Performing and Listening

Regina M. Sweeney
Singing Our Way to Victory: French Cultural Politics and Music during the Great War

Colin Symes
Setting the Record Straight: A Material History of Classical Recording

Steven Taylor
False Prophet: Fieldnotes from the Punk Underground

Paul Théberge
Any Sound You Can Imagine: Making Music/Consuming Technology

Sarah Thornton
Club Cultures: Music, Media and Sub-cultural Capital

Michael E. Veal
Dub: Songscape and Shattered Songs in Jamaican Reggae

Michael E. Veal and E. Tammy Kim, editors
Punk Ethnography: Artists and Scholars Listen to Sublime Frequencies

Robert Walser
Running with the Devil: Power, Gender, and Madness in Heavy Metal Music

Dennis Waring
Manufacturing the Muse: Estey Organs and Consumer Culture in Victorian America

Lise A. Waxer
The City of Musical Memory: Salsa, Record Grooves, and Popular Culture in Cali, Colombia

Mina Yang
Planet Beethoven: Classical Music at the Turn of the Millennium

ABOUT THE AUTHOR

Richard M. Shain teaches African, Caribbean, and Latin American Studies at Thomas Jefferson University. He also taught at the university level in Nigeria and Senegal for nearly ten years.